THE
HISTORY OF CEYLON
FROM
THE EARLIEST PERIOD TO THE PRESENT TIME;

THE
HISTORY OF CEYLON
FROM
THE EARLIEST PERIOD TO THE PRESENT TIME;

WITH AN APPENDIX,

CONTAINING AN ACCOUNT OF

ITS PRESENT CONDITION.

BY WILLIAM KNIGHTON, ESQ.,

COLOMBO.

GYAN

Published by

Gyan Publishing House
5, Ansari Road
Daryaganj, New Delhi-110002
Phone: 011-47034999, 9811692060
E-mail: books@gyanbooks.com

Distribution Network
gyanbooks.com
India, USA, Canada, UK, Australia, France

ISBN : 978-81-212-3511-2 (PB)
First Published, 1845

2nd Impression 2020

Printed at: Gyan Press, Delhi.

The
History of Ceylon from the Earliest Period to the Present Time;
Author: William Knighton

THE

HISTORY OF CEYLON

FROM

THE EARLIEST PERIOD TO THE PRESENT TIME;

WITH AN APPENDIX,

CONTAINING AN ACCOUNT OF

ITS PRESENT CONDITION.

BY WILLIAM KNIGHTON, ESQ.,
COLOMBO.

Πρὸς ταῦτα κρύπτε μηδὲν, ὡς ὁ πάνθ' ὁρῶν
καὶ πάντ' ἀκούων, πάντ' ἀναπτύσσει χρόνος.

Sophocles, apud. Clem. Stromat. iv. p. 742.

LONDON:
LONGMAN, BROWN, GREEN & LONGMANS;
SMITH, ELDER & CO.; AND MADDEN & MALCOLM.
EDINBURGH:—BELL & BRADFUTE.

MDCCCXLV.

TO THE

REV. JOHN G. MACVICAR, D.D. &c.

AUTHOR OF

"THE BEAUTIFUL, THE SUBLIME, AND THE PICTURESQUE,"
"THE CATHOLIC SPIRIT OF TRUE RELIGION,"
&c. &c. &c.

THIS WORK

IS RESPECTFULLY DEDICATED

BY HIS AFFECTIONATE AND GRATEFUL FRIEND,

THE AUTHOR.

PREFACE.

"EVERY year," said Southey, "adds to our ample stock of books relating to the manners of other nations, and the condition of men in states and stages of society different from our own; and of such books we cannot have too many." If this be granted, no apology will be needed for the publication of the present volume.

The labours of Mr Turnour * and Mr Upham † in the field of Ceylonese antiquities opened up materials for a continued history of a peculiar Asiatic people for upwards of 2000 years. The progress of that people to refinement, the causes of their decline, and the effects of European interference, cannot, I flatter myself, be without interest to a cultivated mind. The student of human nature will find that the History of Ceylon adds another to the arguments commonly adduced to prove that the character of a people is the natural result of its government, its laws and its religion.

I cannot close these remarks without mentioning, that the present volume owes its origin to the advice of the gentleman to whom it is inscribed, and that without his assistance it could not have been completed.

* Author of a translation of "the Mahawanso."

† Author of "The Sacred and Historical Works of Ceylon."

COLOMBO, CEYLON, 1845.

NOTICE BY THE PUBLISHERS.

The Author being resident in Ceylon, has not had an opportunity of revising the proof sheets of this work. The indulgence of the reader is therefore requested for any errors of the press which may have escaped notice in the printing.

CONTENTS.

CHAPTER I.

CHAPTER II.

CHAPTER III.

CHAPTER IV.

CHAPTER V.

CHAPTER VI.

CHAPTER VII.

CHAPTER VIII.

CHAPTER IX.

CHAPTER X.

CHAPTER XI.

CHAPTER XII.

CHAPTER XIII.

CHAPTER XIV.

CHAPTER XV.

CHAPTER XVI.

CHAPTER XVII.

CHAPTER XVIII.

APPENDICES.

INTRODUCTION.

GEOGRAPHICAL NOTICE OF CEYLON.

The island of Ceylon lies between 5° 56′ and 9° 50′ north latitude, and between 80° 4′ and 82° east longitude. Its climate, its vegetable, mineral, and marine riches have ever ranked it as one of the finest portions of the earth. In shape it faintly resembles a pear, and it has been elegantly compared to a pearl-drop from the brow of India, It stretches about 270 miles in length, and has an average breadth of nearly 100. Its superficial extent is upwards of 24,600 miles, and its circuit 750. The Gulf of Manaar separates its north-eastern coast from the shores of the Continent, whilst on all the other sides it is washed by the Indian Ocean. The sea-shore is in general level and monotonous, but the greater part of the interior is diversified by mountains. These approach on the southern, eastern, and western sides, to within about forty miles of the sea, whilst, in the northern part, the level district extends for about seventy or eighty. By the mountains on the one side, and the ocean on the other, the breezes which fan the island are kept continually cool, and the suffocating winds of the Continent are consequently unknown. Few countries enjoy the same variety of climates as Ceylon, and, in consequence, few can exhibit the same variety of useful and ornamental plants. On the mountains the thermometer * frequently falls to 50°, and is seldom above 65°, whilst, on the coast, 80° or 81° may be taken as an average. Its highest mountains reach an elevation of from six to eight thousand feet, and form a circular barrier to the interior, which rendered it impregnable to European arms for nearly three hundred years. Several rivers take their rise in the elevated district, of which the Mahawelli-ganga, the Kalu-ganga, the Welawe, and the Guidora are the most considerable; and although there is not a natural lake of any extent in the entire island, few countries are better provided with water.

The sandy soil of the coast is admirably adapted for the growth of the cocoa-nut, and the cinnamon, with which the entire line of shore is almost literally covered. In the interior, magnificent forests clothe the mountains, containing a variety of beautiful and useful trees, perhaps unequalled elsewhere; but the dark groves of satin, ebony, jack, suriya, areka-nuts, and banyan trees are gradually yielding before the axe of civilisation; and where these ancient forests formerly stood for hundreds, possibly for thousands of years, the coffee shrub and the sugar-cane are now appearing.

* Fahrenheit's.

HISTORY OF CEYLON.

CHAPTER I.

First settlement of Ceylon—Its various names—The Ramayana—Gotamo Buddhu—Wijeya—Panduwasa—Abhayo—Rebellion of Pandukabbayo—Pandukabhayo's reign—Ganatissa—Mutasēwo—Tisso—Arrival of Mahindo and Sanghamittha—Establishment of Buddhism—Tisso's religious erections.

The desire of a renowned ancestry is not more common amongst individuals than the assumption of the early celebrity of their forefathers amongst nations. The wild races of the west did not celebrate the heroic deeds of their early progenitors with more enthusiasm than do the more effeminate inhabitants of the east; and China and barbarous Europe, although so dissimilar in customs, habits and national character, yet agreed in this. Nor does Ceylon differ from other nations in this respect. Every class of its inhabitants, whether Ceylonese proper, Malabars or Mohammedans, is equally positive as to the extreme antiquity and early celebrity of the island which they inhabit. Thus the first assure us, that the successive regenerators of mankind—the long line of Buddhas—frequently resorted hither to instruct and elevate its debased inhabitants. The second assert, that here the supreme Vishnu vanquished his enemies, and that the favoured island was the scene of th beautiful Seeta's confinement by Rawāna, the Paris c eastern mythology. Nor are the third less certain, tha here the human race had its primeval habitation, and tha in Ceylon Adam first enjoyed his terrestrial Paradise and subsequently endured his painful penance.

Few nations can distinctly point to the period at which and to the place from which, its aborigines arrived, an Ceylon is not of the number. Probability and tradition however, equally point to the extremity of the Indian peninsula as the country whence it first derived its inha bitants, and the striking resemblance between the Singh or Rajpoots of the continent and the natives of the island may lend, if not certainty, at least additional probability to the conjecture. But this is not the only conjecture on the subject; another, and that adopted by the Portuguese historians, asserts that China was the parent of the Cey lonese, and that a vessel of that nation, wrecked upon the coast, was the origin of its inhabitants. "The Chinese," says Ribeiro, "having been, at a very remote period, the masters of Oriental commerce, some of their vessels were driven upon the coast near the district which they subse quently termed Chilau, the mariners and passengers saved themselves upon the rocks, and, finding the island fertile and prolific, soon established themselves upon it. Shortly after wards the Malabars having discovered it, sent hither their exiles, whom they denominated Galas. The exiles were not long in mixing with the Chinese, and from the two names one was formed, at first Chingalas, and afterwards Chingalais *." This fanciful etymology, however, will not support the hypothesis; as the more common and natural opinion de-

* Historie de Ilgha de Zeilan, Introducaó.

ives the modern title of Singalas or Chingulais from the Indian King *, whom we shall soon find conquering it, and who was famed to have been descended from a lion, (Singha,) whence the name of the island and its inhabitants is now generally conceived to have been derived.

The account of the Dutch historians, Baldæus † and Valentyn ‡ differs somewhat from that of the Portuguese, and represents the Chinese ship as having given, not its inhabitants, but a sovereign to the island, the natives having very generously elected the captain of the vessel as

* Wijeya. † Beschryving van het groote en zeer beroemde Eiland Ceylon. Door Philippus Baldæus. Folio, Amst. 1672.

‡ The following is the title of Valentyn's valuable and extraordinary work, contained in five volumes folio, and as yet untranslated into English :—

"Keurlyke beschryving van Choromandel, Pegu, Arrakan, Bengale, Mocha, van 't Nederlandsch comptoir in Persien: en eenige fraaje zaaken van Persepolis overblyfzelen. Een nette beschryving van Malaka, 't Nederlands comptoir op 't Eiland Sumatra, mitsgaders een wydluftige landbeschryving van 't Eiland Ceylon, en een net verhaal van des zelfs keizeren, en zaaken, van ouds hier voergevollen; als ook van 't Nederlands comptoir op de kust van Malabar, en van onzen handel in Japan; en eindelyk een beschryving van Kaap der Goede Hoope, en 't Eiland Mauritius, met de zaaken tot alle de voornoemde ryken en landen behoorende. Met veel Prentverbeeldingen en landkaarten opgebeldert. Door François Valentyn, Onlangs Bedienaar des Goddelyken woords in Amboina, Banda enz. Te Amsterdam by Gerard Onder de Linden, 1726."

"An accurate description of Coromandel, Pegu, Arrakan, Bengal, Mocha, of the settlement of the Dutch in Persia, with a few interesting particulars of the ruins of Persepolis. A detailed account of Malacca, the settlement of the Dutch in Sumatra, *with an extensive geographical account of the island of Ceylon; its emperors and its antiquities. Lastly,* A description of the Cape of Good Hope, and the island Mauritius, with various incidents of all these kingdoms and countries. Embellished with illustrations, &c. By François Valentyn, late minister of the gospel in Amboina, Banda, &c. Amsterdam, 1726."

their king, a tradition which may remind us of the Manco Capac and Mama Ocollo of Peru *.

If India was peopled before Ceylon, there can be little doubt but that, on the occupation of the entire line of coast on the continent, the island which lay so near its southern extremity could not long be undiscovered, whilst its fertility, salubrity and richness, would make its discovery coëval with its occupation. When this discovery first took place, we have now no means of ascertaining; and it is useless to search in the shallow waters of the imagination, for what has long been lost in the ocean of antiquity.

Like most other countries, also, Ceylon has been described by a great variety of names. The earliest of these is most probably Lanka, (or Lanka-diva,) the Sanscrit and Pali name, although, from the manner in which the country so designated was honoured by Buddha, the natives of India † of that persuasion assert, that the modern Ceylon is but an island adjacent to the ancient Lanka, which now exists no longer.

To some of the Greeks it was known by the name of Σαλικὴ, and the inhabitants Σαλαι, but its most usual appellation amongst classical writers was Taprobane. Under this title it is mentioned by Dionysius ‡, as being famed for elephants; by Strabo §, as being as large as Britain; by Ovid ||, as exceedingly remote; by Pliny ¶, as the commencement of a new continent; by Ptolemy **, as stretching from north to south more than fifteen degrees; by Pomponius Mela ††, as either a continent, or an immense

* Robertson's America, book vii. † Colonel Tod. ‡ Periegetes, v. 593. § Lib. ii. 124, 180. || Ex. Ponto, 5, 79. ¶ Hist. Nat. vi. 29. ** Lib. vii. c. 4. †† De situ Orbis, lib. iii. c. 7.

island; and, finally, by Agathemerus *, as the largest of all islands.

The authors of the west in the middle ages, such as Arminanus Marcelinus and Cosmas Judicoplenstes, together with the greater number of Orientals, called it Serindib, Serinduil, and Σιελεδιβα, from the latter of which it is probable the name of Zeilan or Ceylon has been derived. The natives, in their vernacular Singhalese, call it Singalà, whilst, in their more important Elu, Pali, or Sanscrit works, it is invariably styled Lanka.

The earliest notice which Oriental literature affords us of this island, is that contained in the Ramayana, an epic poem, which celebrates the actions of Rawāna and Rama; the former king of Ceylon and southern India, who, having been insulted, and his relations abused by the latter, Prince of Yodhya or Oude, revenged himself by carrying off Seeta, the beautiful wife of Rama. This eastern Helen being confined by her ravisher in the woody parts of the island, Rama, like another Menelaus, at once proceeded with a powerful army to revenge his wrongs, and again obtain possession of his lawful spouse. The poem we have just mentioned relates the mighty deeds of the future gods in verses, some of which would not disgrace Homer himself, and over which an additional interest hangs, when we reflect that it is probably the oldest epic in the world. The Singhalese annals fix the date of Rawāna's death at 2387 B. C., whilst that eminent orientalist, Sir W. Jones, informs us that Rama about 1810 B. C. conquered *Silan*, a few centuries after the flood. At this early period, then, when the island was much more exten-

* Lib ii. c. 8, *apud* Hudson.

sive than it now is, Rama, entering it with a numerous army, laid siege to Rawāna's capital, (Sri Lanka-poora.) As, however, the sober pen of history cannot receive imagination as its guide, we can merely state, that after a tedious and bloody war of twelve years, Rawāna was slain, and the triumphant Rama, happy in the renewed possession of his lovely wife, left the conquered country to the care of Webeeshana, and returned to his native land "to live a king, and die a god '*debellata colebat* India."'

Respecting the state of the island at this early period, we have no information at all amounting to certainty, being merely informed respecting Rawāna's capital, that it had many noble and extensive palaces, and that it was fortified with seven walls, protected and strengthened by numerous towers; besides this, it was surrounded by a deep ditch supplied with water from the ocean.

But the Lanka which then existed was not the Lanka of the present day. At that period, we are informed, it was an extensive region of some thousand miles in extent, since reduced by various inundations, and especially by one shortly after Rawāna's death, to its present size. Nor is it at all improbable that such inundations and gradual diminutions of the island may have taken place, since we know that an ancient city on the Coromandel coast of India, called Maha Balipoor is now half imbedded in the ocean; a circumstance indisputably proving, that there at least, its destroying waves have been stealing from the land. Besides this, we also know, that Sri Lanka-poora, the meridian of the Eastern astronomers, was in 75° 53′ east longitude, whilst the western extremity of the present island scarcely reaches 80°. Taking these things into consideration with the accounts of the early writers formerly mentioned, it is no imaginary idea to assert, that the ancient Lanka was a much more extensive country than the modern Ceylon.

From this early period, 1800 years B. C., we must pass over, at one huge step, a period of nearly 1300 years *, during which we know nothing of the island except that at the end of that period it was inhabited by a gentle and unwarlike people.

Before proceeding, however, with the proper history of Ceylon at that period, we must say a few words in explanation of the religion about which we shall afterwards have so much to relate.

Those who hold the tenets of Buddhism maintain, that at an immeasurably remote period, during a time of wickedness and depravity, a man, supremely eminent by his exemplary virtues, raised himself to a degree of holiness far above that of other mortals, and, propagating morality and piety by preaching, was finally translated to the superior regions, where he enjoys endless beatitude and infinite happiness. Passing on through the lapse of ages, others gradually attained the same virtues, and finally obtained the same reward, at vastly remote periods of time. In this manner twenty-four Buddhas had passed away, filling up a space of many hundreds of thousands of years. At length, about 1800 years † after the wars of Rawāna, the last and greatest regenerator of mankind appeared in the person of Gautama Buddha. This individual, the son of Suddho-Lana ‡, sovereign of Magadha, a part of north-

* According to Sir W. Jones.

† According to the chronology of Ceylon.

‡ Vulgar tradition asserts that for *eleven* months his mother " ἤνεγχ' ὑπὸ ζώνην."

ern India, lived there in submission to his parents for sixteen years, under the name of Prince Kumara or Siddharta. He then married *, and, living in peace with his wife till his twenty-ninth year, at that period forsook her on the very day on which she produced their first-born son. Having resolved on a life of penance and holiness, he remained for six years in the wilderness of Corawella, in the modern Bahar, subsisting on whatever the trees or the earth produced, occasionally aided by alms. Having, in this manner, thoroughly subdued his passions, we are informed, that before again returning to the society of men, he had a fearful struggle with several demons, personifications, as it would seem, of evil passions. Over these, however, he finally prevailed; and having fasted forty-nine days, proceeded on his mission of reforming the world and establishing his own deityship. He spent the remaining forty-five years of his life in propagating his doctrines and attaining the Buddhaship. The first region in which his principles were openly propounded was that adjoining the modern Benares, where, having taken up his residence in a grove, he daily taught his numerous disciples those pure and excellent moral laws which distinguish his religion from that of most other superstitions.

Having thus assumed the character which future ages willingly assigned to him, he passed over to Ceylon, then inhabited † by a race called Yakkhos, or evil spirits, at whose capital Mahawelligam, (near the modern Binturne,) he propounded those doctrines which the inhabitants of the island have ever since received as the revelations of

* Some accounts allow him also 40,000 concubines. See Upham's Buddhist Tracts, p. 122.

† According to Ceylonese history.

the Almighty. At this period he was distinguished by the appellation of Gautama Gotamo, or Gaudma Buddha*. From the circumstances related respecting the wars of Rama and Rawāna, and particularly from the description given of Rawāna's capital, we cannot suppose that even at that early period Ceylon was sunk into a state of barbarism, nor yet can we suppose that Gautama Buddha, a man who evidently possessed great powers of mind, would have proceeded to an insignificant and barbarous island to propagate his tenets; but, on the other hand, how are we to suppose that Ceylon could have been civilised, when we learn, that at the period of Buddha's death, it was invaded by 700 men and conquered? Lest we should be thought to represent the island as more advanced than it really was, at that early period, we think it right to call the reader's attention to the manner in which it was conquered by Wijeya and his band, which was not by open violence, but by policy, intrigue, and perfidy.

The first visit of Buddha to Ceylon is distinguished in the literature of that religion by many notable miracles.

* His names in different countries are most numerous, from which will at present be selected only those titulars connected with their doctrine. By the Japanese and Chinese he is termed Xaca-Sacya, also Abbutto and Buto. His special name Boodh, or Budhu, or Budha, is often called Boudh, Bod, Bot, and, by the arbitrary substitution of the B and P to the F, Fo or Fho, arising from changes in the cognate letters of B, P, T and D; the Siamese call him Saman, Samana, Somon, whence the Samaneans, a strictly Buddhist sect, described by Clemens Alexandrinus, and strictly practising the ascetic austerities, so constantly commended in the doctrine. Gaudma is the derivative of Godam, or Codam. In the celebrated inscription found at Gonja Bahar, Budha is addressed as Sacya and Thacur. Amaracosha, the philologist and supposed author of this inscription, has eighteen names for Budha: Muni, Sastri, Dherma Raja, Sacya, Sinha, Sandhodana, &c.—Moor's Hindoo Pantheon, 234.

At this period we are informed, he preached to the gods and devils, driving those of the latter who were still obdurate out of the island.

At the expiration of five years spent in his native land of Dambadiva, (the modern Berar,) he again visited the garden of the east. On this occasion he acted the part of mediator between two rival princes who had deluged the country with blood in the course of their contentions. Great numbers were converted to his tenets on both occasions.

A third and last time he visited it, three years after the former, at the request of one of the native princes, an evident proof that his doctrines were fast gaining ground on the minds of the people. On this occasion, he is said to have left the mark of his foot on the mountain called Adam's Peak, an object of peculiar sanctity amongst his followers *. During these three visits, he had sat upon,

* This "faint exaggeration of a footstep" has been claimed by all the various inhabitants of Ceylon as a memorial intrinsically belonging to their own religion. Thus, the Buddhists call it the impression of Buddha's foot, the Moors or Mohammedans claim it for Adam, (stating that it was worn into the rock by the long-enduring penance of our great progenitor, who remained standing there on one foot for many years,) whilst the Malabars assert that Siva planted the footstep.

"This venerated memorial is five feet seven inches in length, two feet seven inches in breadth, and the very slight resemblance which it has to the shape of a foot is given by a margin of plaster coloured to resemble the rock; it is upon this moulding that the metal case which we had seen at Palabadoolla is fitted, before the usual time when pilgrims are expected to arrive. A temple built of wood surmounts the rock, and is retained in its elevated position by many strong iron chains fastened to the stone, and also to the trees which grow on the steep sides of the cone." Forbes' Ceylon, vol. 1, ch. 8.

The inhabitants of Mexico exhibit "an immense block of porphyry, call-

and thereby hallowed, sixteen places in Ceylon *, on all of which some remarkable structure was afterwards erected.

Shortly before Buddha's death, Singhabahu, famed for having been descended from a lion, (whence his descendants obtained the patronymic of Singha,) had obtained the throne of the modern Bengal, then designated Wango. The eldest of his two sons, Wijeya, became a lawless character, and, attended by a train of followers as reckless as himself, committed numerous deeds of violence and wickedness. The people, wearied at length by his repeated misdeeds, loudly clamoured for justice, and Singhabahu, willing to save his life, and yet afraid to oppose his subjects, sent him away with seven hundred followers to seek his fortune on the sea.

Having unsuccessfully attempted a landing on the coast he proceeded to Ceylon, and landed in a district subsequently called Tampabansir, near the modern town of Putlam.

This event is stated by the Ceylonese historians to have occurred in the same year as the death of Gotam, (B. C. 543,) but there is sufficient reason for supposing that the one is antedated, and the other postdated, in order to make an unnecessary coincidence †.

ed 'Piedra del Monarcha,'" which they affirm to have been indented by Montezuma's foot from extreme pressure, after severe fatigue. This stone, like the summit of Adam's Peak, has a natural indentation, "somewhat resembling the print of a naked foot."—Lyon's "Republic of Mexico," vol. 1, p. 284.

* Raja Ratnacari, chap. 1, sec. 4.

† This appears from the fact of every other Buddhist nation assigning a date previous to 1000 B. C. for the death of Gotamo, except Ceylon, Professor Wilson in the Oriental Magazine for 1825, quotes eleven authorities, every one of which makes the era of Buddha more than 1000 B. C.,

On his arrival in the island, Wijeya conducted himself with moderation and craftiness. He formed an alliance with a native princess named Kuwani, and by this means insinuated himself into the favour of the reigning sovereigns or petty governors. He was not long, however, in unmasking his designs, and his wife was not averse to aid him in their execution. By her influence he and his followers were introduced, (probably disguised,) to the marriage feast of one of the superior chiefs of the island, and in the midst of the revels, rising upon their entertainers, unsuspicious, as they were, of danger or treachery, Wijeya and his band succeeded in ridding themselves of those who could alone oppose his projects.

The authority of the invader gradually spread throughout the island, and in a short time it was recognised over all the inhabited part of the country.

But the infamous Kuwani was not long allowed to reap the fruits of her perfidy in peace. Wijeya soon became disgusted with her, and, having resolved on obtaining a more noble consort, dispatched an embassy to the king of Pandi *, requesting his daughter in marriage. The embassy was successful, Kuwani was repudiated, and, with a large train of female attendants, the princess arrived upon the island. An effort was made by the rejected queen to revenge her disgrace, but it was totally unsuccessful, and ended in her death.

In the district where Wijeya had first landed, he found-

the earliest being 1336, and the latest 1027. Most of these accounts agree in fixing it at about 1085 B. C.

* Pandi was composed of the southern provinces of the Peninsula of India; of which Madura was the capital. Turnour's Epitome of Ceylonese History.

ed a city called Tamana *, doubtless intending it to be the capital of his successors. In this, however, he was disappointed; for, on his death, which took place after a long and prosperous reign of thirty-eight years, dying childless, his prime minister Upatissa, having ascended the throne temporarily, removed the seat of government to a city founded by himself, and called after his own name.

Shortly before his death, Wijeya, perceiving that the fair kingdom which he had so unjustly obtained was about to depart from his house, had sent an embassy to his father, requesting his younger brother to be sent as his successor. In the meantime, however, Singhabahu had died and left his throne and kingdom to his second son Sumitto, who, willing to preserve the possession of Ceylon in his own family, sent his youngest son, Panduwasa, to assume its crown.

On the arrival of Panduwasa, Upatisso surrendered to him the sovereignty, having possessed it but for a single year.

Like his uncle Wijeya, he sent to the continent for a consort, and obtained a cousin of Gautama Buddha for his wife. She, accompanied by thirty-two attendants and six brothers, arrived in Ceylon, and was immediately raised to the throne. The six brothers dispersed themselves over the island, and founded principalities, some of which afterwards, on numerous occasions, attempted to shake off the yoke of the descendants of Panduwasa.

The chief of the cities which were founded by these brothers, and those to which we shall afterwards have

* The ruins of this very ancient city have been discovered and described by that indefatigable labourer in the field of Ceylonese literature,—Mr S. Casie Chitty. *Vide* Journal of the Royal Asiatic Society for May 1841.

most frequently to refer, were Rohona, by a prince of the same name, a city and district which afterwards became the fertile source of tumults and seditions; Anuradhapoora, founded by Anuradha, afterwards the capital; and Wijittapoora, founded by Wijitta, celebrated for the siege it underwent during the wars of Elala and Dutugaimono, in the second century before Christ *.

During this reign a large tank and palace are said to have been constructed at Anuradhapoora, the former being the first of those remarkable structures mentioned in the Singhalese annals.

Panduwasa, after a prosperous reign of thirty years, died in peace, 474 B. C., leaving ten sons and one daughter, the eldest of the former, Abhayo, succeeding to the government.

Abhayo's reign was disturbed by the jealousy of his brothers, and by the ambition and rebellion of his nephew, Pandukabhayo, the son of Panduwasa's daughter, Unmansit. Certain Brahmins having prophesied that the son of this princess should destroy his uncles and dethrone the king, his brothers wished her to be put to death. This, however, Abhayo refused, but consented to have her confined alone to prevent the prediction from being fulfilled. The old proverb respecting love and locks was in this case verified. A nephew of Panduwasa having seen the princess, who is represented as having been exquisitely beautiful, found means to carry on a correspondence with her, which, being intimated to the king and his brothers, they consented to the marriage, resolving that should the

* Mahawanso, chap. ix. Rajawalli, part i. p. 178. Mr Upham's Translation.

offspring prove a son it should be immediately put to death. Unmansit (also called Chitta, and Unmada Chitta,) found means to deceive them; and, having obtained a female infant lately born, by the substitution saved the life of her son Pandukabhayo.

The brothers of the reigning monarch having at length heard of the deception, used their utmost endeavours to put the dreaded youth to death, but, failing, they doubtless brought about by their hatred the fulfilment of the prophecy which they feared.

Pandukabhayo was taken under the protection of a wealthy Brahmin named Pandulo, and, being supplied with the "sinews of war" by him, levied an army and entrenched himself in some fastnesses near the Mahawelligama river.

From this position his uncles, the generals of Abhayo's army, were unable to dislodge him, and he remained here, in consequence, seemingly content with that partial success, for four years. At the end of that period his opponents endeavoured to anticipate and prevent his future advance, by erecting a fortification on the Dhumarrakho mountain, (probably the present Dumbara peak, near Kandy.) This proceeding seems to have irritated the pretender to the throne more than their former attacks. He immediately left his entrenchments, marched towards those of the adversary, and, after a short conflict, succeeded in carrying them, obliging the royal army to recross the river with precipitation.

A singular apathy seems to have possessed Pandukabhayo immediately after his successes. Instead of marching direct upon the capital he remained in the fortifications, which he had just taken, for two years, wasting that period in idleness, which, had he acted with decision, would have sufficed to gain him the sovereignty.

In the meantime Abhayo, fearing the result of the conflict, sent a secret embassy to him, proposing that he should reign over that part of the kingdom which he already possessed, and that thus a partition of the island should be made into two sovereignties. Of the answer of Pandukabhayo to this proposal we are not informed, but, from the rage of his uncles when they heard of the proposal, we may conclude that it was likely to prove favourable. They, more offended perhaps that the embassy had been sent *without their approval*, than that it *was* sent, revenged the neglect of Abhayo by dethroning him and conferring the sovereignty on their brother Tisso.

Tisso's advancement to the government, however, was but the prelude to his dethronement. Pandukabhayo once more took active measures to bring about the desired consummation, and, being assisted by the aborigines or yakkhos, at length succeeded in utterly destroying the army of his uncles, and in putting eight of the most violent of them to death. Thus, after a long and tedious struggle of seventeen years, he at length ascended that throne which had, during all that period, been the object of his aspirations, B. C. 437.

It has been before noticed that the town of Anuradhapoora, at this time an inconsiderable village, had been founded by one of the brothers-in-law of Panduwasa; hither the new monarch removed the seat of government from Upatissa, and, by his improvements and exertions, made it a capital not unworthy of the rich and beautiful Lanka.

Nor was Pandukabhayo unmindful of those by whose

assistance he had been enabled to reach the elevation which he desired. Chando, a son of the rich Brahmin who formerly supplied him with money and troops, he raised to the rank of a chief minister; his uncle Abhayo, to whom he was indebted for life and protection, he appointed to the sovereignty of the capital, a step equally judicious and politic; for, whilst it gave him an employment of honour and emolument, it, at the same time, kept him continually under the eye of the monarch; the Yakkhos, who had befriended him in his struggle for the throne, he supported in dignity and honour from the public revenues, and thus, by granting his favour to all who deserved it, he established more firmly his own dominion and made his person an object of attachment to all.

The improvements and exertions of the king were not, however, confined to selfish motives. He constructed these large and capacious tanks, the Jaya, Abhaya, and Gamim tanks—structures of the first utility in a tropical country like Ceylon. The embellishment and civic jurisdiction of his capital seem to have occupied much of his attention; he appointed five hundred people of the lower classes to attend to the cleanliness of the city; two hundred others took charge of it at night, whilst one hundred and fifty others superintended the burial of the dead and their removal from the city to the cemetery which his foresight had provided for their interment. He caused "the whole island to be divided into villages, fields and gardens, and caused the lake Bengaw Waiwa to be inclosed *. This lake, the Singhalese history called Rajawali informs us, was eighteen leagues in length, and that along the sides of it he caused stone pillars to be set up,

* Raja Ratnacari, chap. ii. p. 29.

which pillars were engraven with the figures of lions * (the animal, from which, as we formerly noticed, the royal race was fabled to have been descended.)

These are the scanty accounts which the native annals afford us of this eventful and highly important reign, one which must have left its effects, from the improvements made, to the most distant period; and one distinguished as well by its extraordinary length, as by its peace, happiness, prosperity and renown.

Respecting the successor of Pandukabhayo there is some slight confusion. In most of the native chronicles, that king is represented as having associated his son Ganatissa with himself in the government; but it would seem more probable that Ganatissa succeeded his father, and, as the Rajawali asserts, reigned for thirteen years, being succeeded by his son Mutasēwo, who, however, is generally represented as the son and successor of Pandukabhayo. This last assertion seems quite inconsistent with the accounts which we have received of the length of their respective reigns. Pandukabhayo is stated to have reigned seventy years, whilst his son Mutasēwo succeeds and reigns sixty years, a period of time quite inconsistent with the ordinary duration of human life. By interposing the reign of Ganatissa, the difficulty, if not removed, is at least greatly diminished.

Of the reign of Ganatissa we are left altogether ignorant, and in that of his successor, Mutasēwo, nothing is mentioned, save that he constructed a royal garden, named Mahamego, so called from a very heavy shower of rain which occurred at the period when it was being laid out. This garden was provided with all kinds of fruit and flower,

* Part 1, p. 182.

bearing trees in the utmost profusion. Although we are thus left in ignorance of the actions of Mutasēwo, we may reasonably conclude, that the energetic and excellent reign of Pandukabhayo would cause his immediate successors to reign in happiness and peace over prosperous subjects, and this may account for the silence of the native chronicles respecting the reigns of his son and grandson.

Mutasēwo left ten sons and two daughters, of whom Tisso was chosen as the most worthy to succeed him. He is represented as an exceedingly pious prince, and, on this account, was surnamed Devananpiatisso, that is, Tisso the delight of the devos *. On his succession to the throne, many wonderful miracles are related to have occurred, such as, that the precious gems and stones formerly buried in the earth rose to the surface by their own energy; treasures also rose from the ocean and cast themselves on the shores of Lanka, on account of the piety of its monarch; bamboos reared themselves from the earth bearing gems, precious metals, and flowers of the richest and most delightful hues; with a host of other wonders equally extraordinary and equally true.

What was the state of religion in Ceylon at this period we cannot positively state; but as we know Wijeya to have been a relation of Gautama Buddha, we cannot suppose that he would have been ignorant of the Buddhist faith; nor is it consistent with the general practice of human nature to imagine, that he would have neglected to inculcate such a religion on his followers, when he was aware how much credit it reflected on himself. On these accounts, as well as from the favourable reception which

* The devos are the heavenly spirits or angels of Buddhism.

the author of that religion met with himself, when he visited Ceylon, it seems erroneous to state that Buddhism was first introduced during the reign of Tisso. Such, however, is the general assertion of European writers on the subject.

The religion of the aborigines of the country, (doubtless the ancestors of the present Veddahs,) seems to have been a superstition of the most low and debasing kind, consisting merely of propitiating rights offered to evil demons, and of the worship of serpents. However revolting, or however absurd a religion may be, yet the history of the world assures us, that it will never want professors and apologists; and thus the fact, that such a religion did prevail after Buddha's death in this island, is very far from being a proof that the great majority of its inhabitants did not profess that of the Indian saint. The very fact of Buddha's invitations to the island, of the reverence with which he was treated, and of the honour paid to the relics which he left *, shews us that his religion had taken a deep hold on the minds of the native chiefs and their subjects even at that early period.

Considering it then as altogether improbable that the mission which came from India during Tisso's reign had for its object the promulgation of Buddhism for the first time in Ceylon, we must suppose that, although Buddhism existed previously in the island, yet that it was in such a corrupt and unsystematic form, as to render its establishment on a proper footing expedient and necessary.

Tisso, being an intimate friend of Dammasoko, king of Dambadiva or Maghada, sent to him a valuable present

* The dāgobah of Kalany, situated four miles from Colombo, was erected by the Yakkhos to enshrine a throne on which Buddhas himself had sat.

of gems and fruits, borne by four of the chief men of Ceylon, viz. Maha Aritto, as the chief of the mission, the Brahmin of the Hali mountain, Malla, the minister of state, and Tisso, the chief accountant. These embarking near the modern Jaffna, reached Dambadiva in seven days, and, proceeding directly towards the capital, presented the gifts to the king. Dhammasoko, desirous of reciprocating the friendship of Tisso, received his ambassadors with great honour, and sent them back, accompanied by ambassadors of his own, laden with gifts. An enumeration of the gifts which he sent, as related in the Mahawanso *, may not be uninteresting,—a diadem, sword of state, a royal parasol, golden slippers, an ornament for the head, a golden anointing vase, water taken from the sacred Ganges, asbestos towels, and many other articles of less note. The pious Dhammasoko accompanied his costly presents with an advice to Tisso "to take refuge in Buddho, his religion and his priesthood." The king of Dambadiva did not content himself, however, with merely sending such a message to his contemporary. He had, at this period, a son named Mahindo, a prince of great piety and virtue, and a priest of Buddho; he, sent forth by his father, departed to the favoured Lanka, to establish there, on a permanent and firm footing, the religion to which he had devoted his life.

His reception by Tisso was, in the highest degree, encouraging. That king not only treated him with kindness and respect, but also complied with all his requests, and gave him the most convenient places in which he could preach. But the chronicles of Buddhism are not

* Chap. xi. Mr Turnour's Translation.

content with merely giving to its apostle every opportunity and convenience in preaching its gospel; they also ascribe to him the power of working miracles, such as flying through the air, finding out by instinct the places hallowed by the presence of the Buddhos, making the earth quake, and such like. He at length established himself in the pleasure garden (Mahamego) constructed by Tisso's father, and there, to vast multitudes of hearers, he propounded the doctrines of Buddho, ordained priests, and established ceremonies.

It is not to be supposed that the female sex would have been behind the other in enthusiasm at such a time.

They came in crowds to hear the divine messenger, and, headed by the king's sister-in-law, they demanded to be made priestesses of the faith of Buddho. Mahindo professed himself unable to comply with their demand; at the same time informing them that, in the capital of his father's kingdom, there was a celebrated priestess, named Sanghamittha, who was also his sister. Her, he added, they might induce to come, by an embassy despatched for that purpose. Aritto, the minister of Tisso, was, in consequence, a second time despatched to Dambadiva, and having communicated to the priestess the wish of Mahindo, awaited her resolution. She immediately repeated the message of her brother's ambassador to the king, and he, deeply lamenting the loss of his son, would have dissuaded her, with parental tenderness, from the enterprise. His words on the occasion were affecting. "Honoured priestess and daughter," said he, "bereft of thee, and separated from my children and grandchildren, what consolation will be left wherewith to alleviate my profound affliction." Sanghamittha's devotion to her religion was, however, greater than her affection for her aged parent. She represented to him the necessity there was for obeying her brother's injunctions, the good that might be done, and the injury which might be inflicted on their religion by her refusal. With a heavy heart the monarch resigned his daughter, and she, taking with her a branch of the trees which was sacred to Buddha *, proceeded to Ceylon. This branch which accompanied her was a gift of the very highest importance; it was placed in a vessel highly ornamented for the purpose, and numberless miracles, which occurred on its passage, attested the divine protection. The vessel bearing it, we are informed, skimmed briskly over the water by the power of its protector; for nearly twenty miles on every side the water was hushed to stillness; flowers were scattered on its path in rich profusion, whilst the enchanting melodies of heavenly and seraphic music wafted the sacred vessel on its course.

Such is the picture Buddhists hand down to us of the removal of a branch of their deity's sacred tree from the Ganges to Lanka. Nor was its reception in Ceylon less honoured or less miraculous. With all the magnificence and ceremony which the magnificent and ceremonious Tisso could exhibit, the sacred branch was conveyed from the sea-shore to Anuradhapoora, whilst Sanghamittha, its bearer, (we are left to suppose,) merely mingled with the crowd, all their attention and all their thoughts being occupied with the hallowed relic.

The ceremonies and offerings being concluded, Sanghamittha entered upon the office of ordaining and convert-

* The bo-tree. Each Buddho attained the heavenly state whilst reposing under a tree which afterwards became sacred to him. That of Gotamo was the one mentioned.

ing with zeal and success. Numbers of devoted females, headed by the queen, presented themselves as candidates for the female priesthood. Nunneries were established, and, at length, Sanghamittha, satisfied with the amount of her labours and their effects, retired to spend the remainder of her life in seclusion and retirement, devoting herself to the exercise of her religious duties.

Thus, by the united exertions of Mahindo and his sister was Buddhism firmly rooted in Ceylon, and, as a plant in a congenial soil, flourished luxuriantly. Dāgobahs and wihares * were erected; rock temples and priest's chambers overspread the island, and every means were taken to root the religion of Buddho fast and deeply in Ceylon.

The chief of the religious structures erected during Tisso's reign were Toeparamaya dāgobah, sixty-eight rock temples, with thirty-two priest's chambers, on a mountain called Mihintallai, the Maha wihare (or great temple,) the Issaramooni wihare, the Saila-chetiya dāgobah, and the Tisso-ramaya dāgobah and wihare, besides a large tank or reservoir named Tisso-wewa—structures, the remains of which assure us that Ceylon was at this early period arrived at no inconsiderable degree of civilisation and refinement.

The remaining events in the reign of Tisso are few and unimportant. Anula, his queen, dreading lest the king's brother, Mahanaya, would usurp the kingdom on his death, to the exclusion of her infant son, attempted to poison him, by sending a present of a poisoned fruit. Tisso's son was, at the period, residing with his uncle, and being

* Both of these are religious structures, the former, however, being built merely to enshrine a relic, the latter being a place of worship, containing idols, &c.

by him unwittingly offered the intended instrument of his own death, the youth ate it and died. Mahanaga, fearing the resentment of the Royal Family, fled to the wild southern division of the island, called Rohona, and there founded a subordinate principality, called Magama, carrying with him, at the same time, a firm reliance on the religion of Buddho.

In this reign also an encroachment of the sea is recorded, on the western coast, which submerged nearly fifty miles of country in a direct line east and west, inundating upwards of nine hundred villages of fishermen, and four hundred belonging to the pearl-divers. Such a subsidence of the land cannot surely be considered as entirely imaginary, however we may suppose that it is exaggerated; and the numerous inundations which the Singhalese annals and traditions relate will easily account for the apparently absurd statements of its size at more remote periods.

CHAPTER II.

Utteya—Deaths of Mahindo and Sanghamittha—Mahasēwo—Suratisso—Rebellion of Sena and Gutika—Aséla—Invasion of Elala—Birth and youth of Gaimono—His war with Elala—He obtains the sovereignty—His religious erections—His celebrity and death—Sali's romantic love—Saidatisso—Toohl and Laiminitisso—Kaluna—Walagambahu—Invasion of the Malabars—Rebellion of the prince of Rohona—Walagambahu flies—is restored—The doctrines of Buddhism committed to writing—Mahachula—Chora Naga and his wickedness.

Before investigating the state of Ceylon during the period whose history we have just related, it will, perhaps, be better to carry that history down to the Christian era, and then, reviewing it under the Singha race, observe the evidences these exhibited respecting its civilisation, manners, religion and government. The pious and devoted Tisso was, after a prosperous reign of forty years, succeeded by his brother, Utteya, (B. C. 266.) As the Buddhist historians of this early period filled the account of Tisso's reign with the acts and sayings of Mahindo, so, during that of his successor, little else is recorded than that in the eighth year of it the great Mahindo died, "a luminary," as one account states, "like unto the divine teacher (Gautama) himself, in dispersing the darkness of sin in Lanka."

The description of his funeral solemnities is, like every other event connected with him, described with much circumstantiality. The king, overpowered with grief, had the body embalmed in scented oil; it was then placed in a golden coffin, filled with exquisite perfumes; this coffin was again encased in one of sandal wood. Having been then placed on a gorgeous hearse, it was borne, accompanied by an immense procession, through the streets of Anuradhapoora in silence and grandeur, until, finally, having reached the Mahawihare, it was there deposited, and, amidst the tears of a whole nation, the funeral pile was lighted by the king himself.

Mahindo was followed in the ninth year of Utteya's reign by his sister, Sanghamittha, who, in the enjoyment of a good old age, "was taken by the Lord, whom she had imitated, to exchange an earthly priesthood for a heavenly paradise *."

No one, who regards for a moment the lives of Mahindo and Sanghamittha, can possibly doubt their extreme devotion to the principles which they had embraced. The one resigned a kingdom for a priesthood, the other left friends, relatives, wealth and comfort, to propagate her opinions in a foreign land with which she was otherwise unconnected. Nor do we find, in the characters of these amiable enthusiasts, any thing of that overbearing priestly pride, so common to those who imagine themselves the bestowers of heaven upon their unworthy fellow-mortals; they assumed neither the political influence of a Wolsey, nor the insolent haughtiness of a Thomas a-Becket.

Mahindo continued to act as he had done at first; that is, went about preaching the mild tenets of Buddhism, and doing good of no despicable character, in establishing

* Absorption into the divine principle of all things appears to be the paradise of Buddhism. From its extreme mysticism, and from the ambiguous terms in which it is frequently described, many have been led to believe that it is a mere nonentity.

these tenets where beastly ignorance, and the most grovelling superstition had before reigned. Sanghamittha, on the other hand, when she had fulfilled the object of her mission, by ordaining the numerous band of females who offered themselves as candidates for the priesthood, retreated, as befitted her sex and character, to a retired station, where, in the practice of the precepts which her brother preached, she presided over a convent of female devotees, who, like herself, had abjured the world, its vanities and sins.

There is something surpassingly engaging in this amiable picture of a brother and sister (and these, too, the son and daughter of a powerful monarch,) leaving their native land to propagate what they believed to be the truth amongst a foreign people, and there devoting their lives, their energies and their talents, to win this nation from the paths of error into the ways of truth.

Utteya reigned ten years, during which nothing is recorded but the death of the apostles of Dambadivà. The Mahawanso has a curious reflection on his death, which is perhaps worthy of our notice. The purport of it is, that if man would but reflect on the "irresistible, relentless, and all-powerful nature of death," instead of sighing on earth for a hopeless immortality, he would, by contemplating his speedy end, be led into a virtuous line of life, and thus, that virtue upholding him, he would, in reality, obtain the only eternity allowed to him *.

Scanty as the record of Utteya's reign is, that of his successor, which also extended to ten years, is yet more brief. Mahasēwa, the younger brother of Utteya, ascended

* Chapter xx. Conclusion.

the throne 256 B.C. He erected a beautiful wihare in the eastern quarter of Anuradhapoora, which rivalled, as the historian informs us, the queen of beauty (Angana) herself. Suratisso his successor, a prince eminent for his piety, erected numerous temples in the provinces, but committed a fatal error in taking into his service two Malabar chiefs named Sena and Gutika. These princes were at the head of a body of mercenary cavalry, which Suratisso took into his service in a period of profound peace. What his object might have been in this step we cannot determine; but whether he was actuated by a desire to keep in awe the tributary chiefs, or merely instigated by a principle of foolish and extravagant pride, we know that the step was the cause of great evil and bloodshed,—immediately, by the murder of Suratisso himself by the two adventurers, and remotely, it is probable, by creating in the Malabars a desire of obtaining settlements in the rich and beautiful Lanka. That this desire was the pernicious source of innumerable evils, and of much bloodshed, the subsequent history will most abundantly prove.

Not a syllable is recorded respecting the reign of Sena and Gutika, which was prolonged to twenty-two years, save that, with extraordinary good fortune, they maintained peace between themselves; and although they had obtained the crown by injustice and murder, yet their succeeding acts were those of just and excellent princes.

Having for that long period enjoyed a peaceful throne, the two princes were at length dethroned and put to death by a member of the royal family named Aséla.

In the meantime the evil effects of Suratissa's ill-advised measure became apparent. Elala, a Malabar prince, who came from the kingdom of Sollee, on the

Coromandel coast, having, we may suppose, heard of the success of Sena and Gutika, resolved to try his fortune in the same field. Having arrived, with a great army, at the mouth of the Mahavelli-ganga river, he there landed his troops, and marched directly upon the capital. There he was met by Aséla, who, without success, disputed his entrance. Elala was victorious; and, having ascended the throne, found little difficulty in getting his authority acknowledged by the native chiefs. Respecting the reign of Elala two very opposite accounts have reached us: The one representing him as an impious monster, who destroyed, without remorse, the temples erected by his predecessors, and who reigned in injustice and cruelty *: The other admitting, indeed, that he destroyed many temples, and that he was not a follower of Buddhu, but still claiming for him the character of a good and just prince who administered the laws with impartiality and justice †. Perhaps these conflicting accounts will not surprise us so much, when we recollect, that, with the historians who present to us the dark character of Elala, to be a heretic and a monster of iniquity were inseparable characters. In his reign it came to pass, says one historian, that the holy and beautiful city of Anuradhapoora became a sepulchre filled with filth and corruption. The holy temples were not only overthrown, but were also made seats of defilement and profanation; the images of Buddha were destroyed; and the wicked savages resembled ravenous wild beasts more than men. Another account states that he kept his army to destroy the

* Raja Ratnacari, chap. ii. p. 37. Rajawali, part ii. p. 188, Upham's Translation.

† Mahawanso, chap. xxi.—Mr Turnour's Translation.

temples and dāgobahs, and concludes with the pithy sentence, that he reigned wickedly for the space of forty-four years. On the other side, the more liberal Mahawanso, although it censures severely his enmity to Buddhism, styles him a friend to justice, and states that he administered equity with impartiality to friends and foes.

Elala, however, although nominally sovereign of Ceylon, was, in reality, but the governor of a part. The southern division, called Rohona, was still governed by a branch of the Royal Family.

We have before mentioned that the consort of Tisso, fearing lest (on that monarch's death) his brother should ascend the throne, to the exclusion of her son, had attempted to poison him, and that, in consequence, he had fled to Rohona. There he governed as a tributary prince, and was succeeded by his son, whilst Tisso was still reigning over the kingdom. The successor of that son, Kakawanatisso, had two sons, Gaimono and Tisso, the former of whom was an energetic warlike character, who, regarding the usurpation of Elala with envy and detestation, resolved to try the event of a contest, and either perish himself or establish the lawful dynasty. The manner in which he collected his army is curious enough, in that it so closely resembles the account given by Xenophon of the enrolment of Cyrus' army, when he went to succour his uncle Cyaxares *. In the first place

* Οὕτω δὴ δεξαμένου τοῦ Κύρου, οἱ βουλεύοντες γεραίτεροι αἱροῦνται αὐτὸν (Κῦρον) ἄρχοντα τῆς εἰς Μήδους στρατείας. Ἔδοσαν δὲ αὐτῷ διακοσίους τῶν ὁμοτίμων προσελέσθαι· τῶν δ' αὖ διακοσίων ἑκάστῳ, τέτταρας ἄνδρας ἐκ τῶν ὁμοίων ἔδοσαν προσελέσθαι· γίγνονται μὲν δὴ οὗτοι χίλιοι· τῶν δ' αὖ χιλίων τούτων ἔδοσαν προσελέσθαι ἑκάστῳ ἐκ τοῦ δήμου τῶν Περσῶν, δέκα μὲν πελταστὰς, δέκα δὲ σφενδονήτας, δέκα δὲ τοξότας, &c. Cyropædia, 1. v. 5.

he associated with himself ten warriors of celebrity and confirmed excellence: each of these was then ordered to enlist ten men. The hundred which were thus chosen in like manner enlisted each ten others, and similarly each of the thousand having chosen other ten, thus formed an army of ten thousand men. With these the impatient Gaimono would have at once proceeded against the enemy, but was dissuaded for a short time by his father, who feared the issue of a contest with a warrior so renowned as Elala.

The impatience of Gaimono, however, could not be long restrained by the timid counsels of his parent. Having sent three distinct embassies to his father, desiring that the army might be allowed to proceed, and each message having been met with a firm denial, enraged at the timidity of his parent he at length sent to him some female ornaments, desiring that he would assume with them the garments most suited to his character. The king, enraged at his insolence, threatened revenge, but was disappointed by the flight of his son, who, having heard of his intentions, fled to Kotta, the present Kotale, in the mountainous district of the island, and, from this act of disobedience, obtained the prefix of Dutu, "the disobedient." He had not been long there before he heard of his father's death, upon which he immediately left his mountainous retreat and advanced to Māgam, the capital of Rohona. Whilst there, intelligence was conveyed to him, to the effect that his brother Tisso had assumed the sovereignty at Dighawapi, the modern Dhigawewa, in the Batticuloa district. Gaimono was not a prince who would allow his rights to be infringed with impunity. He marched with promptitude against the usurper with what troops he could hastily collect, and defeated him in a bloody and well-contested battle. A second battle, in which a personal conflict between the two brothers is described with the usual exaggerations, had the same issue, and Tisso, perceiving the futility of his designs, was, by the intercession of the priests, reconciled to the conqueror.

It has been formerly mentioned, that, on Gaimono's first entertaining the idea of disputing with Elala the sovereignty of the whole island, he had associated with himself ten celebrated warriors of acknowledged excellence and bravery. These, however, were not associated with him in the contest with his brother; for before his father's death, that prince, who had probably foreseen the contest which would arise between his sons, had, with politic prudence, obtained from the ten leaders a solemn promise that they would not aid either of his sons in opposing the other. This promise they had religiously kept; and, now that they perceived the renewal of peace, they at once offered their services to Gaimono against whatsoever enemy he pleased.

The enterprising monarch finally determined to put his long-intended scheme in execution; and, having reviewed his forces, which consisted, we are informed, of riders on elephants, riders on chariots, riders on horses and infantry, he went forth to war. The river Mahavelli-ganga having been crossed, and some inconsiderable generals of Elala having been overcome, his further progress was stopped by a fort called Wijittapoora, which was strongly fortified and no less strongly manned. This town we have formerly noticed as having been founded by Wijitta, the brother-in-law of Panduwasa, three hundred years before.

The siege of Wijittapoora is variously represented as

having occupied six and four months, although the former is the more probable period. It was protected by three lines of lofty battlements and iron gates, a circumstance which shews us the advancement of the military art in Ceylon even at that early period. At length a general assault was determined on, and the four chief gates of the fort were simultaneously attacked by various divisions of Gaimono's army. The outer fortifications were forced, but the immense and ponderous iron gate which guarded the inward passage resisted, for a long period, the utmost efforts of the invaders. An enormous elephant, trained from an early period to war, and which had the honour of bearing the monarch himself, rushed forward against the gate with the utmost fury, but was repelled by showers of molten lead and huge stones hurled on him by the besieged. The furious animal became ungovernable with pain, and rushed for protection into a neighbouring tank. The smarting pain of the wounds, however, was assuaged, and, a covering having been made for him of buffaloes' hides, he once more advanced to the attack, and with irresistible violence rushed against the gate, and dashed it open. In the mean time the others had not been idle; a breach was made in the walls, and entering the city sword in hand, the unbelieving Malabars were cut to pieces.

Several places of inferior note yielded in a short time to the prowess of the army of Gaimono. Girilako was taken and destroyed—Casaw Totta was taken after a siege of two months and Mahaw-wetta after four months. Mahelo, a fortification near the capital itself, was next invested, and, after four months spent in fruitless assaults, it was at length taken by stratagem.

The attack of Anuradhapoora seems to have been the

next object of Gaimono, and, in order to commence this with due precaution and circumspection, he commenced the erection of a fort or place of retreat on which he might fall back in case of repulse. Elala, however, who seems to have regarded, with supercilious contempt, the efforts of Gaimono, and to have imagined it an easy task for his generals to repel the youthful rebel, was at length obliged to regard the matter with more seriousness and respect. His generals were convened, an immediate attack determined upon, and the plan of the campaign sketched out by the over-confident monarch. He disdained, however, to attack his rival without giving him full intimation of his intention, and a messenger was accordingly despatched to him, desiring him to prepare for the encounter.

Gaimono, who had already raised a great part of the forts, hastened their erection, and soon saw himself surrounded by a fortification containing thirty-two distinct redoubts. In the mean time the army of Elala appeared advancing against the invaders: Gaimono, supported by the valiant Nando Mittrago (one of the celebrated ten) on the right, and by Nermalagaw on the left, advanced, leading on the centre of his army in person.

Elala, mounted on his elephant, and accompanied by his most renowned warrior, Digajantu, led on his army to the sound of innumerable trumpets. A fierce attack, headed by the warrior last named, was made upon the line of Gaimono, which received it no less fiercely. The obstinate valour of the Malabars, however, could not be withstood, and, step by step, the army of Gaimono retraced the way to the towers. There a stand was made which well nigh ended fatally for the prospects of the young aspirant. The headlong valour of Digajantu carried every thing before it. Redoubt after redoubt was occupied and lost, and, to all human appearance, the hopes of Gaimono were speedily to be overthrown. Such, however, was not the case. Suranimilo, one of the generals of the young prince, intercepted the course of the raging warrior, and, by a fortunate stroke, ended his success with his life. The contending armies, hearing of the event, were variously affected, the one with hope renewed, the other with terror and amazement. The precipitate valour of the Malabars was imitated by the Singhalese, and, headed by Suranimilo, they drove the invaders headlong from the fortification into the open plain; their retreat became a flight, and, but for the timely interference of Elala, all had been lost. Gaimono advanced to meet his rival and end the contest by single combat. Mounted on two equally renowned and famous elephants, the rival monarchs drew near to contest the sovereignty of the ocean's fairest island. Elala, seeing the youth approach, hurled his spear; Gaimono, by a dexterous movement, avoided it, and urging on his elephant with fury, the two noble animals engaged each other, and, in the struggle, that of Elala fell, and with it fell the dominion of the Malabars.

Without further opposition the victorious Gaimono entered Anuradhapoora, and once more established the Singha race, in his own person, on the Singhalese throne. In the midst of his rejoicings, however, Gaimono did not forget what was due to his brave opponent. With every ceremony which could add lustre to the circumstance, the body of Elala was burned on the spot where he had fallen, whilst a decree was made that royalty itself, in passing by the tomb, should silence its music and dismount,—honours which were most religiously observed up to the British occupation of the Kandian territories *. A monument and pillar erected by the fortunate conqueror further marked the spot where his rival fell. (B. C. 164.) Gaimono had not long enjoyed his new found kingdom ere another competitor appeared to dispute the prize. Balluko, variously reported as the brother and nephew of Elala, having been informed of the war which was waging in Ceylon, collected an army of 30,000 men † with all haste, and at once embarked for the scene of hostilities. Having landed at Matura, he marched directly towards the capital, hoping, doubtless, to find the victorious monarch inactive and rejoicing at his recent victory. In this, however, if such was his expectation, he was disappointed. Gaimono, with his elephants, cavalry, chariots and infantry, marched with equal expedition to arrest his progress; and, having taken up a favourable position directly in Balluko's line of march, there awaited his approach. The invader, rushing on with headlong impetuosity, fell in the first attack, and his army, thus deprived of its leader, became an easy prey to the doubly victorious Gaimono. Festivals, ceremonies and rejoicings were the natural followers of his success, and, amidst these, suitable rewards were not wanting for the brave partners of his dangers and triumphs. The restless mind of Gaimono, however, although the great object of his early ambition was attained, found not peace in inactivity. Like most other

* In 1818, Pilamé Talawé, the head of the oldest Kandian family, when attempting to escape, after the suppression of the rebellion in which he had been engaged, alighted from his litter, although weary and almost incapable of exertion; and, not knowing the precise spot, walked on, until assured that he had passed far beyond this ancient memorial.—Forbes, vol. i. p. 233.

† Rajawali.

celebrated characters, his happiness consisted not so much in reaching the goal the first, as in running the race, and, when the race in one place was concluded, it was but to commence it again elsewhere *.

He had now surpassed his predecessors in military fame and in doughty deeds of war; but he was not yet equal to the renowned Tisso in piety. His next pursuit was, therefore, to rival him in the more peaceful, but not less difficult task of signalising himself as a Buddhist king. Besides the ambition which hurried on Gaimono to signalise himself by the erection of numerous religious edifices, another, and (if possible) a more selfish motive, had at least equal influence with him. This was his anxiety respecting his welfare in another world; for, when reflecting on the innumerable lives which had been sacrificed in his wars, he became anxious lest the cause of this destruction would be deemed unworthy of future happiness. Influenced thus, the monarch applied all his resources and all his leisure to the erection of priests' houses, temples and pagodahs. The chief of these erections was the Marichawatti temple, including a temple proper, a residence for the officiating priests and a dāgobah enshrining a relic. The Ruanelli Saye, an enormous pile of massive masonry, was also erected by this persevering monarch. It was 270 feet in height, standing on a square mass of building 2000 feet in circumference, and containing numerous relics of the Indian saint. Gaimono, however, persevering as he was, was unable to finish this immense erection, and it was reserved for his successor to add the

* The three stages of Gaimono's life, his wars, his political projects, and his religion, afford us a practical illustration rarely met with of the sublime verse of Hesiod. *Εϱγα νεῶν, βουλαισι μέσων, ἰυχαισι γεϱόντων.*

spire. These works, massive as they were, were yet surpassed by another of still greater size, extent and magnificence; this was a place for the priests, called the Lowa Maha Paya, (the great brazen palace.) It was 120 cubits, or 270 feet square, and the same in height. The apartments were elevated on 1600 granite pillars, the remains of which attest to the present day, that here, at least, there has been no exaggeration. On these were erected nine stories, containing 900 apartments, the whole roofed with metal, whence the name (the brazen palace.) The interior of the building was magnificent in proportion to the extent of the exterior. A spacious hall occupied the centre, adorned with gilt statues of lions, and elephants, whilst, at one end, an ivory throne of beautiful workmanship was raised, on one side of which a golden emblem of the sun appeared, to which, on the other, a silver one of the moon, corresponded *.

The reflection which the religious Mahanāma (the author of the Mahawanso) makes, after describing these various erections, may well engage our attention. "Thus do the truly wise obtain for themselves imperishable and most profitable rewards from their otherwise perishable and useless wealth †."

The fame of Gaimono's exertions in the cause of religion spread far and wide. Numerous priests, renowned for their piety, came from the continent of India, to behold

* The account of this building given us in the Mahawanso is circumstantially confirmed by F. Hian, the Chinese traveller, who, visiting Ceylon in 412, A. D. had the best opportunities of viewing the structure, and had no temptation to exaggerate its greatness. See Notes on Ancient India by Col. Sykes, in the Journal of the Royal Asiatic Society for May 1841.

† Chap. xxvii.

the erections of the powerful monarch, and to enhance their sanctity by their own presence. This was precisely the object of that prince's wishes; and having thus been gratified in the two species of fame which most men desire, (military and religious,) he died a happy and satisfied king, in the twenty-fourth year of his reign, and the hundred and fortieth before the Christian era.

A minute account is handed down to us, in the native histories, of the last moments of Gaimono. Whilst stricken on what he perceived would be the bed of death, he had the record of his religious acts brought forth and read in his hearing, whilst ever and anon, as something of more than usual excellence was repeated, he stopped the relation to address the priests around him, and, having finally received an account of the heaven to which he should go, on separating from his mortal tenement, he expired in the pleasing hope of shortly seeing and reigning with the future Buddho Metteyo.

Thus died this persevering, indefatigable, energetic, warlike and religious prince, beloved by his people, honoured by his contemporaries, and extolled by posterity, as the deliverer of his country, the embellisher of Ceylon, and the prop and support of Buddhism itself. Nor was it without reason that Gaimono received these extraordinary honours. His life had indeed been one of uncontrolled selfishness and audacity *, at least entirely so in the subsequent part of his history; but, fortunately for his future character, that selfishness ran parallel with the interests

* Animus paratus ad periculum, si sua cupiditate, non utilitate communi impellitur, audaciæ potius nomen habeat, quam fortitudinis. Cic. Offic. I. 62.

of his country, and thus the motives of his actions were overlooked in their effects *.

The ambition of Gaimono did not descend to his son. That prince, Sali by name, having become deeply enamoured of a beautiful maiden of a low caste, preferred retaining her as his wife to ascending the throne. Such was the alternative, and Sali hesitated not to enjoy his love and violate his ambition, in consequence of which he was superseded by Saidatisso, his uncle, who assumed the government on the demise of Gaimono.

Saidatisso ascended a peaceful and well-established throne, and found, on his accession, no rival able or willing to oppose him. He carried out the religious designs of his predecessor, finished the imperfect temples, established others at regular distances from Anuradhapoora, and, in the practice of these and similar undertakings, passed a peaceful and prosperous reign of eighteen years.

The two sons of Saidatisso, Toohl or Thulathanako and Laiminitisso were at the period of his death in possession of principalities under their father. The younger son, Toohl, having been accidentally in Anuradhapoora, when Saidatisso died, at once assumed the sovereignty, and found his usurpation seconded by the priests. For the period of a year and a few days, the usurper found his authority recognised by the kingdom, but, at the ter-

* Some works of public utility, which, perhaps, it would be unfair not to mention, are also ascribed to Gaimono; such as hospitals well-appointed with physicians, medicines, and wholesome food; astronomers and priests to preside over various districts, and such like. These, however, are only mentioned in one of the native annals to which we have access, and as they are omitted in the Mahawanso, which gives a most minute account of his meritorious actions, they are, at least, suspicious.

mination of that brief period, an end was put both to his life and power by the treachery of his elder brother. Whilst inspecting the erection of a dāgobah in the vicinity of his capital, an assassin, hired by Laiminitisso, gave him a fatal blow, of which he soon after expired. The author of the murder immediately ascended his rightful throne, stained, however, with the blood of a slaughtered brother. This event, the murder of Toohl, was the cause of numerous evils in the subsequent history, inasmuch as the descendants of either brother frequently aspired to the throne, by following the example of Laiminitisso.

Laiminitisso and his successor Kaluna occupied their reigns, of nine and six years respectively, in adorning and enlarging the erections of Gaimono. Of the inferior princes, the royal family or the state of Ceylon during their reigns we have no information, and, save that Kaluna, having irritated his minister Maharantaka, was murdered by him, we are left in complete ignorance of the events of both these reigns.

The first act of Walagambahu, the successor of Kaluna, (who ascended the throne 104 B. C. and 439 after Buddha,) was one of justice. He had the murderer of Kaluna brought to trial for that offence and executed. The reign of Walagambahu was one of trouble and commotion. In the fifth month of it, (one account states the fifth year *,) a prince of Rohona, instigated by a prophecy, which stated that he should be a future king, took up arms against the reigning sovereign; and very shortly after, an army of Malabars from the Coromandel coast, headed by seven chieftains, landed in different parts of the island, and

* Raja Ratnacari.

having united their forces, also marched against Walagambahu. Thus threatened on both sides with destruction, the situation of the monarch seemed to be desperate. He acted, however, with prudence and circumspection. Apparently yielding to the Rohona chief, he gave that leader every mark of submission and respect, finally succeeding in urging him to march directly against the Malabars. This the Rohonian did, whilst Walagambahu made every exertion to attack the victor vigorously on the termination of the combat. The result of the struggle was what might have been expected; the well-disciplined army of the Malabars routed the new raised levies of their adversaries, taking the commander prisoner, and it was now Walagambahu's turn to face the powerful invaders.

The warlike talents of that monarch were, however, very inferior to his diplomatic abilities. In an engagement fought near Anuradhapoora, the wily king was, with ease, overcome by the well-trained Malabars, and he, flying precipitately before them, took refuge in a forest in the vicinity of the capital. The conquerors entered the city, and two of the chiefs, content with the plunder which they had obtained, returned to their native country, leaving the rest to fight for the sovereignty as they pleased.

When the conquering army was divided into five parts, each governed by a leader equal to the others, and entirely without control, it was not to be supposed that unanimity could long prevail. The first retained the sceptre for three years only, and was deposed and murdered by another who reigned two; and, in this manner, murders, depositions and usurpations succeeded each other with frightful rapidity. In this period of anarchy and confusion, which lasted for upwards of fourteen years, we are not informed of a single effort having been made by Walagambahu to presume his lawful seat, until that (at the end of that period) which was successful. Dathiyo, the last of the Malabar usurpers was, however, at length overthrown, and the weak hand of Walagambahu again seized that sceptre which he had been formerly obliged to relinquish so hastily.

The reign of which we are now treating is highly distinguished in the history of Buddhism, from its having been that in which the religious works of that system were first committed to writing. Previously to this period, the doctrines of that religion, its history and ordinances, had, in Ceylon, been orally transmitted from one generation to another. This, which was doubtless the cause of much interpolation, admixture and corruption, seems at length to have become so inconvenient, that the priests themselves found the necessity of committing the discourses of their saint to writing, and thus preventing further inconvenience. Five hundred of the most learned priests were assembled by the king at a cave (where he himself had passed part of his exile) in Mátalé *. There the Buddhist scriptures or Banapota, the discourses of Buddhu called Pitakattaya and their commentaries, the Atthakatha, were, in the Pali language, committed to writing, and formed the esoteric doctrine of the instructors of the Singhalese, a doctrine pure, patriarchal and religious, but very different from that attention to external ceremonies and unmeaning ordinances, which formed the bulk of their exoteric doctrine. This important event occurred 92 years B.C.

Walagambahu was not content with this piece of service

* This place was visited by Major Forbes, and is described in his work, vol. i. chap. 15.

to the religion which he had embraced. Like his eminent predecessors, Tisso and Gaimono, he resolved to leave erections behind him, which should commemorate his reign amongst future ages. The Abhayagiri dāgobah and temple which he erected in Anuradhapoora was one of the most extraordinary temples in that very extraordinary city. It was 180 cubits (405 feet) in height, and the length of the outer wall at the present day is one mile and three quarters. When we reflect on the massiveness of these buildings, their extraordinary height, and the immense mass of masonry which they contain, we must be blind indeed, if, regarding this, we measure the ancient power and population of the kingdom of Ceylon, by its present debility and desolation. The Abhayagiri temple, either from its size or sanctity, was peculiarly reverenced. It seems, indeed, from the frequent mention made of it in the succeeding history, to have become the chief resort and centre of the Buddhist priesthood.

How little the monarchs of Ceylon reflected on the labour or cost of their stupendous works is evident from the fact, that Walagambahu, on the occasion of recovering his queen, who had been carried away by one of the marauding Malabars, commemorated the event by erecting one of the largest dāgobahs in Anuradhapoora, the Suwana-ramaya. This building, which has not since been identified, was, we are informed, 140 cubits, or 315 feet in height.

The reign of Walagambahu, which, from the attention to architecture, and improvement exhibited in it, must have been prosperous and peaceful, lasted for twelve years, and, in a good old age, he left the throne to the son of his predecessor, and his own nephew, B.C. 77, and in the year of Buddhu 466.

The doctrines of Buddhism had now taken such a hold on the inhabitants of Ceylon, that every other consideration was neglected. The successor of Walagambahu, Mahachula, (properly Mahachulamahatisso,) having heard that the merit of offerings procured by personal labour was very far superior to that of offerings made from hereditary wealth, disguised himself in the character of a husbandman, and cultivated, with his own hands, a field of rice, of which he bestowed the produce on the priesthood. On another occasion, he waited, in the same way, on a sugar mill, for three years, offering, at the end of that period, the whole produce, as before.

However extravagant the encomiums which the Buddhist historians may lavish on such conduct, we may surely doubt, whether, under any circumstances, such proceedings could be really commendable, knowing, as we do, that the government of a kingdom is an employment, which least of all will brook intermission and neglect.

The reign of Mahachula, which extended to a period of fourteen years, was undistinguished by any thing save his extravagant piety, and by the contrast which it makes compared with that of his successor Chora Naga.

That prince, the son of Walagambahu, having been excluded from the throne on account of his wickedness, had spent the period of his predecessor's reign at the head of a lawless band, with which he committed numerous depredations, and now, finding the throne empty, seated himself on it in defiance of the people's wishes. The religion of Buddhu, which had been the rule of his predecessors, had no influence over Chora Naga. Eighteen temples were, by his orders, levelled with the dust; a melancholy example of the fickleness of that prosperity which depends on regal favour. It is not to be supposed that a character so wicked would be allowed to rest in peace by the bigotted historians of Buddhism. Not content with telling us, that, after a depraved reign of twelve years, he met with a merited death from the hands of his offended subjects, they pursue him beyond the grave, and assure us, that, in the depths of the lowest hell, he now receives the punishment due to his flagrant crimes, and that there he shall remain till the end of the world. Fifty years before our Saviour's birth occurred the murder of Chora Naga; and before proceeding farther in the history, it will perhaps be profitable for us to take a view of the state of Ceylon in that period whose history we have just related, observing, from the indications which we there meet, its civilisation, improvement and condition.

CHAPTER III.

STATE OF CEYLON BEFORE THE CHRISTIAN ERA.

Early Civilisation of the East—Developement of Civilisation different in the East and West—Castes introduced by Wijeya—Origin of Castes—Wijeya's Government—Remains of early Ceylonese Edifices—The Dăgobahs—Anuradhapoora—Excellent Carving.

As the East was the cradle of the human race, so in the East the arts of civilisation and refinement were first cultivated with success. Whether we ascribe to the early empires of India and China that excessive antiquity which the inhabitants of these countries claim for them, or not, yet we must allow that, long before Europe had shaken off the ignorance and degradation of barbarism, these nations were advanced much above mediocrity in the arts of refinement. When Greece was but the seat of rapine and savage life; when it was as yet but divided into a number of petty and independent states, too insignificant in themselves to attract the attention of other nations, and too barbarous to unite for common purposes, the empires of the East had, even then, attained a high degree of splendour and refinement, whilst some of them were already sinking in the debility of old age. Rome and Carthage were then unheard of places, whose very existence, as cities, had not commenced. Britain was either altogether uninhabited, or peopled by the most wretched and ignorant of the human family, whilst the north of Europe was a *terra incognita*, known only to the freezing blasts of heaven and their attendants, frost and snow.

At this early period, then, when Europe was thus involved in obscurity, man, under the more genial sun of India, had exhibited himself as a rational being, capable of mental exertion and of mental enjoyment. There the respective ranks and occupations of society were not only duly marked out, but separated by an insurmountable barrier from each other—the distinction of castes; a distinction, certainly, most impolitic and most paralyzing to improvement, but nevertheless a distinction which could nowhere exist but in a regular society, considerably advanced in civilisation and the arts. There also men were governed by established laws and a settled constitution,—laws so framed as to meet many of the contingencies which occur in civilised life alone, and which decided with equity their various litigations. The arts and sciences, those sure indications of a nation's advancement, were cultivated with a zeal and success which merits more praise from their followers than they have ever received. Not only, however, were the rougher and more substantial arts cultivated with success, but also the more refined and elegant sciences of poetry, logic, metaphysics, ethics and natural philosophy. These were advanced by the ancient Hindus to a degree which bespeaks, if not a very refined, at least an improved, and, to a certain degree, a civilised condition.

Civilisation, in a European mind, is so naturally connected with extensive commerce, vast manufactures and wonderful machines of various kinds, that, with these alone, such a mind imagines civilisation can exist. Europeans are, in this, however, totally deceived. In a country such as India, where nature almost spontaneously produces every requisite of wealth and luxury, what need is there (might not the Indian argue) of building vast ships and undertaking perilous voyages, to bring those things which we do not require, and to exchange our superior productions for the inferior or useless ones of other countries? Or, again, why spend our wealth and strength in manufacturing those things of which we feel not the want, and know not, till taught, the use? Thus we see that the development of civilisation is essentially various in different situations. That which marks refinement in the coldness of Europe, may be but an useless encumbrance or uncomfortable appendage in Hindostan, whilst, on the other hand, the luxury of the latter would be but idleness and waste of time in the former.

In reading the history of the island of which we are now treating, these considerations are peculiarly necessary to be borne in mind; *with* them, we shall view things in their natural and proper light; *without* them, we will despise what is far from being despicable, and undervalue virtues of which we cannot experience the benefit *.

What the state of Ceylon was prior to the arrival of Wijeya (for of any earlier period we disclaim all *historical* knowledge) cannot, from the very obscure hints respecting it which remain, be either actually or fully ascertained. The visits of Buddha, however, shew it to have been, even at that remote period, a place of some importance; an importance, doubtless, derived, as well from the advancement of the people, as from the obscure hints and tradi-

* The same or similar considerations may be found more eloquently expressed in the preface to Wilkinson's 'Ancient Egyptians,' vol. i.

tions respecting the visits of former Buddhas, and the miracles performed by them in it.

The country from which Wijeya came (the modern Bengal) was at that period considerably improved. It had a settled government; justice was administered by recorded laws; and, altogether, its state was similar to that which we have just described as the state of India generally at an early period. Such a state of civilisation was doubtless superior to that of Ceylon six centuries before the Christian era; and as Wijeya, coming from such a country, employed the slow, but sure methods of diplomacy, treachery and stratagem, we should not be surprised at his having ultimately obtained the sovereignty.

The system of castes was, we may suppose, introduced by Wijeya. This institution, an extraneous graft upon the tree of Buddhism, is stated by the founder of that faith to have been brought into existence very shortly after the fall of man. That fall, which we shall afterwards have occasion more particularly to describe, consisted in a change from immortality to mortality; from infinite happiness to pain and sorrow; from spotless purity to corruption; and from a condition of miraculous power to the present state of debility. Such was the result of gradual decay through innumerable ages. "Desire," (we quote Gotamo's own words,) "desire had introduced sin, sexual passions came into being, private property was now first acquired; then men assembled and deliberated, saying, most assuredly wicked actions have become prevalent amongst us; every where theft, degradation and punishment will prevail. Let us then elect some one individual who may eradicate that which should be eradicated; who may degrade those who should be degraded; who may expel those who should be expelled, and we will assign to him a share of our produce *:" a Maha-Sammatta, or Great Elected, was accordingly appointed, and, from his possessing lands, he was called Khattiyo or Kshatrya; such (according to Gautama) was the origin of the highest or royal caste. "*He was*," (however,) "*of a perfect original equality with the people* †." As utility was the foundation of the setting apart of the first caste, so was it also of the succeeding. Men soon found that others to investigate the conduct of the people were necessary, and, accordingly, the Brahmins, or Bamino caste,—the eradicators of vice—were constituted the second class.

Next to these, necessity compelled them to provide for the little conveniences of life, and forthwith the Wessa,—or Vaisya—artificers, workmen and merchants—became the third division.

Fourthly, The great body of servants, labourers and inferiors were comprehended in the last great caste.

From any of these the Sumannos Samanéans, or priests, might be appointed, so that they could not form a distinct caste, as has been frequently asserted, being bound by the vow of chastity, which would oblige their order to be constantly recruited from the ranks of the before-mentioned castes ‡.

* The Suttra pitaka, section Dighaniko. † Idem.

‡ It may not be amiss to notice the description of Arrian with regard to the castes of India in his time. He states that there were seven; and the description which he gives of their several occupations may afford us an excellent idea of the existing state of society in India at that time.

First, He enumerates the sophists or learned men (*οἱ σοφισταί*,)—these were the sacrificers to the gods, the diviners, the astrologers, and so forth. They went naked, (*γυμνοὶ διαιτῶνται οἱ σοφισταί*,) whence their name of gymnosophists.

That the introduction of the system of castes would be of material advantage to Ceylon at that early period we can scarcely doubt, however unsuited and prejudicial to later times. That wandering propensity too common amongst unsettled people would be prevented: every man finding himself born into the world in a particular station, from which he could scarcely emerge, would make up his mind to his lot, set his ambition at rest, and prepare to fulfil the duties of his station. A large part of the aborigines, however, appear to have been incapable of this settled life; accustomed to roam the forest for prey, or search the streams for food, they knew no

Second, The husbandmen, (*οἱ γεωργοί,*)—these, says Arrian, do not engage in war, and, in civil commotions and convulsions, their plantations are preserved.

Third, The shepherds, herdsmen, and all who lived neither in villages nor cities, (*οἱ νομέες, οἱ ποιμένες, τε καί Βουκόλοι, καὶ οὗτοι οὔτε κατὰ πόλιας, οὔτε ἐν τῇσι κώμῃσιν οἰκέουσι.*)

Fourth, The artificers and tradesmen, (*τὸ δημιουργικόν τε καὶ καπηλικὸν γένος,*) forming the great body of the inhabitants in the towns.

Fifth, The warlike tribe, (*οἱ πολεμισταί,*) forming the only class obliged to defend their country, and who were supported from the public treasury.

Sixth, The inquisitors, punishers of offences and public censors, (*οἱ ἐπίσκοποι.* These, says Arrian, overlook all things done either in the city or country, and report the evil to the king or magistrates.

Seventh, Those who consulted on public affairs, (*οἱ ὑπὲρ τῶν κοινῶν βουλευόμενοι,*) the leaders of armies and fleets, provincial magistrates and superintendents of rural affairs.—(Historiæ Indicæ, chap. xi. and xii.)

That this enumeration is not set down in the order of precedence of the respective castes is evident, and it requires no ingenuity to perceive that the second, third, fourth and fifth are all included in the third and fourth of Buddha's division, whilst the seventh would be variously distributed between the first and second. The reader must decide for himself which he thinks the most natural, as that, whichever it may be, would certainly be the most ancient.

other occupation, and they wanted none; and, accordingly, betaking themselves to the boundless forests and wastes, they pursued their occupation, uncontrolled by foreigners, and undisturbed by innovation. Such was probably the origin of the Veddahs of Ceylon, a wild, uncultivated race, preferring the wild life of the hunter to the tamer one of the agriculturist, and finding in the woods all that was necessary for subsistence, whilst the skins and ivory of their prey were then, and are still, exchanged for foreign luxuries.

Having thus seen the introduction of civilisation, let us now observe in what that civilisation consisted. Wijeya became king by force of arms; and doubtless constituted himself, in reality, if not in name, an absolute monarch *. But as the country was too extensive to be occupied throughout by his followers and those who subsequently arrived, he seems to have adopted the politic measure of establishing various chiefs in different situations, who, in subordination to himself, should keep the districts around them in subjection and security. This measure, although at first perhaps necessary and useful, was afterwards the cause of much disorder. These tributary princes, finding their situation hereditary, and hoping to transmit their authority to their sons, as they themselves had received it from their forefathers, gradually considered themselves as of more importance than mere subordinates, and assumed, in their various districts, an authority all but absolute; sometimes, indeed, in direct opposition to the power of their sovereign. Whether that power was limited by any

* To found a government well, one man is the best,—once established, the care and execution of the laws should be transferred to many. Machiavel. Discor. lib. i. ch. 9.

other is a question which the native annals do not afford us the means of answering; for the mere mention of certain ministers, and of the influence which they possessed over the kings, is not sufficient to enable us to decide that these ministers were regularly constituted officers, expressly appointed to curtail the sovereign's power. In every monarchy, weak princes, whether absolute or limited in power, will be influenced and sometimes controlled by favourites whom they have raised to authority, either from personal friendship or the influence of accidental causes. Reasoning, however, from analogy, we may conclude that the sovereignty of Ceylon, like that of the great majority of eastern nations, was absolute and unlimited. The monarchs of India, a country which bears in its manners so great a resemblance to Ceylon, were completely uncontrollable by any inferior authority in the state, and, in the same manner, it is but natural to suppose, (since we have no contrary evidence,) that the sovereigns of Ceylon were equally so. In one respect, indeed, the power of the latter was much greater than that of the former, inasmuch as they could, if they pleased, control the priesthood, whilst the Indian kings were completely at the mercy of that body. This difference arises from the different division of the castes on the continent where Brahminism had already gained the ascendant. The priesthood formed a class distinct from all others, and superior to that from which the sovereigns were derived, whilst in the island the ministers of religion were selected indiscriminately from every caste, except the lowest, and thus, unless by the consent of the king, they could not assume authority superior to his. That the despotic power of the monarchs of Ceylon was not, in the majority of the early reigns, hurtfully employed is evident from the accounts of them. Considering religion as the great object of their lives, they employed, for the most part, all their energies and exertion to promote it. Hence arose those stupendous piles of architecture entitled dāgobahs and wihares; and as they imagined their happiness in the future world depended on their zealous advocacy of Buddhism in this, we cannot be surprised, that, reign after reign, we read of dāgobahs and wihares in endless succession having been erected, and of offerings to the priests far more numerous than of attention to the politics of their country. Besides this, another reason, of perhaps greater weight, conduces to the frequent repetition of such accounts. The native historians were all Buddhist priests, and therefore we cannot wonder at their dwelling on the good acts of the kings towards the priesthood more than on their legal acts. Stupendous, however, as the religious erections were, they will yield in importance to the vast tanks, or artificial lakes hollowed out by several kings in various parts of the island. On the utility of these under a tropical sun we need not dilate. With a fertile soil, calculated for producing almost every vegetable, the want of water was severely felt and nobly remedied. Such, then, was the government of ancient Lanka, and such were the works which that government executed; may we not therefore conclude, that a country in which the monarch was so truly the father of his people, would be both happy and prosperous?

Of the laws of Ceylon at this early period we are left almost entirely ignorant, but we may reasonably conclude that they were not totally dissimilar from those which regulated the kingdom at a later period, and which we shall hereafter have occasion to consider more particularly.

Of bodies or codes of laws we shall find frequent mention in the succeeding narrative, but unfortunately none of these entire codes have as yet been made accessible to the English reader. From a paper to be found in Bertolacci's "View of Ceylon *," however, we may form some idea of the systems of government and justice prevalent amongst the natives from the earliest period. Thence we learn that, in certain cases, the crown was elective in the family of the king—that a court of justice, consisting of Adigars, Dissauves and other chief officers, received and decided appeals from all the lesser courts—that the moral laws of Buddha were esteemed superior to all others—that the king could, in certain cases, be opposed and controlled by his ministers, and that the sanctity of marriage could only be annulled by a regular divorce. These appear to be institutions for which we would hardly look in an eastern despotism, but as we purpose hereafter to examine Ceylonese jurisprudence more particularly, we shall, for the present, be content with examining the marks of civilisation apparent in their arts, their literature, and their religion.

Before considering the religion of the ancient Ceylonese, which formed perhaps the most important element in their civilisation, let us view the state of the arts and sciences, in so far as that state is exhibited to us in their histories.

The despotic sovereignties of ancient times, whether in the coldest or warmest climates, in the eastern or western worlds, seem to have devoted their energy to the erection of buildings, or the accomplishment of undertakings which

* Appendix A. Answers given by some of the best informed Candian Priests to questions put to them by Governor Falk, A. D. 1769, respecting the ancient laws and customs of their country.

should transmit the evidence of their power to future times. Hence arose the vast and stupendous pyramids of Egypt, the lofty walls and massive palaces of Babylon and Nineveh, the excavated caves and pagodahs of India and Burmah, the temples and canals of China, together with the mighty ruins of America, which bespeak, amidst the desolations of barbarism, a nation civilised and powerful.

If, then, from the remains which still exist of these early works, we are justified in concluding that the nations which raised them were numerous, united, powerful and civilised, we are surely also justified in applying the same conclusions to similar evidences in the island of which we are treating, and by the superiority of the work judging of the degree of refinement which existed amongst the people.

We have already noticed the enormous size of some of the works erected by Tisso, Gaimono, and others, affording at least evidence of a numerous and united people. But it is to the way in which these works were executed, to the decorations with which they were embellished, and to the excellence of their materials, that we must look, in order to be convinced of the existence, at that period, of a degree of refinement much removed above mere absence of barbarism. What these works were in their original perfection we cannot attempt to decide : it is to their ruins that we must look for the evidence of what they once were ; and whilst regarding these ruins, let us remember, that the influence of time, destructive to erections everywhere, is peculiarly so amidst the fertility and warmth of Ceylon. There the parasitic creepers cling pertinaciously to every part of the ruin ; whilst even lofty trees erect themselves upon the very summit, thus combining with the elements to destroy the fated building.

The stupendous erection, called the Lowa Maha Paya, or brazen palace of the priests, built by Gaimono, has been formerly mentioned ; and the following description is an account of its present state, as published in the Colombo Journal of 1832.

" These ruins consist of sixteen hundred stone pillars, forming nearly a square of forty feet on each side ; the length of these pillars appears to have been equal, and even now they only differ by a few inches. They are generally eleven feet in height, and those in the corners, centres, and gateways, two feet square. The rows of pillars are parallel and at right angles to each other, but are not equidistant. The distance between the pillars varies from two and a-half to three and a-half feet." The writer then proceeds to mention that they were formerly built upon, and were intended as a habitation for the priests, &c.

Major Forbes' account * of this ruin is substantially the same as that just quoted ; he mentions, however, that the inner pillars are ornamented, whilst the exterior are plain, which may be accounted for from many of the exterior having been split when repairing the devastations caused by Mahasen, a wavering monarch, who, from enmity to Buddhism, at one period destroyed it, and, at another, wished again to restore it.

" To the north of these ruins, at various distances within a mile, are six dāgobahs, the most remarkable structures certainly in the vicinity of Anuradhapoora.

* Forbes' Ceylon, vol. i. chap. x.

The effect of the proportions of these buildings exemplifies, in a very remarkable manner, the truth of an observation of Burke in his Treatise on the Sublime and Beautiful, viz. that ' height is infinitely more imposing than length or breadth.' The dāgobahs appear to be at least the height of the diameter of their bases, whereas we are informed that, from an accurate measurement, their height is just equal to half such diameter. Each dāgobah may indeed be considered as half a sphere with a spire built upon it. The height of the two larger ones is about the same, viz. 270 feet. They are solid structures of brick, at one time covered with chunam, which, however, has fallen off from the whole of them except Lanka Rama *." The following general rémarks on dāgobahs will, perhaps, be read with interest.

" Amongst the ruins of this city (Anuradhapoora) the dāgobahs †, or monumental tombs of the relics of Buddha, the mode in which they are constructed, the object for which they are intended, above all, their magnitude, demand particular notice. The characteristic form of all monumental Buddhistical buildings is that of a bell-shaped tomb, surmounted by a spire, and is the same in all countries which have had Buddha for their prophet, lawgiver, or god. Whether in the outline of the cumbrous mount, or in miniature within the laboured excavation, this peculiar shape (although variously modified) is general, and enables us to recognise the neglected and unhonoured shrines of Buddha, in countries where his religion no longer exists, and his very name is unknown. The gaudy

* Colombo Journal, November 1831.

† From Dhatu-garba, the womb, or receptacle of a relic.

Shoemadoo of Pegu, the elegant Toopharamaya of Anuradhapoora, the more modern masonry of Boro Budor in Java, are but varieties of the same general form; and in the desolate caves of Carli, as in the gaudy excavations and busy scenes of Dambool, there is still extant the sign of Buddha,—the tomb of his relics." * * * "These monuments in Ceylon are built around a small cell, or hollow stone, containing the relic; along with which a few ornaments and emblems of Buddhist worship were usually deposited, such as pearls, precious stones, and figures of Buddha: the number and value of these depended on the importance attached to the relic, or the wealth of the person who reared the monument *."

From the earliest period at which Europeans have travelled through Ceylon, the ruins of Anuradhapoora have been celebrated as exhibiting indisputable evidence of its former greatness, and of its fitness to have once been the capital of a powerful monarchy. In the year 1679, Knox, when making his escape from the Candian provinces, where he had been for twenty years detained a prisoner, met with the ruins of this ancient city, and thus describes them. "Here and there, by the side of the river, is a world of hewn stone pillars," (very probably the remains of the Lowa Maha Paya,) "which I suppose formerly were buildings; and in three or four places are the ruins of bridges built of stone, some remains of them yet standing upon stone pillars †." Speaking of Buddha and these remains, he says, "they report ninety kings have reigned there successively, where, by the ruins that still remain, it appears they spared not for pains and labour

* Major Forbes, *ut supra.*

† Historical Relation of Ceylon, part iv. c. 10.

to build temples and high monnments to the honour of this god, as if they had been born only to hew rocks and great stones, and lay them up in heaps: these kings are now happy spirits, having merited it by these their labours."

In the finer and more delicate arts the Ceylonese seem never to have made much advancement; with perspective they were totally unacquainted, and, of course, their finest paintings are but rude masses of colouring. Statuary they cultivated with better success; and in several of the images of Buddha, gigantic as well as miniature, the features are chiselled with precision and delicacy. The following is extracted from an account * of the Maha wihare, built by Tisso the First, in the third century before Christ. "The angles of these steps (those leading to the entrance,) are in perfect preservation, and the basso-relievos on their depths, and on the stones in the landing place, are almost as well-defined as if fresh from the sculptor. The elephant horse, lion and ox, are here represented with very considerable fidelity and spirit. Some of the small ornaments in stone are also in admirable taste."

That most diligent researcher into the ruins of ancient Ceylon, Major Forbes, has left us, in his work, the following account of the Toophárámaya dāgobah, which we have before noticed as an erection of the same monarch. "Toophárámaya, although inferior to many in size, yet far exceeds any dāgobah in Ceylon, both in elegance and unity of design, and in the beauty of the minute sculptures on its tall, slender and graceful columns. This dāgobah is low, broad at the top, and surrounded by four lines of pillars, twenty-seven in each line, fixed in the elevated

* Colombo Journal, 24th Nov. 1832.

granite platform, so as to form radii of a circle, of which the monument is the centre. These pillars are twenty-four feet in height, with square bases, octagonal shafts, and circular capitals; the base and shafts, fourteen inches in thickness, and twenty-two feet in length, are each of one stone. The capitals are much broader than the base, and are highly ornamented." Of the ancient sculpture, the same diligent and accurate observer gives the following just and meritedly high character: "Although simplicity is the most distinguishing characteristic of the ancient architectural remains of the Singhalese, yet some of the carving in granite might compete with the best modern workmanship of Europe, (in the same material,) both as to depth and sharpness of cutting; whilst the sculptures at Anuradhapoora and places built in remote ages are distinguished from any attempts of modern natives, not less from the more animated action of the figures, than by greater correctness of proportion."

Such, then, are the remains which the Ceylonese of the five centuries preceding our era have left us; and surely in these we may perceive the traces of early civilisation and continued refinement, not less than from the accounts which western authors, and eastern histories, afford us of its extensive commerce and numerous exports at that remote period. Nor can any sensible reflecting person, we imagine, resist the evidence of two proofs so totally unconnected and accidental.

CHAPTER IV.

BUDDHISM, AND ITS INFLUENCE ON THE PUBLIC MIND.

There seem to be few better criterions of the state of a nation, than the spirit and nature of the religion which it adopts. If universally promulgated, whether refined or gross, whether elevated or low, it must have a powerful influence on the minds of its professors. It may be absurd or incomprehensible; it may involve the grossest inconsistencies, or inculcate the most troublesome ceremonies; but, nevertheless, if accident or talent favour its growth over a nation, the history of the world assures us, that the great bulk of that nation will be its professors, whilst the sceptics will be few and powerless. If adopted, then, as the national faith, its moral code becomes the standard of perfection, its saints the object of imitation, and its devotees the subjects of praise and envy. From these and other causes, we generally find, that the character of a nation is precisely such as its religion would lead us to expect. Can the history of man reveal to us a fiercer or prouder, or a more valiant race than that of the ancient Huns? Every thing about them was barbaric indeed, in the fullest acceptation of the term, but no people were ever distinguished for a fiercer spirit, and a greater contempt of death. And what was their religion? Their temple was the open air; the sky was their roof; their god was a naked scimitar, and their worship was prostration *.

Few nations have surpassed the ancient Scythians in cruelty and fierceness ; and amongst what people was there ever a system of religion more barbarous and savage? † And, again, is not the simple and high-minded adoration of the Great Spirit by the tribes of North America fully characteristic of their contempt of danger, their unalterable attachment and their free and roving lives?

Nor does the analogy between the character and the religion alter, if we advance to more improved countries, and more enlightened nations. In proportion to the nobility of the native character, we find the religion simple and pure; in proportion to its degradation we find it likewise debased and corrupt.

The system which we are now about to examine has exercised a powerful influence over an extended region of the mass of humanity. India, Thibet, China, Burmah and Ceylon, were all at one time subject to its influence and its control. Even at the present day, hundreds of millions bow with superstitious reverence before the decrees of its prophets, and profess obedience to its code of morality.

As to when and where Buddhism was first propagated we are equally ignorant. Tradition and history, however, point to a region of northern India, now included in Bengal, whence, it is probable, its professors and teachers first emanated. That country was called Maghadha, and, from

* Nec templum apud eos visitur, aut delubrum, ne tegurium quidem culmo tectum, cerni usquam potest; sed gladius barbarico ritu humi figitur nudus, eumque ut Martem regionum quas circumcireant præsulem verecundius colunt. Arminan. Marcelinus, xxxi. 2.

† *Vide* Herodotus, lib. iv. cap. 62.

the name of the district, came also that of the language in which it was first promulgated. Now, however, that language is more frequently styled Bali or Pali, the origin of which designation is obscure. For this language, the sacred books of Buddhism claim the highest honour, assert its extreme antiquity, and that it is the root of all languages. *Sa Magadki ; mula bhasa, narayeyadi Kappika, trahmanochassuttalapa Sambuddhachapi bhasare.* "There is a language which is the root of all languages ; men and brahmins, who never before heard or uttered a human sound, spoke it at the commencement of the creation. The Buddhas themselves spoke it,—it is Magahdi *."

We have said that the era of the introduction of Buddhism into the world is lost in the gloom of antiquity, but there cannot be a doubt of its having been one of the earliest of human religions. This religion, according to the belief of its votaries, has been handed down, through an infinite series of ages, by successive prophets appearing at vast distances of time. Twenty-four of these godlike men or Buddhas had already appeared, when, in the sixth century before Christ, the son of a king of Northern India raised himself by his merit and piety to the same rank, and, having reformed the world by his exertions, revived the old and pure religion, and left teachers to extend it, he too departed, to be absorbed into the first principle or "architect" of all things.

Whether the preceding Buddhas had a personal existence or not cannot now be decided ; but we can scarcely doubt of the humanity and substantiality of the two last—Kassapo and Gotamo, inasmuch as the faith of the first

* Kachayano's Grammar of Pali, Mahawanso, Introd. p. xxii.

had extended to China before the appearance of the second, whilst the latter was in fact unknown in that vast empire till about the second century after our era *.

According to the tenets of Buddhism matter and mind are equally immortal and eternal; they have come into their present condition and connection by a series of transmigrations extending back through an incomprehensible period of time, and they shall continue thus to progress throughout eternity. Whether Buddhism maintains or denies the existence of a Supreme Almighty Being has been frequently disputed; and although we cannot pretend to settle the question definitely on either side, probability seems to incline to his exclusion, inasmuch as there seems nothing for such a being to do in the system of Buddhism. The following verses, ascribed to Gotamo on the occasion of his becoming a Buddha, would, however, lead us to conclude that such a being *was* recognised by the founder of the modern system.

> Through various transmigrations
> I must travel if I do not discover
> *The builder* whom I seek ;—
> Painful are repeated transmigrations !
> I have seen *the architect* (and said)
> *Thou* shalt not build me another house †.—

If it be asked who this "builder" and this "architect" is, no satisfactory answer can be given to the question. On this point, then, much uncertainty still exists, an uncer-

* This interesting fact is proved by the account of Buddhism as then existing in China, given by Fa Hian in his collection of Buddhist tracts, more especially, however, in the " Chin i tian," p. 26-8. This collection was partly translated into French by M. Remusat Landresse and others, some years since.

† The Friend, April 1839.

tainty which will not probably be cleared away, before the voluminous sacred books of the faith shall have been translated *. The following is the chain of existence as delivered by Gotamo himself in one of his discourses: "On account of ignorance are produced merit and demerit; on account of merit and demerit is produced consciousness; on account of consciousness, body and mind," and so on—but if there be ignorance there must be also *beings* to be ignorant. Amongst the professors of the faith at the present day, the existence of an Almighty Eternal Being is certainly denied; "for" said a college of priests in answer to the questions of a Dutch governor, "if there were such a being how could pain have entered into the world? †"

Gods, however, are maintained in sufficient abundance. These appear to be immaterial spirits of a nature superior to man, but limited in power, in knowledge, and in existence. Thus the greatest of these deities, Maha Brahma, is a being of wonderful power, and of vast comprehension, but inferior to the successive Buddhas in wisdom,

* These works are the three "Pitakas"— The Wineye, Abhidharma, and Suttra pitaka, with their respective commentaries, entitled the Attakätha. These works contain the sermons of Buddha, and, of course, his doctrines at length.

† Did the supreme God make the inferior ones? was the question—"God can neither create the inferior gods nor any other kind of soul. There is no necessity for such a creation, for, if a soul were created that soul must of necessity endure pleasure and pain, but no god that is all-merciful would create a soul that must endure pain. The gods and all other creatures receive their birth or formation by means of the power emanating from their own kusula or akusula (merit or demerit:) such a thing as the creation of new souls by God does not appear in any of the books of Buddhism. If it be said, in the books of any religion whatever, that God creates souls, such a statement may easily be proved to be false." Friend, April 1842.

purity, excellence, and knowledge, although superior in strength. That spirit, like all the higher orders of beings in Buddhism, rose from a common station to his present exalted one, by his virtue; and, after existing thus for some thousands of years, will either attain Nirwana, (an extinction from all impurity and defilement) or relapse into his original obscurity. Four of these deities are supposed to have a peculiar influence on mankind, others are employed in guarding the other parts of the universe, whilst an innumerable host of subordinate demons (yakkhos) fill the air and the central regions.

Into this part of Buddhism it will not be necessary for us to enter; as the chief object of our attention is the moral code and the probable influence of that code, and the ceremonies enjoined on those professing the religion.

We have already stated that the eternity of matter is one of the dogmas of the faith of the Buddhas. The world is consequently supposed to have always existed, and to have in itself the principle of continued existence for ever. It is declared also to be destroyed and reproduced at certain vast intervals of time, the principal agents in this destruction being water, fire and air. Sin, misery and death, were not always inhabitants of our planet, however, and they were produced, according to Buddhism, as according to a purer faith, by the desire, covetousness and folly of man.

Living beings (said the last of the Buddhas,) first appeared by an apparitional birth, subsisting on the element of felicity, illuminated by their own effulgence, moving through the air, delightfully located, and existing in unity and concord *. Such was the condition of primeval man,

* Suttra pitaka, section Dighaniko.

but he did not always remain so—by the influence of desire and covetousness sin entered into the world and "death by sin," until at length they had degenerated into the present perverse and sinful race. The world was not allowed to degenerate thus however, without an effort having been made for its reformation. Twenty-four beings of infinite purity and unsullied holiness had appeared upon the earth in the revolutions of countless ages, to arrest the progress of its decline, and had preached righteousness and purity to the world not without effecting wonderful improvement, before the last of the Buddhas, Gotamo himself, appeared upon the earth. One more is yet to come; and then shall cease the present order of things, when "a new heaven and a new earth" shall come into existence. *Aggo hamasmi lokassi* (said Gotamo;) *jettho hamasmi lokassa; settho hamasmi lokassa; ayamantimājāti nathidāni punabbhewo.* I am the most exalted in the world; I am the chief in the world; I am the most excellent in the world; this is my last birth; hereafter there is to me no other generation.

The birth and parentage of Gotamo have been formerly mentioned, according to the most received account; but the traditions on the subject are various and conflicting. Some represent him as born from a virgin's side, others as having been preternaturally conceived in the womb of Suddhódano's wife, but, as we have just observed, the account of his life already given is that best authenticated and most commonly received. The rise and progress of a later faith may convince us that there was nothing improbable in his assuming the character of a prophet, and still less in his being received as such. In the prime of manhood the son of a powerful monarch renounces "the pomps and vanities" of the world, retreats to an unfrequented forest, and there submits to want and privation, regardless of the hopes of ambition or of the softer feelings of affection. *Such* was the foundation of the faith; can we then wonder at the superstructure?

Mysticism and voluntary mortification will ever pass with the vulgar for the influences of heaven; and if the professor of them assumes a divine character, they are already more than half persuaded to believe him.

The assumptions of Gotamo were not less favourably begun than they were afterwards happily executed. He resorted to no violence; his life was strictly moral and consistent with his pretensions *; he propagated his doctrines orally, going with his attendants from village to village; he wrote no books, but allowed his disciples freely to copy out his conversations, and in these he preferred the language of parable and simile to direct assertions. He preached reliance upon the gods, faith in the Buddhas, and confidence in good works—he hinged the very universe, in fact, upon the piety of his followers. Simple and austere in his manners, he courted not the adoration of the great, nor did he despise their invitations if he thought he might be an instrument of good.

Apart from the numerous miracles ascribed to him, the history of his life is monotonous and uncheckered, whilst his disciples seem to have vied with each other in ascribing to him the most amazing feats. His discourses shew few pretensions, however, to superior power or strength; in knowledge, and the subjection of his passions he de-

* Amongst his (Gotamo's) tribulations upon earth, even after he had attained the rank of a Buddha, was that of being accused by a young lady of incontinence with her. Notes on Ancient India, p. 264.

sired to be, and he appears to have been, superior to his age. The following, one of his moral discourses, may give us a good idea of his doctrines, his style and his morality. Having been asked to declare what actions were of superior excellence to all others, the substance of his answer was :—" Not to serve the unwise but to attend on the learned, and to present offerings to those worthy of homage ; to live in a religious neighbourhood ; to be a performer of virtuous actions ; to be established in the true faith ; to be well informed in religion, instructed in speech, subject to discipline and of pleasant speech ; to honour one's father and mother ; to provide for one's wife and children ; to follow a sinless vocation ; to give alms ; to act virtuously ; to aid relatives and lead a blameless life ; to be free from sin ; to abstain from intoxicating drinks, and to persevere in virtue ; to be respectful, kind, contented, grateful, and to listen, at proper times, to religious instruction ; to be mild, subject to reproof ; to have access to priests, and to converse with them on religious subjects ; to have a mind unshaken by prosperity or adversity, inaccessible to sorrows, free from impurity, and tranquil ; these are the chief excellences. Those who practise all these virtues, and are not overcome by evil, enjoy the perfection of happiness, and obtain the chief good *."

Attended by a large train of priests and followers, Gotamo wandered from town to town, receiving alms from all who offered them, but neither requesting any, nor allowing his followers to do so. Having in this manner passed a lengthened life, it was closed in peace, and the

* Discourse, entitled Mangala, The Friend, May 1839.

"ruler of the world" left the earth to attain the much controverted Nirwana *. "The Buddhas" (said the college of priests before noticed,) "are now entirely free from birth, decay, sickness, death and sorrow, or, in other words, they have attained the imperishable, immortal, ever-during Nirwana." This Nirwana is the object of Buddhistic desires, the paradise of the faith; and if we deny it to have been an absorption into, or an intimate union with that "architect" formerly referred to, we must suppose it to have been a "complete cessation of existence,"—an annihilation † or nonentity.

The priesthood instituted and incorporated by Gotamo very much resembled those initiated into the esoteric tenets of Pythagoras. They lived in communities and had a common table; they were doomed to poverty and celibacy; they shunned luxuries of all kinds, whether intended to delight the imagination or to please the body; they were enjoined (as were all the Buddhists) to shun the destruction of animal life as they would of human; they were to eat at certain seasons of the day; they were prohibited from all exciting and intoxicating liquors, and they were to content themselves with low and unadorned seats. The enthusiasm of kings frequently provided for all their wants, but the simple and austere character of their lives remained, and, although residing in palaces, they maintained the manners of the hermitage.

Having thus rapidly glanced at some of the character-

* This state is generally represented as a complete cessation from existence.

† Abhorred annihilation blasts the soul, says Young; yet here we perceive it (according to the accounts of the missionaries,) the object of the highest aspirations of a prophet, a philosopher, and a future God.

istic features of Buddhism, and at the life of its reviver, we come now to consider its morality and its ceremonies, on which, as being more immediately connected with the history of Ceylon, we shall more largely dilate.

The ten fundamental prohibitions delivered to priests and laity were the following:—

1st, A prohibition of unjust suspicion.
2d, A prohibition of coveting in every form.
3d, A prohibition of evil wishes to others.
4th, A prohibition of all falsehood.
5th, A prohibition of betraying the secrets of others.
6th, A prohibition of slander.
7th, A prohibition of all foolish conversation.
8th, A prohibition of *all* killing.
9th, A prohibition of stealing.
10th, A prohibition of fornication and adultery.

The great fundamental doctrine of the metempsychosis was one of the distinguishing features of Buddhism. By this doctrine, as is commonly known, the transmigration of the soul after its separation from the body into that of some other animal is inculcated *, that animal being high or low in the scale of creation, according to the character of the soul in its present existence. Here, then, was a full incentive to ambition, inasmuch as, by the piety of the man, his soul might subsequently become an inhabitant of one of the superior heavens; but there was in it little discouragement from present gratification, from all recollection of its previous exaltation being expelled in its subsequent debasement. Can we wonder then that kings

* Some elaborate essays have been written by the Rev. D. J. Gogerly, to prove that it is not the same but a new soul which receives punishment or reward for the conduct of some soul here!—*Vide* Friend, vol. 2.

and priests vied with each other in holiness in the hope of so exalted a reward, or that a few baser spirits let loose all their evil passions, like a torrent, without restraint or control?

Gotamo's discourses, so far as they have been translated, exhibit the reflections of a powerful, equable and cultivated mind, and appear as far removed above the absurd tales and precepts of Brahminism, as the simple tenets of Socrates above the mysticism of the priests of Egypt. "There are seven sections of moral science" (said he *,) "which have been fully taught, meditated on, and practised by me, and which are necessary for the attainment of knowledge, wisdom, and deliverance from transmigration. These seven are, contemplation; the ascertainment of truth; persevering exertion; contentment; extinction of passion; tranquillity and equanimity."

The duties enjoined upon the priests consisted chiefly in reading a portion of the sacred books on stated days, to which they added exhortations and explanations. They were prohibited, as we have stated, from the most innocent indulgences, no less than from the more wicked, with the most ascetic rigidity. Priestesses, however, have been mentioned in the preceding narrative; and, doubtless, the practices of the nuns and friars, with their irregular pleasures, will occur to many, as being probably similar to those of the priests and priestesses of Buddha. The slightest communication, however, was strictly forbidden between the two classes, and the following prohibitions will convince us that Gotamo had studied the mind of man with no ordinary acuteness. The following is the

* In the Kassapa Bojjhangan—Friend, July 1839.

list of crimes "punished with suspension and penances, the offender not to be restored except by an assembly of twenty priests." A priest touching a woman in any way; his holding libidinous conversation with a woman; his praising sensual pursuits, thus,—saying, "Sister, the most meritorious action a woman can perform is to gratify the desires of so virtuous, so pure, and so excellent a person as I am;" his making known "the desires of a woman to a man," or the opposite *. The two following acts made the priests "liable to exclusion, suspension, or censure, according to circumstances;"—his sitting privately on a seat with a woman, secluded from observation; or his sitting on a seat with a woman, which, if not so secluded as to allow of his breaking one of the fundamental laws of his faith, was yet secluded enough to permit of his holding, unheard by others, improper conversation. Such were the more heinous offences; but even the avenues to vice were guarded with the most rigorous prohibitions. Thus, at the risk of public confession, and public forgiveness granted on contrition, no priest could recline in the same place with a woman; nor could he speak to her more than five or six sentences without an intelligent witness; nor could he visit the abode of the priestesses under the pretence "of delivering exhortations;" nor could he travel with a priestess; nor could he sit down to converse with her during a casual interview †. These facts may serve to assure us that no precaution, which could possibly be taken, was omitted to ensure regularity and pureness in the colleges of either

* Friend. Laws of the Priesthood, December 1839.

† Friend. Laws of the Priesthood, January and February 1840.

sex. Gotamo was aware, however, that "all men could not receive" and practise the rigid rules binding on the priesthood; and he accordingly enjoined that all who should find themselves incapable of keeping their vow of perpetual chastity, might put off the yellow robes and marry.

We now come to the moral precepts enjoined upon all men, and we shall find abundant proofs in those precepts of the vast superiority of their lawgiver to those around him at that early period. Gotamo was eminently a practical philosopher, and spent his time, not in curious investigations into mind and its influence, but in deducing rules from nature for the government of man.

In the "Damma Padan *," or the "Footsteps of Religion," we have exemplified a code of morality, and a list of precepts which, for pureness, excellence and wisdom, is only second to that of the Divine lawgiver himself. To transcribe the entire of this beautiful series of apothegms would occupy too much of our space; and we shall probably render a more acceptable service to our readers, by culling the rarest and most beautiful flowers from this garden of eastern exotics.

"Anger is not to be appeased by anger, but by gentleness.

"The worldly-minded man who applauds religion and understands its precepts, but does not practise them, is like the herdsman of another's cattle,—he tends the flock, but receives not their produce.

"Religion is the path of immortality; irreligion the

* Translated by that indefatigable orientalist, the Rev. D. J. Gogerly, and published in the Friend, vols. iii. and iv.

path of death. The righteous die not, but the irreligious are even as now dead.

"The wise man so establishes himself, in industry, perseverance, prudence and mental control, that he is not carried away by the floods of sensuality.

"Live not in the practice of irreligion, neither cleave to sensuality; for the meditative and the religious man experiences great happiness.

"As a man elevated upon a mountain surveys in calmness the plains below, so does the virtuous man behold without envy the actions of the sinful multitude.

"As the fletcher makes straight his arrows, so the wise and virtuous man rectifies his mind.

"Mental control, and the subjection of the passions, is the path to happiness and eternity.

"The mind that repays injury by injury, and wrath by wrath, wanders ever further in the mazes of error.

"True nobility is not of one's parentage, but of a virtuous and noble soul.

"As the bee collects nectar and departs without injuring the beauty or the odour of the flowers, so the sage sojourns among men; he views their ways, and learns wisdom from their folly.

"Be not anxious to discover the faults of others, but jealously watch your own.

"As the lily, growing from a heap of manure accidentally cast upon the highway, delights the soul with the delicacy of its fragrance, so the wise, the disciples of the all-perfect Buddha, shine amongst the foolish, and are grateful to the gods.

"The wise man becomes so by the consciousness of

his own folly, but the foolish is rendered more so by his pretensions to wisdom.

"Let man perform those actions of which futurity will never cause him to repent.

"He who reproves, instructs, and restrains from evil, will be loved by the wise, and hated by the foolish.

"The conduit-maker guides the streams of water; the fletcher forms his arrows, and the carpenter bends the wood to his purpose, but the wise man performs what is more difficult,—he directs himself.

"*As the solid rock stands unshaken by the storm, so the wise man is unmoved by contempt or applause.*

"One verse, which, when heard, causes us to subdue our passions, is better than a thousand poems destitute of profit.

"*He is a more noble warrior who conquers himself, than the warrior who, in the field of battle, overcomes thousands of thousands.*

"One day of that man's life who lives virtuously is of more worth than a thousand years of sin.

"Sin is frequently clothed in the garb of virtue, but its effects unclothe it.

"Avoid sin with no less care than the merchant who, with few attendants and great wealth, avoids a dangerous road.

"Nothing is sinful to the pure.

"Think not that going naked, or being defiled with dirt, or fasting, or lying on the earth, or remaining motionless, can make the pure impure; for the mind will still remain the same.

"Let him who wastes all his attention on the body,

consider the skeletons of those departed, and then decide whether the body is worthy of his care.

"Kings, and their pride, and their splendour decay, but truth is immutable and eternal.

"He who has entered on the road to Nirwāna is superior to the greatest monarch of the earth.

"All the religion of Buddha is contained in these three sentences:—Purify the mind; abstain from vice; practise virtue.

"That man is the most skilful of charioteers who can guide the chariot of his own anger.

"*Conquer anger by mildness, evil by good, covetousness by liberality, and falsehood by truth.*

"Men *have* ever been, and *will* ever be, subject to unjust censure, and to unjust praise.

"Cultivate mildness of speech; let your every word be guarded; abandon all improper language, and let your speech be altogether virtuous.

"The wicked man is like a withered leaf; the messenger of death is near, and yet he stands at the gate of death without provision for his future life.

"Your evil passions you cannot eradicate all at once: it is the work of time, and must be done slowly, just as the jeweller removes the rust of gold.

"Know, O man, that sinful actions cannot be hid, but that pride, covetousness and wrath will bring long sufferings upon you.

"There is no fire so fierce as lust; nothing has a grasp so pertinaceous as hatred; no net can be compared with folly, and no flood is so rapid as desire."

These examples of the moral verses of Gotamo may serve to convince us that purity of life, consistency of conduct, and, above all, *mental control*, were the objects of his lessons, and may serve to convince us that few systems of ancient morality, if indeed there is one, can be compared with that of the Maghadic philosopher. Nor must we forget that the man who delivered these maxims was the son of a powerful monarch, who had left his hereditary throne to obtain a mental and a moral superiority over his contemporaries, instead of a factious or a political pre-eminence. He acquired power, indeed, but he used it for benevolent purposes; his influence was employed, not in ministering to his passions, as was that of Mahomet, but in the persuading of others to renounce sin and embrace virtue.

So far as the volumes of Gotamo have been opened to us, we know of no ceremonies which he enjoined, save the simple preaching of his doctrines. No religion could ever exist, nor has any ever existed amongst the great mass of mankind, in such a state as this. Ceremonies *must* be instituted, however pure the doctrines of the faith may be, and, without such ceremonies, the faith would at once lose its hold on the public mind. Men must have *something to see* in their religion, there must be *some* outlet for enthusiasm; and whether this outlet be the gorgeous pageantry of Rome, or the enthusiastic "revivals" of American Christianity, it will equally affect the minds, and attract the feelings of the "profanum vulgus." The pure and beautiful edifice of Buddhistic faith did not long endure, therefore, without the addition of gaudy and unmeaning ornaments, which are now too often mistaken for the inventions of Gotamo himself—inventions which his eminently intellectual mind would have scouted as absurd. These ceremonies, however, were a part of the faith as introduced into Ceylon, and, however unpleasing the mixture, we must add them to the doctrines just recited. But even in these, corruptions, as they were, of the religion of Gotamo, we shall find nothing of a decidedly immoral or pernicious tendency—they are of that simple and gentle nature which become additions to so intellectual a faith.

The estimation in which Gotamo was held by his contemporaries and disciples during his life was naturally transferred, on his death, to those things hallowed by his touch. In this the religion of Buddha differed not from that of most others; and if we find a branch of the Christian church itself hallowing the relics of those whose lives were, in many instances, far from blameless, (as was the case with many of their saints,) we cannot wonder at the unenlightened inhabitants of Ceylon regarding the tooth of their prophet as "the most precious thing in the universe." This, then, the worship of the relics of Gotamo, was the first addition made by his followers to the religion which he delivered to them.

Buildings of vast dimensions, and lavishly ornamented, were erected to contain these hallowed relics, and, attached to these pagodahs was generally a temple (or wihare) for the priests, containing an image of the prophet, in which his doctrines were expounded at certain stated times. Here, at the hours of morning and evening prayers, the religious inhabitants of both sexes assembled, and, kneeling before the image of their god, they repeated, after the priest, some passages of their religious books, in a language which, (in later times at least) was entirely unknown to them. Others, and especially the pious females, came with their simple offerings of odoriferous flowers in their hands, and laid this bloodless sacrifice on the altar of their peaceful deity. Such was the only worship required by their faith.

The ceremonies with which the Dalada or tooth-relic was received by Tisso, may exemplify the natural disposition of the kings to exhibit, in the ordinances of their religion, their own power and greatness. Succeeding monarchs were not disposed to let the ostentatious parade thus exhibited be discontinued; and, accordingly, we find that in future times the exhibition of the same relic at stated periods was the signal for fresh exhibitions of their own power, and of the wealth of their kingdom. The people flocked from all quarters to the capital to behold the precious relic; elephants were caparisoned, horses decorated, and vehicles of all kinds exhibited, containing each their respective owners. The king himself with the royal family attended; and, on the elevation of the sacred deposit in the hands of the highest of their priests, to be faintly seen by those assembled, the vast multitude was moved like the waves of the ocean to and fro, and a loud burst of "Sadhu" rose from that mighty throng, caught up, as it died away, by the more distant, until the whole air was filled with the notes of adoration. Games, festivals, plays and rejoicings succeeded, and having thus given vent to the enthusiasm so long confined, the multitude departed to their respective villages.

One of the earliest superstitions amongst mankind appears to have been that of devils or demons of great power inhabiting the air, whom it was necessary for man to appease by sacrifices and offerings. This superstition was also introduced into Buddhism, and devil-dances to appease those spirits were not long in making their appearance. The origin of these we shall hereafter have an opportunity of noticing; and as they were not introduced into Buddhism till the third century after Christ, we cannot possibly suppose them to have been the institutions of Gotamo, as is, however, commonly asserted. "The reverse of this," says the Rev. D. J. Gogerly, "is the case; for he has declared such practices to be, at the best, useless, and, where an animal is killed to appease the demon, decidedly sinful." The power of these demons was, nevertheless, a tenet inculcated by Gotamo, and as he asserted their power, he also took care to provide his followers against it. This provision consisted in the recitation of a number of his maxims, and in the reading of certain of his sermons, a procedure doubtless propounded by him as a relief to the pious mind, in a full conviction of the strength and power of the imagination; for we cannot conceive him to have supposed that any real influence would have been exerted by the ceremony. This ceremony, when performed for the advantage of a district or a village, lasted for seven days, during which time two pulpits were continually filled, and on the seventh a procession was formed, a particular sermon read, and thus the farce was ended. No proofs have as yet been given us, however, that this was really an institution of Gotamo, and, considering the stress he lays on mental control, and the futility of ceremony, there appears quite sufficient reason to make us doubt the fact. Probability seems to designate that it was introduced by some follower of his, who was anxious to comply with the wishes of his people, and yet careful not to transgress the commands of his superior. Otherwise we must suppose that Gotamo had before him a written copy of all his sermons, whilst these sermons themselves appear not to have been transcribed either by his own command, or with his knowledge.

It would be tedious and unprofitable to recount the various puerile ceremonies in use amongst the Singhalese on almost every domestic occasion of importance. The birth of a child, the marriage of a relation, the death of a parent or a friend, had each their appropriate ceremonies, chiefly performed with a view to the conciliation of the evil demons whom they imagined to fill the air. These no one will contend to have been institutions of their religion, foreign as they are to its whole spirit, and to the precepts of its founder. If we take a survey of the various religions invented by mankind, we shall find few, if any, that can be advantageously compared to that of the Maghadic prophet. It seems to approach as near, indeed, to that purer faith delivered by the Almighty himself, as it was possible for a human system to come. Its defects are many, and its faults obvious; but to cover these defects, and to hide these faults, we may abstract from its excellence, to clothe its deformity. Equally distant from the barbaric rites of Brahminism, and from the gross materiality and sensuality of Moslemism, Buddhism stands prominently forward as a system enjoining no immoral rite, and luring men into the path of religion by the prospect of none of the gross pleasures of sense. Its code of morality is no less eminently suited for this world than its system of rewards for the next, and although so defective in its theology it is equally distinguished for the simplicity of its worship, as for the peaceful tenor of its doctrines. War in any and every shape, and under whatever pretence, is, by this system, absolutely and morally sinful, a point in which it approaches nearer to the sublimity of

Christianity than in any other of its doctrines. "Overcome evil with good" is the beautiful precept of the gospel, and "conquer evil by good" is one of the precepts of Gotamo. The whole system, indeed, wants the impress of divinity as a whole, but in its ethics it is an embodiment of the spirit of Christianity.

The effects of Buddhism, when propagated as at first, in a pure and unadulterated form, must have been wonderfully salutary on the minds and lives of its professors *. To its influence there is every reason to suppose we may ascribe the prosperity of Ceylon in the period whose history we are treating of, and to its deterioration and loss we may also ascribe much of its subsequent decline.

If, then, we consider collectively the evidences transmitted to us in Ceylonese history of the early refinement of its people,—if we consider the ruins of its ancient buildings, the nature of its government, the power of its sovereigns, and, above all, the influence of its admirable religion,—the mind must be blind indeed which cannot trace here the footsteps of civilisation and the proofs of early refinement †.

* Salvation is here (in Buddhism) made dependent, not upon the practice of idle ceremonies, or the repeating prayers, or hymns or invocations to pretended gods, but upon moral qualifications, which constitute individual and social happiness upon earth, and ensure it hereafter. Notes on Ancient India, p. 266.

† *Vide* Appendix I. for the connection of Buddhism with the Philosophy of Greece.

CHAPTER V.

HISTORY FROM B. C. 51 TO A. D. 800.

Koodatisso — Anula — Her depravity and debauchery — Makalantisso — Batiatisso—Maha Dailiya—Addagaimono—Kanijani Tisso—Choolabhayo —Seewali—Ellona—His expulsion and return—Chando—Yasa Siloo—Subho—Wasabho's insurrection—His reign and death—Wankanasiko—Invasion of the Solleans—This invasion revenged by Gajabahu—Batiatisso II.—The Wytoolian heresy—Abhayo—Sangatisso—Glass used as a preservative against lightning—Gotabhayo—Mahasen's inconstancy—Kitsiri Majan—Jetta-tisso—Budhadaso—His reforms—Upatisso II.—Mahanamo—Civil wars—Pharindo and the Malabars—Dutasewo's success—Kassapo—Mogallano—Kumara Dhas and the poet Kalidhas—Upatisso III.—Sila Kala—Bonaya—Assigahaka—Siri Sangabo II.—Detutisso—Kassapo—Dalupiatisso—Kassapo — Dalupiatisso II. — Hatthadatha—Mahalaipam—Aggrabodhi—Mihindo—Dapulo.

On the death of Chora Naga, 51 years B. C. Koodatisso, the son of his predecessor, ascended the throne. His reign was short, and terminated unfortunately in his being poisoned by his wife, a woman whose wickedness cannot perhaps be paralleled in the history of the universe. Having ascended the throne which she had thus rendered vacant, in order to gratify her own lust, she raised an obscure individual, named Balat Sewana, to her husband's seat and condition. With him, however, she quickly became disgusted, and fixing her eyes on a gigantic Malabar, named Wattuka, she cut off Balat by poison, when he had possessed and *enjoyed* the sovereignty for one year and two months. Wattuka was raised to the vacant dignity, but failed to please the insatiable Anula for a longer period than thirteen months. To wish him removed was, with her, but the prelude of his assassination. Poison was again administered, and again her victim perished. Warned by these examples, we would imagine, that even the madness of headlong ambition would have paused before occupying the fatal seat. Such, however, was not the case,—Prohitta, a Brahmin, was the next whom she desired; he satisfied her for six months, and was then buried. Two more, Sukkū and Balla Tisso, were mad enough to follow his example, and did so but to fall, the former in eleven and the latter in fifteen months.

Anula now found, however, that the world was thoroughly weary of her. Not another victim could be induced to share her crown and bed; and, after a wretched loneliness of four tedious months, a period was at once put to her wickedness * and her life.

Makalantisso, her son by Koodatisso, who had formerly fled to escape her violence, now returned with a numerous and determined army from concealment. Anula resisted, but was defeated, and the capital, Anuradhapoora, was besieged and forced. The queen would not, however, even yet yield, and, defending herself in her palace, was with it consumed by fire. Such was the miserable end of this fearfully wicked monster.

And here let us remark the partiality and unfairness of

* She was not quite so bad, however, as the Roman matrons alluded to thus by Juvenal.—Sic fiunt octo mariti, quinque per autumnos. Sat. vi. 228. Again, non consulum numero, sed maritorum annos suos computant. (Seneca de Beneficiis, 3. 16.) Whilst Martial (lib. 4, epi. 6.) mentions a wife who had ten *husbands* in one month!

priestly history. The character of Chora Naga is represented in the blackest and most hateful characters, and, after his death, he is said to have descended to the lowest hell, merely because he destroyed the temples, whilst the infamous Anula, who set all rules of decency and order at defiance, is allowed to escape without a single condemnation * !

Makalantisso found the kingdom, as we may readily suppose, in frightful disorder. The task of recomposing it was difficult, but he accomplished it, and, having done so, he proceeded to the strengthening of the fortifications of his capital. This he accomplished by erecting a stone rampart † seven cubits (10½ feet) high completely round

* A still more curious instance of this unfairness occurs in the history of France, and in the case of Charles Martel, the vanquisher of the Moors. "It might have been expected that the saviour of Christendom would have been canonized or at least applauded, by the gratitude of the clergy, who are indebted to his sword for their present existence. But, in the public distress, the mayor of the palace had been compelled to apply the riches, or, at least, the revenues of the bishops and abbots, to the relief of the state and the reward of the soldiers. His merits were forgotten, his sacrilege alone was remembered; and in an epistle to a Carlovingian prince, a Gallic synod presumes to declare that his ancestor was damned; that on the opening of his tomb, the spectators were affrighted by a smell of fire and the aspect of a horrid dragon; and that a saint of the times was indulged with a pleasant vision of the soul and body of Charles Martel burning, to all eternity, in the abyss of hell." Gibbon, vol. vi. p. 473.

† The following is the account of the present state of this rampart, as given in the explanatory notes appended to Turnour's Epitome of Ceylonese History. "Lieutenant (now Captain) Skinner's plan (of Anuradhapoora) is on too limited a scale to admit of the delineation of the city walls, which are said to have encompassed a space of four square gows or 244 square miles, that area being a square, each side of which was sixteen miles long. That officer notes, however, that the wall described to have surrounded the city, is to be seen near Aliaparté, running north and south, and forming the

the capital; and if the account which is handed down to us of the extent of this rampart be true, Anuradhapoora must have been a prodigious and gigantic city. A stone dāgobah at Mihintallai, and the construction of several tanks are also ascribed to him, in which is contained the history of his long and prosperous reign of twenty-two years.

Makalantisso was succeeded by his son Batiatisso, a prince remarkable for his deep humiliation of himself before the priesthood. He caused certain lands to be appropriated to the continual repair of the public edifices. To one thousand priests who officiated on a particular mountain he daily sent provisions, besides supporting numbers at his own table. He ascended the throne twenty years before the Christian era, and having reigned twenty-eight, died in the year 8 A. D.

On the demise of Batiatisso, his brother, Maha Dailiya, ascended the throne, in the eighth year of the Christian era, and the five hundred and fifty-first of the Buddhistical.

Nothing worthy of note is recorded of him, except that he built a dāgobah, called Saigiri, approached by 1800 stone steps, upon the summit of Mihintallai, a sacred mountain in the immediate vicinity of Anuradhapoora *.

west face. Aliaparté is about seven miles from Anuradhapoora, which confirms the account given of the extent of the wall, Mihintallai being about the east face. I had not sufficient time to make a minute exploration. The old place was situated about a quarter of a mile north-west of Lankaramaya; the foundations of the wall are so perfect that the ground plan may be traced throughout."

* The rocky mountain of Mihintallai is situated on the east about eight miles from the centre of Anuradhapoora, and was either included within, or formed part of the walls of that city. The extent of labour bestowed,

After a reign of twelve years he was succeeded by his son Addagaimono (also called Amanda Gaimous,) distinguished by his piety alone. He interdicted the taking of animal life, and, that the inhabitants might be supplied with food without doing so, he caused great *numbers of fruit trees* to be planted. He was dethroned and put to death by his younger brother, Kinihirridaila or Kanijani-tisso. This monarch is styled by Mr Turnour * " a cruel and impious prince." That he was a man of little virtue appears from the means by which he obtained the throne; but the most faithful of the native annals lay nothing more to his charge than this, and had he deserved the title of " impious," doubtless the Mahawanso would not have left us in doubt as to his true character. The following is the account of his reign, according to that rigidly religious work, as translated by Mr Turnour himself; " His younger brother Kanijani-tisso, putting him to death, reigned in the capital three years. This raja decided a controversy, which had for a long time suspended the performance of the religous ceremonies in the apósatha of the Chetiyo, (the Giri wihare,) and forcibly seizing the sixty priests who

and the different stages of decay visible on the ruins of Mihintallai, even in the steps cut in the solid rock, confirm the accounts given of them in Singhalese history, and render probable the traditions which connect the sanctity of this place with the visits of Buddhos who preceded Gotamo, (the last Buddho.)

The great number and breadth of the steps leading up to Mihintallai, and the summit, (where the Atta Dāgobah stood,) particularly attract attention; the dāgobah containing the Aurua Ruma, the Ambasstella Dāgobah, and the perilous bed of Mihindo, situated on a pinnacle, and overhanging a precipice, are amongst the monuments which procured for Mihintallai the name of Solosmastana. Colombo Journal, 24th November 1841.

* Epitome of the Hist. of Ceylon, page 19.

contumaciously resisted the royal authority, imprisoned *those impious persons* in the Kanira cave, in the Chetiyo mountain." (Chap. xxxv.)

Kanijani-tisso was succeeded by Choolabhayo, the son of Addagaimono, who reigned one year and was succeeded by his sister Seewali, who, after a reign of four months, was put to death by Ellona, (also called Ilanaya.) Ellona having by this act of wickedness obtained the crown, found it anything but a peaceful possession. Having interfered with the system of castes, by appointing an inferior one as the judge of a superior, a general rebellion was excited. Ellona was obliged to fly, and, having reached the western coast of the island, he embarked, in order to collect a foreign army to chastise his rebellious subjects. At the end of three years he returned, bringing with him a formidable force, and landing at Rohona, his army was increased by numerous volunteers. Nor were his enemies idle; Anuradhapoora was fortified, an army collected, and everything put in a posture of defence. Ellona advanced directly towards the capital, and was met in a plain near it, by the opposing army. Numerous conflicts took place, with various success. In one of them, however, the king's troops were on the point of defeat, when he, by a timely exhibition of himself, charging with fury on his elephant, restored the fortune of the day. A dreadful slaughter ensued, and, immediately afterwards, the victorious monarch entered the capital in triumph. After a reign of six years, Ellona was succeeded by his son Chando, (or Chandamu Khosiwo,) a prince distinguished alone by his having constructed a tank, which he dedicated to the wihare named Issarasumano; and his consort, we are informed, dedicated the village which supplied her personal retinue to the same wihare. From this we may suppose, that the same custom prevailed amongst the Ceylonese, as that of which we read amongst the ancient Persians, viz. that a particular city or village was appointed to yield a certain part of each prince's necessaries. Thus, when Themistocles delivered himself up to the Persians, three cities in Asia Minor,—Magnesia, Lampsacus and Myus —were appointed to supply his wants; one with bread, another with wine, and the third with other provisions or clothing *.

Chando was put to death by Yasa Siloo, (also called Yasalalako Tisso,) at an aquatic festival celebrated at the Tisso tank; who was himself dethroned by Subho †, a person of low birth, who usurped the kingdom. Several wihares are attributed to this monarch. Having heard that a person of the name of Wasabho was to put him to death, he resolved to extirpate all of that name in his dominions, and, for this purpose, commanded all the governors of the provinces accordingly. One of this name in the service of a chief in the north of the island, hearing of the king's command, and its cause, fled to Maha Wihare for refuge. Having remained there for some time, he at length ventured on bolder measures, and drawing together an army of resolute, determined men, commenced by reducing the province in which he then was. Thence

* Plutarch in vita.—Cor. Nep. c. x.—Plato also mentions the same custom. 1. Alcibiades.

† The manner of his death is thus related in the Mahawanso: Subho, being remarkably like the king in personal appearance, was frequently invested by the latter with the royal robes, whilst he, taking Subho's staff of office, stood as porter at the gate. On one of these occasions Subho resolving to act the king in reality, found fault with the porter, and had the disguised king at once put to death. (Chap. xxxv.)

proceeding to the Rohona district, the fostering place of every insurrection, he gradually advanced towards the capital. Nor are we to suppose that all these events took place at once; the accounts of these transactions have come to us so meagrely and concisely, that in very few cases are the particulars stated. We are informed, however, that he was engaged for some years in these enterprises and petty engagements, before the final one took place.

Subho advanced with a powerful army against his rival, but was defeated and slain, after a reign of six years.

As if to atone for his injustice in usurping the throne, Wasabho devoted himself entirely to piety, pious acts, and the erection of buildings for pious purposes. The building of three wihares, and the formation of eleven tanks are ascribed to him. But besides these, he repaired dilapidated edifices, erected houses for the priests; and, in order to make the capital a properly fortified city, he raised the walls all round to the height of eighteen cubits. In the erection of these stupendous works a long, happy and prosperous reign of forty-four years was spent, and, unlike his two predecessors, he left a peaceful throne to his son Wankanasiko.

The good fortune of Wasabho, however, did not descend to his son Wankanasiko. During his reign, the island was invaded by the Solleans, who, landing in the north-west, proceeded to ravage the country, and, advancing almost to the capital, retreated with an immense booty, and 12000 of the inhabitants. These they conveyed to their own country; and the task of revenging the invasion was left to Gajabahu, Wankanasiko's son.

He, at the head of a large army, invading the Sollee

country, retaliated on its inhabitants the evils endured by those of Ceylon from their invasion. Besides bringing back those of the Ceylonese who had been made prisoners, he carried off an equal number of the Solleans, and, on his return to Ceylon, settled them in that part of it called the Aloot-Kurakorla *. A warrior much celebrated for his prowess in Singhalese annals, called Nela-Yodhaya, accompanied Gajabahu in this expedition, and is represented as having performed the most extraordinary feats of valour. This expedition took place about the year 112 after Christ.

We are now entering upon that part of the history of Ceylon, which is, perhaps, the most uninteresting; little, indeed, is recorded of the reigns of each successive monarch, except the manner of his death, and that such and such a dāgobah or wihare is ascribed to him.

Gajabahu was succeeded by his son Mahallako-Naga, so called from his great age on ascending the throne; he reigned six years, and is said to have constructed seven wihares.

He was succeeded by his son Batiatisso the Second, who also built several wihares, and formed many tanks. Of his successor we may say what Pliny said of Trajan, "Idem tam parcus in ædificando, quam diligens in tuendo." Nothing being recorded of the next sovereign worthy of notice, we shall pass on to the reign of Wairatisso, the era of the introduction of the Wytoolian heresy into the Buddhism of Ceylon. He and his prime minister Kapilo,

* "The 12000 Ceylonese were sent to their respective homes, and the 12000 captives were allowed to reside in Aloot-Kūrakorla, a district to the northward of Colomba, *the inhabitants of which, to this day, retain many marks of their continental origin.*" The Friend, vol. iii. p. 42. A ceremony called the Parahara or procession was annually performed at the capital to commemorate this event.

being both enemies of the heresy, used all their influence to suppress it, and, for this purpose, punished the priests who adhered to it, besides having the books containing it publicly burned. This event (an important one in Buddhistical theology,) occurred in the 209th year of the Christian era, and the 752d of the Buddhistical.

Wairatisso had a younger brother who was found to be criminally attached to the queen, named Abhayo, who, on this discovery, fled towards the sea-shore, having first formed a league with the queen's father, Sabhadewo, in which it was decided between them, that he (Subhadewo) should remain at court, and so carry on his intrigues as to cause dissatisfaction amongst the people, at the same time informing Abhayo of how matters stood. Subhadewo was perfectly successful; dissatisfaction was every where apparent, and the whole kingdom ripe for a revolt. A messenger was then despatched to Abhayo, informing him of this, and he, having collected a large force in Malabar, landed quickly on the coast, and marched directly towards the capital.

Wairatisso found the instability of greatness; he was unable even to collect an army, and was obliged to fly with precipitation.

In the meantime Abhayo having entered the capital, proceeded immediately in pursuit of his brother, who had taken the queen with him, and succeeded in overtaking and killing him. He then returned to the capital, where, with the former queen, he reigned for eight years.

Abhayo's reign was undistinguished by any remarkable event, and that of his successor was equally uninteresting to the historian. The latter was dethroned by the commander of the army, named Sangatisso the First. We are informed that he raised a glass pinnacle on the spire of the Ruanello dāgobah as a protection against lightning, a circumstance which shews the advanced state of the arts and sciences amongst the ancient Ceylonese. During the reign of his successor, Siri Sangabo, a great famine, succeeded by a destructive plague, occurred. These were attributed to the malignity of an evil spirit, styled the red-eyed demon, to appease whom a rite, called the devil dance, was instituted, which remains even to this day *. His

* The following is the account given by Major Forbes of one of these devil-dancers whom he had seen:

"The Kapua, (or devil-dancer,) an athletic and very active man, danced to the noise of the tom-toms which had accompanied our party, and kept excellent time with his feet and hands, on which, as well as on his neck, arms and ankles, he wore large, hollow metal rings, called Salamba. Occasionally, he appeared in the highest state of bodily and mental excitement; his flesh quivering, and his eyes fixed, as if straining to distinguish forms in the gloom of the surrounding forest. In this mood, advancing towards the person for whom his incantations were performed, and while continuing one long respiration, he predicted the fate, or prescribed for the complaint of the demon worshipper.

"The scene I had just witnessed was impressive from its mysterious wildness; the banian tree, which stretched its huge branches on one side above the frail temple, and 300 natives of different ranks, on the other side, extended far over the stream, while the Yakadupha torch (formed of resin and nitre) of the exorcist, threw over the scene an indistinct light and livid colouring, in which his wild figure, long dishevelled hair, and frantic gestures, could be decerned and contrasted with the mute and motionless body of the spectators, or the intensely anxious look of the one who stepped forward to hear of "coming events," and pry into his future fate. Anon the torch blazed for an instant, then sank into a dull, blue flame, which blended with the halo formed around it by the dank fog that rested on the slimy stream. With such a light, and in such a chilling stagnant atmosphere, the gigantic trees, even the people amongst whom we stood, had an unearthly semblance, as if the spirits of past ages were shadowed forth,—those who had known these woods and wilds ere death had gained exclusive dominion over man, or the face of nature had been obscured by forests."

minister having conspired to dethrone him, Sangabo yielded the throne without a struggle, and retired to a wihare, where he remained for some time in safety. A price, however, had been laid on his head, by the usurper, Gotabhayo, and he was in consequence killed and beheaded by a peasant, (A. D. 240.)

In Gotabhayo's reign the Wytoolian heresy was revived, and its doctrines embraced by the Abhayagiri priests, whom the king, in consequence, degraded and punished, sixty of the more contumacious being banished from the island.

Gotabhayo intrusted the education of his two sons, Jetta-tisso and Mahasen, to a priest of the name of Sangamittra, a distinguished admirer of the Wytoolian doctrines, who endeavoured to inculcate these doctrines on the minds of his pupils. In the former case he was unsuccessful, Jetta-tisso remaining throughout his whole reign of ten years firmly attached to the established religion, but with Mahasen he was more successful. Having ascended the throne, Mahasen resolved to render his favourite doctrines the established religion of the island, and for this purpose ordered that no alms should be bestowed by his subjects on the orthodox priests. These, having no other means of support, wandered about in a state of great destitution, and finding no sustenance near the capital retired to the Rohona division of the island, a district to which the heterodox dogmas had not extended. The king, finding that his endeavours were vain to force them to renounce their tenets, changed his plan of operations, and proceeded to the demolition of their finest edifices. He pulled down the brazen palace, and demolished 363 other edifices of a religious nature; this he did in order to obtain materials for building others, in which the Wytoolian priests might officiate. Those priests, banished by Gotabhayo, were recalled, and every means adopted which priestly cunning could plan, or royal authority execute, to establish firmly the heretical doctrines. Sanghamittra, however, was soon to learn how unstable a support the royal favour was. A minister of Mahasen, who had formerly been a confident of his, being enraged at the revolution which the king was effecting in religion, resolved to strike a blow in favour of his ancient faith. For this purpose, flying to the mountainous district surrounding Adam's Peak, he there entrenched himself, and resolved to bring about a change in the king's sentiments by force of arms. Mahasen, dreading a popular revolt, preferred altering his religion to losing his crown. The favourite minister was recalled, Sanghamittra beheaded, and a counter revolution commenced.

That he might atone for his former impieties, the king re-erected the sacred edifices which he had destroyed, recalled the scattered priests, and used every exertion to render those doctrines firmly established, which, but a short time before, he had endeavoured to extirpate; a melancholy proof of the instability of that favour which is founded not on conviction but on caprice.

The violence of his religious views, however, did not entirely prevent his turning his attention to the improvement of his country. The formation of sixteen tanks and of a large canal, by means of which 20,000 fields were irrigated *, is ascribed to him. He seems to have been

* Six miles beyond Paecolom we passed through a low range of hills; on one of which, Nuwara Kande, (the hill of the city,) Mahasen Raja resided in

a man of singular energy and impetuosity, but wanting greatly fixedness of purpose and stability.

Mahasen was succeeded by his son Kitsiri Majan, (also called Sirimeghawanno,) whose reign seems to have been almost entirely occupied in rebuilding the edifices destroyed by his father. During his reign the celebrated tooth relic (the right canine tooth of Buddha) was brought to Ceylon by a Brahmin princess, from a part of Northern India, A. D. 310, and in the 853d year of the Buddhistical era *.

Kitsiri Majan was succeeded by his brother Jetta-tisso, celebrated for his skill in painting and carving. He executed several images with his own hands, but particularly a statue of Buddho, which is represented as having been wrought with the most exquisite skill, insomuch that we might almost believe him inspired for the work.

The successor of Jetta-tisso, Budhadaso, seems to have devoted himself almost entirely to the study of medicine and the regulation of the villages. He was (says the Mahawanso) a mine of virtues and an ocean of riches. Many wonderful cures are related which he performed, and, we are told, that he appointed to each district, contain-

the third century while superintending the formation of the neighbouring tank of Minneria, whose glassy lake and radiant plains soon burst on our view. From the great extent and irregular form of the lake of Minneria, I could hardly imagine it a work of art; and although its waters are now confined to little purpose, and the neighbouring plains contain but a few sickly inhabitants, better government will gradually restore cultivation, and health, with increasing population, smile on the "20,000 fields" which the magnificent and royal architect formed together with the lake which was to render them productive.—Forbes.

* The history of this relic has been written in a work still extant, called the Dathadhastu-wanso, the relic itself being styled the Dathadatu.

ing ten villages, a medical practitioner, an astrologer, a devil-dancer and a preacher. From this we may, at least, conclude, that the internal administration of the kingdom was not neglected, and that whatever were the disorders in the succession, the Ceylonese kings were perfectly well informed as to their duties. He did not confine himself to the appointing of practitioners, but also wrote a work (still extant in Sanscrit) containing a full account of the chirurgic art. This work is entitled "*Saratthasangabo* *." He also established hospitals, and built asylums for the crippled, deformed and destitute, a proceeding which shews, not only great humanity and wisdom on his part, but that his kingdom must have been in a very advanced state to feel the want and benefit of such establishments. Unfortunately it is merely from such incidental notices that we can conjecture the state of the kingdom; had we a distinct treatise on that subject, it is not going beyond the bounds of probability to say, that it would most probably exhibit a state of society quite as refined as that of Rome in its decaying splendour †.

* From the following remark of Sir William Jones, this would appear to be the only work on medicine and surgery yet known amongst the Asiatics. "There is no evidence that in any language of Asia there exists one original treatise on medicine considered as a science." Asiat. Res. iv. 159. Are we then going too far in claiming for the Ceylonese a degree of civilisation superior to that of most other eastern nations?

† That we are not going beyond the bounds of probability, in this supposition, may be easily shewn, by the fact, that in the reign of Constantine there was not a single artist in Rome who could decorate his triumphant arch; and that after Trajan's had been stripped of its most elegant figures,—to supply the want, the new ornaments, which it was necessary to introduce, were "executed in the rudest and most unskilful manner." — Gibbon, vol. 2, c. xiv.

Budhadaso was succeeded by his son Upatisso the Second, a prince of exemplary piety, who devoted himself to the study of religion and to the protection of its professors. During his reign the island was afflicted with a great famine.

Upatisso was murdered by his consort, who appears to have been attached to her brother-in-law Mahanamo. The latter was raised to the throne, and during his reign, the island was visited by a learned Buddhist who came from India. This person composed some very learned and valuable commentaries on the discourses of Buddho, besides adding some of his own, with commentaries also. His reign is also distinguished as having been that during which Ceylon was visited by the learned Fa Hian of China, who gives us an interesting account of the flourishing state of the island. The city of Anuradhapoora, he informs us, was inhabited by numerous magistrates, nobles, and merchants, engaged in foreign commerce. The houses were handsome, and the edifices well ornamented. The streets and roads were broad and straight; and at all the crossings were built lecture rooms, or rather halls, to preach in. The eighth, fourteenth, and fifteenth days of the moon were dedicated to high service or preachings, and a crowd of all classes assembled to hear the law *. Mahanamo died peaceably after a prosperous and happy reign of twenty-two years. His son, however, was not equally fortunate. Mahanamo's consort was a Malabar, by whom he had two children, Sotthiseno and his sister Sangha. On the day of his accession to the throne, Sotthiseno was put to death by his sister, who raised her husband in his place. Their prosperity, however, was not of long duration; her

* Col. Sykes' Notes on Ancient India.

husband died within a year, and was succeeded by Mittasena, of whose relationship to the other kings we are uninformed. Before Mittasena had enjoyed the title of sovereign for a year, the island was invaded by several Malabar chieftains, who took the capital and put the king to death. The princes and chiefs, however, unwilling to live in subjection to the invaders, fled to the Rohona district, which still remained independent.

A young prince of the royal blood, whose ancestors had concealed themselves on the usurpation of Subho, seeing the condition of the country, determined to make an effort to rescue it. On the death of the first usurper, Pandu, he commenced operations. Pandu's son, Pharindo, was not inclined to relinquish his fair kingdom without a struggle; and as he had the greater part of the country under his command, besides having his trained army of Malabars, the struggle was long, bloody and obstinate, continuing, indeed, till the termination of his life,—sixteen years. Datuseno, the young prince formerly mentioned, appears at this time to have been ruling over the Rohona district, and thence to have drawn his supplies. The Malabars, on their part, were not idle. Immediately on the death of Pharindo, his brother Kuddhaparindo was elected king. In this manner they continued a warfare for three years and nine months after Pharindo's death. The Malabars during that period elected three commanders, each of whom was in succession slain by Datuseno. Immediately on his accession, he proceeded to wreak his vengeance on the Malabars and on the Ceylonese nobles who had formed connections with them. The former he extirpated, and confiscated the estates of the latter *. Thus we are informed

* Perhaps Datuseno would have ended his life in peace, had he followed

he restored peace and tranquillity, reinstated Buddhism in its former magnificence, and diffused contentment and happiness amongst all his subjects. The nobility who had fled to Rohona rallied around him, and particular honours were bestowed upon his followers.

During this prince's reign, and with his assistance, Mahanamo, his uncle, composed the Mahawanso, or history of Ceylon from the period of Wijeya's arrival till the death of Mahasen; and from which the foregoing account has been principally taken. (A. D. 459.)

Datuseno had two sons and one daughter, the latter married to his prime minister. Having heard of some indignities inflicted on her by his son-in-law, he put his mother to death. The minister, naturally indignant at his cruelty, fled, with the intention of attempting to dethrone him. In this attempt he was unnaturally aided by the king's eldest son; and, by their united exertions, he was at length dethroned and beheaded. The Mahawanso contains the following beautiful reflection on this event: "Thus worldly prosperity is like unto the glimmering of lightning; what reflecting person, then, would devote himself to the acquisition thereof?" (Chap. xliii.)

Kassapo, his eldest son, having thus, by the murder of his father, received the crown, found it an unhappy and dangerous possession. His brother, Mogallano, resolving to revenge his father's death, fled to India, in order to collect an army, by means of which he might accomplish his intentions. In the meantime Kassapo, fearing either a general rebellion or the return of his brother, left Anuradhapoora, in order that he might fortify himself on an in-

the Roman Historian's maxim—"Bellorum egregios fines, quotiens ignoscendo transigatur. Tac. An. xii. 19.

accessible rock, which, from its having been decorated with several figures of lions, obtained the name of Sehagiri *. He was not long allowed to retain his new position in peace.

Mogallano, returning with an army from Dambadiva, fortified himself near the modern Colombo, and, by frequent incursions into his brother's territories, at length drew him from his retreat. A battle ensued, in which Kassapo was defeated, and, either maddened by his sudden reverse of fortune, or dreading lest he should fall into the hands of the enemy, he put himself to death.

Immediately on his accession, Mogallano proceeded to take a barbarous revenge on the enemies of his father,—the minister was executed, and upwards of one thousand others shared the same fate. During his reign, which lasted eighteen years, the Kaisadhatu relic, or lock of Buddho's hair, was conveyed from Dambadiva to Ceylon. Mogallano was succeeded by his son Kumara Das, a prince of great learning. During his reign, the celebrated Indian poet, Panditta Kalidhas, visited Ceylon, and is reported to have lost his life in the following manner:

One evening while Kumara Das was in the house of a courtezan, he observed a bee alighting on a water lily, which closed and imprisoned it. Taking advantage of the incident, the king elegantly compared it to his own condition, and, with great readiness, wrote the two following lines:

Siyatambera Siyatambera siyasewane
Siyasapura nidinolaba unsewane †.

This riddle, peculiarly elegant in Singhalese from the

* *Vide* Forbes' Ceylon, vol. ii. p. 1.

† By beauty's grasp, in turmoil, uncomposed,
He's kept a prisoner, with eyes unclosed.

position of the words and letters, was left by the king written on the wall of the apartment where he then was, with a promise beneath, that whoever should complete the verse, by explaining the riddle, should obtain any request he might make. Kalidhas, the poet, observing the lines, completed them, and in consequence awaited the reward. This, however, the courtezan endeavoured to obtain for herself, by having the poet murdered and buried beneath the apartment, asserting afterwards that she herself had added the stanza,—which ran thus :

Wanebambara malanotala ronatawanee
Mahadedera panagalawa giyasawanee *.

The king, suspecting the truth, had a rigorous search instituted, which ended in the discovery of the murder, and the guilt of the courtezan.

The body was exhumed, and a sumptuous pyre erected for the burning of it. A day was appointed when the king and court attended; but scarcely had the flames reached the body, when the king, overwhelmed with grief at so great a loss, rushed into them and was consumed.

The reigns of his two immediate successors being entirely devoid of interest, (of whom we can say no more than that "domi foresque otium fuit,") we shall pass them in silence; nor is that of their successor, Upatisso the Third, distinguished, save by its melancholy character. He himself lost his sight, and Sila Kala, his son-in-law, taking advantage of his distress, became a competitor for the throne. There was, however, one who was generous enough to

* But if all night the manel (the water lily) keeps the bee,
The morn beholds him gay, unhurt, and free.

fight for Upatisso: this was his son. The brave young prince, however, was defeated, and, overwhelmed at the prospect of the evils which awaited him, committed suicide. The king shortly after died of grief, and left the throne to his unworthy son-in-law.

During the reign of Sila Kala, the Wytoolian heresy was revived, and being for some time secretly adopted by the priests of Abhayagiri, was at length ably and openly opposed by a learned and eminent priest, named Jhoti Pali. This schism occurred in the 1088th year of the Buddhistical era, A. D. 545.

History could scarcely have been made more uninteresting than it is in the Ceylonese annals from the period of which we are treating, the sixth century, till the eleventh. Ceylon, however, we must remember, is not a country likely to afford much of the remarkable or revolutionary in its history. Its insulated position, its extreme fertility, and the unenterprising character of its inhabitants, would all combine to render its chronicles filled with repetitions of the same events, and to render its kings content with their government without attempting the conquest of distant nations. But we should be adopting a false conclusion, were we to suppose that it must, on this account, have been a miserable, poor and servile country; on the contrary, although extensive conquest, great power, and long continued or successful wars may contribute to the happiness of a few restless and turbulent spirits, yet it is only in the quiet of inglorious peace that the great body of the people enjoy happiness or prosperity, and, in consequence, that part of the history of Ceylon, of which we are now treating, although dull and uninteresting to the inquirer, may have been its most happy and prosperous period.

Happy is that people (says Machiavel) whose annals are tiresome. Nor would the deposition of a monarch, and the usurpation of his throne by his deposer, be an event likely to disturb this tranquillity amongst the great majority of the inhabitants. Their own petty chiefs were those with whom alone they were connected, and to these alone they would look as their lawful superiors and political fathers. Thus the same deep happiness and quiet would descend from father to son amongst the poorer classes, whilst kings were beheaded, their children persecuted, and their palaces overthrown.

It would be a tedious and monotonous task to name each successive sovereign, with the period of his death and the length of his reign; we shall therefore refer the inquirer to the list of kings which we annex * to the present volume, and now pass on to the reign of Bonaya (or Laimini Bonaya,) A. D. 633, at which period the northern division of the island was afflicted with a general sickness, and, in consequence, so weakened as to become quite defenceless. The governor of the Rohona district, a grandson of the king, whom Bonaya had deposed, perceiving the weakened state of that part of the country which was under the king's more immediate control, resolved to take advantage of it, and accordingly advanced against him with a powerful army. Bonaya could make but a weak defence, and was quickly defeated and slain. Assigahaka having thus obtained the kingdom, found that he had but to turn those arms which had lately vanquished an usurper against a pretender—that pretender being his own uncle, who had escaped from the kingdom immediately on the deposition

* *Vide* Appendix, II.

of his brother by Bonaya. No sooner had Assigahaka heard of his uncle's landing, then he marched to oppose him. The rival armies met, and the new king was once more successful; his uncle was slain, and a great part of his army made captive. These captives Assigahaka bestowed as slaves to the temples. He reigned nine years, and was succeeded by his son, Siri Sangabo the Second. Siri Sangabo, however, was not allowed to retain his throne in peace. A descendant of another branch of the royal family asserted his claim to the throne, and resolved to support that claim by force of arms. Siri Sangabo, in consequence, was, after a reign of six months, driven out of the island, and Detutisso (or Kaloona Detutisso) the usurper, occupied his throne. Brief as the reign of his predecessor had been, that of Detutisso was still more so. Siri Sangabo having fled to the Malabar coast, there collected an army, and with it sailed for Ceylon, to redispute, with his opponent, the possession of the throne. Landing in the northern part of the kingdom, he advanced towards the capital, and was met by the reigning sovereign. Several battles ensued, and the invader was on the point of relinquishing the enterprise, when a large reinforcement of Malabars arrived to his assistance. The report of this addition to his rival's army filled Detutisso with consternation and dismay, and, in a fit of despair, he put an end to his life and reign, after the latter had continued five months. Siri Sangabo, thus a second time raised to the imperial dignity, began to imitate his predecessors, by erecting structures which should cause his name to descend to future years. He was not allowed, however, to enjoy in peace the throne he had twice won. Another member of the royal family, of the same branch as Detutisso, named Kassapo, opposed him; and, after a protracted war, succeeded in again dethroning him. Sangabo again left the country in the hope of reinstating himself by the aid of a foreign army, but was this time unsuccessful, and finally died in the Rohona district, after having spent sixteen years in struggling for that sceptre, which, when he obtained, he was unable to preserve.

Dalupiatisso, on his accession, gave a bad omen of his future government. Several acts of injustice are attributed to him, besides his plundering many temples and dāgobahs, an act quite sufficient in itself to brand his reign as tyrannical and impious in the annals of Ceylon.

In the meantime, Kassapo, the brother of Siri Sangabo, took upon him to revenge his brother's injuries. Advancing from Rohona against the king, he compelled the usurper to quit the country, and on his return with a foreign army, again encountered and defeated him. In this last battle, Dalupiatisso was slain.

Kassapo, after a reign of nine years, appointed his maternal nephew heir to the crown; and this prince, Dapulo, perceiving that most of the disorders of the kingdom were brought about by the intrigues of the Malabars, endeavoured to drive them forth from the capital. The Malabars, however, were not so easily to be dispossessed of their possessions. Dalupiatisso's son was still alive in their native land, and him they invited to Ceylon, promising to give him the throne. The son, (also called Dalupiatisso,) delighted at the offer, immediately prepared for the invasion, and, landing in the southern coast, advanced at once towards the capital. Nor were the insurgents idle; and Dapulo, thus doubly assailed by internal enemies on the one hand, and invaders on the other, was obliged to fly to Rohona, where, after lingering for three years, he died (A. D. 696.)

Passing over the reigns of three monarchs, the successors of Dalupiatisso, being a period of twenty-seven years, we find a sovereign of the original royal family, named Hatthadatha, reigning. At this period there was a scion of the royal blood of Ceylon, in that part of Northern India so frequently mentioned under the name of Dambadiva, who distinguished himself in the military service of the monarch of that country. This young prince gradually acquired more ambitious views, and at length resolved to dispute with the reigning monarch the Ceylonese throne.

Having obtained aid from an Indian king named Naraseeha, he proceeded at once to carry his ambitious projects into execution. Hatthadatha, however, was not disposed to yield possession of his crown without a struggle. Mahalaipamu, the invader, landed, and the king at once proceeded to oppose him. An obstinate and well-contested battle was the result, and Mahalaipamu, notwithstanding his utmost exertions, found himself unable to oppose the fury of his adversaries, and was, in consequence, driven from the island. His ambitious views, however, were not to be overturned by the loss of a single battle. Having repaired to his former patron, he collected a larger force of resolute men, and with these once more proceeded to Ceylon. Fortune that had before frowned, now smiled upon his perseverance; another battle ensued, in which he was perfectly successful. The king's troops were routed, and he himself made prisoner, and, with unnecessary cruelty, was immediately decapitated: respecting Mahalaipamu's future conduct we are left entirely ignorant. Indeed, in the history over which we are travelling, the manner in which the throne was obtained by the successive sovereigns, and the cause of the death of each, seems alone to have engaged the attention, or to have excited the curiosity of the native historians; and, however we may lament the dearth of information, we cannot supply the want. "It is," indeed, "fertile in names, but barren in events *."

On the death of Mahalaipamu, two sovereigns reigned successively forty and six years; during that of the latter of these, (Aggrabodhi,) the seat of government was changed from Anuradhapoora to Pollanarua †. Aggrabodhi was succeeded by Mihindo the First, in the seventy-fifth year of the eighth century. This monarch, we are informed, engaged himself in the erection of a palace and several temples, whilst his son Dapulo was occupied in suppressing an insurrection which occurred in the northern province. In the palace which Mihindo erected, called the Rattana-prassada, we are informed there was a magnificent golden image of Buddho. Besides the erection of

* Hume, History of England.

† The ruins of this ancient and once flourishing city are thus noticed by Major Forbes, vol. i. p. 413. "The temples and buildings of Pollanarua are in much better preservation than those of Anuradhapoora, although very inferior to them in point of size; the extent of the city also corresponds with the diminished resources and decreased population of the island in the twelfth century, when the rampart or fence of Pollanarua was formed, as compared with the power and splendour of Ceylon under the "great dynasty," when Wahapp built the walls of Anuradhapoora in the first century of the Christian era. In several of the buildings at Pollanarua, particularly in two small doors, the proper arch is to be found, but the principle of it does not appear to have been understood by the Singhalese architects.

this and several other buildings, Mihindo caused registers of the kingdom to be composed, which should regularly record the acts of the successive sovereigns.

Mihindo was succeeded by his son, Dapulo, a prince greatly commended for his attention to the welfare of his subjects. Whatever works required repair, there the king took up his residence to see the repairs properly executed. We are informed also, that several hospitals owe their erection to this monarch's anxiety for improvement; and, more than all this, he founded a college for the regular education of medical students. A code of laws is also attributed to him, committed to writing, lest his successors should neglect them. Thus, in a short reign of five years, Dapulo gave proofs of a military genius, combined with an anxiety for internal improvement, and a wisdom in the prosecution of it, unsurpassed, probably, by any of his predecessors.

This great and good man died in the first year of the ninth century.

Before proceeding further with the history, let us now take a brief review of what is contained in the present chapter, and endeavour to discover the condition of Ceylon at this period from the indications here given us.

CHAPTER VI.

STATE OF CEYLON IN THE FIRST EIGHT CENTURIES AFTER THE CHRISTIAN ERA.

In reviewing the history of Ceylon during the five centuries preceding the Christian era, we found that it had advanced to a degree of civilisation quite equal to that of most eastern countries; and in the subsequent narrative we find continual references to customs, establishments and proceedings, which could only have existed or taken place in a well-ordered, civilised and polished country.

Unfortunately, as we have before said, it is but from these incidental allusions that the state of the country can be guessed at; and, in consequence, we cannot arrive at anything like full or certain knowledge on the subject. Enough, however, is apparent to convince us, that the neglect of the antiquities of Ceylon has been both unjust and inconsistent, and that much curious and valuable information might be derived respecting the internal condition of the country, were those antiquities diligently investigated.

From the birth of Christ to the commencement of the eighth century seems to have been the golden age of Singhalese literature. In that period Ceylon's greatest historian lived, and left to succeeding ages the history of his country from the earliest period, respecting which he could obtain authentic accounts, to his own times. In that period, the discourses of Buddho were committed to writing for the benefit of future generations; and, in that period, the greatest poets which the country has produced flourished. Thus, we see that theology, history and poetry, (the three species of composition most cultivated by those states whose literature is yet growing,) were cultivated, and successfully so, by the ancient Ceylonese. Thus, whilst Rome was being overrun by barbarians; and whilst Genseric, with his hosts of Vandals, was destroying its buildings, and rooting out its literature, Mahanamo was celebrating the reigns of the sovereigns of his beloved Lanka, and shewing forth its glory and splendour; whilst shortly after Kumara Dás was enriching his native tongue with his poetry and erudition. In this manner the noble plant of learning, although uprooted in one land, rears its venerable head in another, and there perpetuates its life-infusing seed.

During the period we are now reviewing, the inhabitants of Ceylon appear to have devoted themselves less to military affairs, than to the improvement of the fine arts. Nor was it in this respect different from other countries under the same circumstances. When a certain degree of prosperity and wealth has been achieved by a country, it naturally enters upon the boundless field of luxury, and before its taste has become vitiated, and its inhabitants depraved, it is generally at such a time that nations are the most prosperous, elevated and happy. Such was the state of ancient Greece before the age of Pericles, and such the condition of Rome during the Augustan age. Both had reached the summit of elevation; literature, painting, sculpture and architecture were at their height, and in their perfection; but the seeds of future destruction were even then sown, and gradually entwined themselves round the branches of those mighty oaks, which overshadowed almost the whole world, until they could no longer sustain the weight, and fell. Ceylon never reached the same pitch of perfection. Its insular situation, and the unwarlike spirit of its inhabitants, prevented the establishment of such a mighty and extensive empire as those just mentioned; but, on a smaller scale, we see precisely the same result, modified by the peculiarities natural to each. Thus the rise of Greece and Rome was sudden and electric; that of Ceylon gradual and slow; the former shot far before the latter in the race of refinement, and, in consequence, their fall was sudden and utterly debasing; whilst the other, never having advanced to the same height, never fell so far, and fell as it had risen, gradually and slowly.

Some will perhaps smile at such comparisons, and tell us, that Ceylon is, and ever was, too debased and low to be compared with Greece and Rome. Such, however, we boldly assert, is not the case. Human nature, however different its features, is ever the same, and, under similar circumstances, will always produce the same results. Thus in the histories of Greece, Rome and Ceylon, we see a gradual rise, the height attained, and then the descent accomplished, and all these only differing in each from the force of the varying circumstances under which each successive step was accomplished.

It will be quite unnecessary for us to select every indication of an advanced state of society from the preceding narrative, and thereby to prove the ancient refinement of Ceylon. The state which turns its attention to literature and science cannot be barbarian, and in proportion as it excels in each, is it civilised and refined. But we would direct particular attention to the establishment of hospitals for the sick, asylums for the maimed and lunatic, and medical practitioners for each rural district. The internal administration of the kingdom, and the excellent manner in which that arrangement was conducted, is shewn to us from that simple fact; and although we frequently read of depositions and usurpations, yet these appear to have passed over without much disturbing the inhabitants of the rural districts, who formed, it must be remembered, the great majority of the population *.

The estimation in which the politer arts were held is proved by the kings themselves studying them with diligence and success. Thus Jetta-tisso (A. D. 330) devoted himself to sculpture, and, as we have read, particularly excelled in it; his son and successor Budhadaso was a great and celebrated proficient in medicine; Kumara Dás was celebrated as an excellent poet, and a successor of his, named Aggrabodhi, whom we have not before mentioned, rivalled him in the same art; whilst almost every one of the princes was well learned in the theology of their day, and even the schisms which occurred shew an

* Perhaps the following remarks of Gibbon may help us to account for these disorders. "The superior prerogative of birth, when it has obtained the sanction of time and popular opinion, is the plainest and least invidious of all distinctions among mankind. The acknowledged right extinguishes the hopes of faction, and the conscious security disarms the cruelty of the monarch. To the firm establishment of this idea, we owe the peaceful succession and mild administration of European monarchies. To the defect of it we must attribute the frequent civil wars through which an Asiatic despot is obliged to cut his way to the throne of his fathers." Decline and Fall, vol. i. chap. vii. 8vo edition of 1823.

independence of research and opinion very uncommon in the East. Such being the honour in which the fine arts and sciences were held, we cannot doubt but that they would be assiduously cultivated and improved. But may we not fairly conclude that, if so much respecting these matters can be learned from a work written almost exclusively to record the religious acts of the kings, and to afford us a connected list of them, (*i. e.* from the Mahawanso,) were we to have any thing like distinct and explicit information on the subject, we would find a degree of excellence in their government, and improvement in their civilisation far exceeding what is here claimed?

Another proof of their cultivation of literature exists in their cultivation and study of two classical languages, viz. the Sanscrit and the Pali. It is, however, quite possible that the adoption of these languages by the priests, for their sacred writings, took place only to screen their knowledge from the vulgar, just as the Egyptian priests used the hieroglyphical and enchorial characters. This supposition, however, is improbable, inasmuch as a better reason can be given for the use of these languages, and because we find no traces of exclusiveness in their religion. By writing in the former of these languages they were understood by the Brahmins and Hindus of India, and in the latter by the Buddhists of the Burman empire. On these accounts there is little reason to suppose that Sanscrit or Pali was originally adopted as an exclusive vehicle, although, finally, they would doubtless become so, by being the learned language of the East, and, of course, understood by the learned only.

Works on astronomy, medicine, chemistry, mathematics and natural philosophy were written in Sanscrit;

whilst for those on history, Pali was almost exclusively used. Thus we have seen in the preceding history, that Budhadaso used the Sanscrit for his medical treatise. The principal religious works composed during the period of which we treated in the last chapter are ascribed to Buddho, from whom they descended orally, in the Pali tongue, through succeeding generations, till finally they were committed to writing, as we noticed, in the reign of Walagambahoo, before Christ 89. These consist of the three Pitakas, (or the Pittakattaya,) divided into the Wineye, Abhidharma and the Sutra pitaka. They are in fact the scriptures of Buddhism, containing their doctrines, sacred history and precepts; to these commentaries were added, on the introduction of the first schism, which are called the "Attakātha," to which additions have since been made at various periods, and which were originally written, not in the Pali, but in the vernacular Singhalese; about the fifth century after Christ, however, they were translated into the former. The Mahawanso, from which the following history is principally compiled, was written by Mahanamo, who also added commentaries on that work, called the Tíka. These were both compiled in the Pali language. Before again turning to the history of Ceylon, it will be well to remember that, at the period of which we are writing, its inhabitants consisted of three distinct classes, the native Singhalese, (the Aborigines,) Beddas or Veddahs, and the Malabars.

The former being the more numerous and the proper inhabitants of the island, the second, those designated yakkhos in the native accounts, being those driven into the mountainous and woody parts by the invasion of Wijeya, and who appear never to have mingled with their conquerors, and the latter those who came from the Malabar coast during successive invasions, and who had become a numerous and powerful people, insomuch that we have seen the monarch Dapulo unable to expel them from his capital, and losing his throne, in consequence of attempting to do so. Respecting the customs of each of these classes we shall treat in a future part of this work; but it may not be amiss to remark here, that the Veddahs lived in a wild state, preferring the life of the hunter to the more sedate one of the agriculturist, inhabiting caverns and trees, and depending on the precarious result of the chase for food. The knowledge of this fact will help us to account for the ease with which rebellions were excited, and armies raised in Ceylon, especially when we remember that these savage inhabitants principally occupied Rohona, the south-eastern division of the island, that division which yielded shelter to the traitor, refuge to the rebel, and armies to the pretender.

Keeping in view, then, that such was the state of Ceylon at this period, we will be the less surprised to find the next era of its history one of turbulence, revolution and military glory.

CHAPTER VII.

HISTORY FROM A. D. 800, TO 1160.

Invasion of the Malabars—Suicide of Mihindo—Kasiapo—Pandi invaded—Udaya II.—Rebellion in Rohona—Kasiapo V. and VI.—Sekka Sena—Dapulo—The King of Pandi seeks refuge in Ceylon—Udaya III.—Rebellion—Sena II. III. and IV.—Description of Anuradhapoora—Sena expelled—Ceylon becomes tributary to Sollee—Wickramabahu—Wijayabahu—Embassy sent to Siam for help against the Solleans—Ceylon again independent—Again invaded—Wirabahu—Sollee invaded—Jayabahu—Wickramabahu dethrones him—Prackramabahu's birth foretold—His boyhood and education—His ingratitude—His able policy—Rebellion in Rohona—Quelled—Fate of Subhāla.

On the death of the excellent and energetic Dapulo, the country seems to have been in a state of profound tranquillity. It would be as uninteresting as useless to name his four successors. They each obtained the crown in peace, and peaceably left it to their successors, not one of them having had to quell an insurrection, or having lost his life by violent means. Thirty-eight years after the demise of Dapulo, Sena ascended the throne on his father's death. At this period the continual enemies of Ceylon—the Malabars—again made their appearance, and, accustomed as they were to rapine and war, proved too formidable an enemy to the peaceful Ceylonese. Some time was lost by the sovereign in the enrollment of his army, and, in the mean while, the king of Pandi had fortified himself at Mahapellegama. An attack on his entrenchments there proving unsuccessful, the unfortunate monarch was obliged to seek safety in flight, leaving the task of recovering his kingdom to Mihindo and Kasiapo, his more persevering sons. They advanced with a fresh army against the invaders, but with equal unsuccess, and once more the beautiful Lanka lay at the mercy of the ruthless Malabars. Mihindo, in despair, ended his life by his own hands, and Kasiapo joined his father in the Malaya division of the island. Pollanarua was now invested by the invaders, and was quickly taken; the spoils, amongst which the sacred jewels of the temple, the golden statues, the drum of victory, and the sacred cup * of Buddhu, are particularly mentioned and deplored being sent to Pandi. The country being thus conquered the king of Pandi offered to return to his own country for a suitable ransom. This was eagerly given by Sena, and the conqueror departed in triumph, leaving the throne to its former occupant. After a reign of twenty years, Sena was succeeded by his son, Kasiapo, who found a favourable opportunity for revenging the injuries of his father.

One of the sons of the king of Pandi having revolted against his father, after an unsuccessful attempt to obtain the throne of his native country, fled to Ceylon, where Kasiapo, for political reasons, received him with every

* The following is the usual account given of this sacred cup. When Gautama became Buddhu, it was necessary that he should have a drinking vessel of a particular kind; accordingly the four hill-gods, Pattiny, Wisbesenne, Saman Rajah and Kandi Kumara, having each made a cup, brought it to Buddhu. On this, Gautama told them that one was enough, and had the three accordingly placed one on the top of the other so as to form but one." It was generally composed of blue sapphire, and was intended to last till the next Buddhu, *i. e.* five thousand years.

demonstration of kindness. He espoused the young prince's cause, and they immediately proceeded, with their combined forces, to dethrone the reigning king. On landing in Pandi, the first expedition in which they engaged was against the capital, Madura, and in this they were perfectly successful; the capital was taken, the king put to death, and his rebellious son raised to the throne—thus was the injustice which he had inflicted on Sena more than equalled by that he himself experienced.

Kasiapo, loaded with spoil, returned in triumph to his own kingdom, and terminated a long and prosperous reign in peace. Another heresy, called the Neela-pata-dara (which seems to have had reference to the colour of the priestly vestments) was introduced from the continent during this reign.

His successors, Udaya the First, and Udaya the Second, passed lengthened and peaceful reigns, chiefly occupied in the promotion of internal improvement. During the reign of the latter, his brother, Mihindo, then governor of Rohona, wished to raise that province into an independent kingdom, and, in consequence, renounced his allegiance to Udaya. The king was not long in attempting to chastise him; but, in a battle which ensued on the borders of Rohona, he was defeated, and fell back on his capital, Pollanarua. Mihindo, too impetuous to reap the fruit of his first victory, rashly pursued him, and, entering the capital with a small body of followers, was taken prisoner and executed. The construction of a fertilising canal and several tanks is ascribed to Udaya.

An occurrence very similar to that which took place in Udaya's reign happened to his successor, Kasiapo the Fifth. A prince of Rohona, also called Mihindo, wishing to add the adjoining province of Maya to his territory, was opposed by the king in the prosecution of his design. A battle ensued, in which Kasiapo was perfectly successful; and, with a degree of clemency seldom shewn to rebels in eastern countries, he generously took the defeated Mihindo again into his favour, bestowing on him his former province, and, in addition, the hand of one of his daughters. Nor was his confidence misplaced. Mihindo, admiring his generosity, and fearing his power, applied himself with diligence and success to the improvement of his territory, and to the cultivation of Kasiapo's good-will; whilst the latter having thus firmly established his own power, and finding his kingdom in perfect peace, applied himself to the study of religion, and to the observance of its ordinances.

The prosperous and peaceful reign of Kasiapo was but as the deceitful lull which precedes the tempest. Two of the kings of Southern India, whose predecessors we have so frequently found invading Ceylon, viz. the king of Sollee and Pandi, were at this period engaged in war. The latter, remembering the aid which Kasiapo the Fourth had rendered to a predecessor of his, in endeavouring to attain his father's throne, solicited the new monarch, Kasiapo the Sixth, to grant him aid against the Solleans, whom he was pleased to style the hereditary enemies of Ceylon. Kasiapo was not adverse to the proposal, and sent a powerful force under the command of his son Sekka Sena, to co-operate with the Pandian king. Sekka, embarking at Mantotte, at once proceeded to the relief of his ally, and, landing at Madura, joined his forces with those of the Pandians. That country, oppressed with an invasion which it was unable to oppose, beheld the relief with joy, and, with eagerness, the combined forces marched against the Sollean invaders. The latter, however, fearing to encounter their enemies, evacuated the country, and, ere their invasion could be retaliated, Sekka died.

Kasiapo, fearing that his son had perished by unfair means, recalled the Ceylonese army and gave the command of it to his youngest son, Udaya. Shortly after, the hand of death seized the king, and Dapulo, his son, succeeded to the throne, but enjoyed it only for seven months.

During all this period the war in Pandi was vigorously prosecuted greatly to the disadvantage of the king of that country.

Dapulo having died, as we have intimated, seven months after he had received the crown, was succeeded by a monarch of the same name, of whose relationship to the former kings we are uninformed. In the mean time the king of Pandi, unable to resist effectually the power of his antagonist, was obliged to leave his country, and seek a refuge in Ceylon. Immediately on his arrival at Mantotte Dapulo welcomed him with becoming hospitality to his dominions, and prepared for his reception a palace near Anuradhapoora, the ancient capital. A king, however, even though an exile will still be an object of suspicion to his more fortunate brethren, and so was the Pandian king to Dapulo. Certain dangerous intrigues with the Ceylonese nobility were either discovered to have been carried on by him, or at least were, without hesitation, ascribed to him. The conduct of the reigning prince, in consequence, became so equivocal as to cause the exile's departure from Ceylon, and that with such precipitation, that his crown and regalia were left behind.

Dapulo having reigned ten years, died in the 974th

year after Christ, and the 1517th of the Buddhistical era.

He was succeeded by a tyrant, called Udaya the Third, against whom the chiefs and people conspired. Udaya, however, was powerful enough to defeat the rebellion, and the leaders of it, dreading his resentment, endeavoured to save themselves by becoming priests. The king disregarding the sacred character which they had assumed, seized and decapitated them, at the same time ordering their heads to be cast into the public streets. The populace, enraged at the loss of their favourite chiefs, and still more at the indignities which were perpetrated upon them, rose in a mass, and, besieging the palace, loudly demanded that the same punishment which the rebels had suffered, should be inflicted on the king and his advisers. The king, unable to stem the torrent, endeavoured to avert it by surrendering his ministers into their hands, and they, infuriated at the counsels which they imagined had originated with them, renewed the tragedy by subjecting them to the fate of their favourites. Reeking with blood, and intoxicated with revenge, they had no sooner retaliated thus, than they again rushed to the palace, declaring that nothing but the blood of the king himself would satisfy them.

The priests, fearing lest things would proceed to extremities, resolved on exerting their influence, and acting the part of mediators between the hostile parties. They succeeded in obtaining from the king various concessions, which at length appeased the people, and brought them back to their allegiance.

From the shortness of Udaya's reign, the perpetual troubles in which he was involved, and his tyrannical and cruel conduct, we may infer, without much doubt, that his end was a violent one, although we are not informed of this in the native accounts. This appears the more probable from the amiable character of his successor, Sena the Second, and from his relationship to the former kings being passed over in silence. The only fact of which we are informed in his reign is, that he appointed his faithful friend Udaya the Fourth to be his heir.

In Udaya's reign an embassy arrived from the king of Sollee, requesting the regalia of the exiled king of Pandi; this application Udaya thought proper to refuse, although the refusal, he was aware, would be attended with much trouble to himself.

The Sollean king, resolving to enforce his demand, sent an army against Udaya, which, being opposed by that king, overcame him in the ensuing combat, and obliged him to fly to Rohona. There, uniting his forces with those of the prince of that district, he found himself again able to cope with the aggressors, and, advancing against them, gained a complete victory, driving the invaders from the island.

The reigns of his successors, Sena and Mihindo, are quite unimportant, and undistinguished by any event of consequence, except that, during that of the latter, which continued sixteen years, the religious edifice, formerly erected on Adam's Peak, but destroyed by the Solleans, was restored to its former condition, and that the monarch obtained in marriage a princess of Kalingoo.

The successor of Mihindo was Sena IV., who ascended the throne, A. D. 1013, at the age of twelve. The prime minister of Mihindo (also called Sena,) was appointed regent during the minority of the young prince. A strong party was, however, formed against the regent, and, by their intrigues, his mother and brothers were put to death. The minister was not of so placable a nature as to endure this tamely; and as there were so many foreigners in the island ever ready to fight for money, the establishment of an army was not a very difficult matter.

The youthful prince was put by his dissimulating courtiers at the head of an opposite army, and the result was, that he and they were obliged to fly to Rohona. The Queen Dowager seems to have acted the part of mediator on this occasion; and, by her exertions, a reconciliation was brought about between the prince and his injured minister. The former returned to Pollanarua, where, in the tenth year of his reign, he died from the effects of excessive drinking.

Sena was succeeded by his brother, Mihindo IV., who transferred the seat of government from Pollanarua to Anuradhapoora. Perhaps we cannot interest the reader better than by extracting here the account which a native has left us of this ancient and far-famed city.

" This magnificent city, (says the describer,) is refulgent from the numerous temples and palaces, whose golden pinnacles glitter in the sky. The sides of its streets are strewed with black sand, whilst the middle is sprinkled with white; they are spanned by arches of bending wood, bearing flags of gold and silver; whilst vessels of the same metals, containing flowers, are observed on either side. In niches placed for the purpose are statues holding lamps. * * *

" Elephants, horses, carts and multitudes of people are ever to be seen passing and repassing. There are dancers, jugglers and musicians of all kinds and of all nations; the latter performing on chanque shells, ornamented with gold. The city is four gows (sixteen miles) in length from north to south, and the same in breadth from east to west. The principal streets are Moon Street, Great King Street, Bullock Street and River Street, all of them of immense extent, and some containing 11,000 houses; to enumerate the smaller ones would be impossible."

Scarcely had Mihindo become firmly seated on his throne, when he found himself involved in troubles. Such was the number of the foreigners resident in the country, that the greatest disorder was everywhere apparent. In the tenth year of his reign, his palace was besieged by those who called themselves his subjects, and he was obliged to fly, with precipitation, in disguise to Rohona, where he fortified himself. There he had a son, named Kasiapo, born to him. For twenty-six years the kingdom was in such a state of anarchy and disorder that he was unable to obtain his lawful throne. At the end of that period, an army of Solleans from the Coromandel coast landed to plunder the country and revenge their ancient wrongs upon the unfortunate Singhalese. The capital was taken and plundered; but, not content with that, they followed the dethroned king into Rohona, and made him and his consort prisoners. They, together with a vast amount of booty, consisting of gold and silver and precious stones, and images and shrines, were sent to Sollee, where they ended, in captivity, their miserable lives. In the meantime, their son, Kasiapo, was still in the Rohona district, waiting for an opportunity of regaining his hereditary throne. A Sollean viceroy having been appointed to govern the country during its subjection, he, fearing lest in some of the revolutions (so common in eastern countries) he should be hurled from his throne, resolved to obtain possession of the young prince, and thus secure his own prosperity. His army was, in consequence, set in motion, but such was the alacrity and energy of the young prince and his attendants, that an opposing army was almost immediately on foot, in defence of Kasiapo, and, after many harassing marches, wasting delays, and numerous petty engagements, he was forced to abandon the enterprise, and retreat. Kasiapo, encouraged by this advantage, resolved to make a determined effort to obtain his lawful throne, but, unfortunately, in the midst of his preparations, he was seized with a fatal fit, which terminated at once his hopes and his life.

Ceylon was now divided into two totally distinct provinces, the more extensive, important and populous of which was under the dominion of the Solleans; the other, the wild and rugged Rohona, governed by native princes. It may be easily imagined, that neither the one nor the other was in a state of order or tranquillity; the whole island was in fact one scene of anarchy, owing to the constant invasions and depredations of the Malabars. During this turbulent interregnum of twelve years, four native princes seized the reins of government in Rohona, until at length an infant prince was crowned, who restored the fortunes of his country, repressed its invaders, and once more established it as a free and powerful country. On the demise of Wickramabahu, his infant son Wijayabahu was crowned (A. D. 1071) king of Ceylon, an empty title then, indeed, but one which he afterwards rendered substantial and secure. An embassy was now sent to Siam, which, as being an eminently Buddhist country, it was hoped would send assistance to the suffering Buddhists of Ceylon. The embassy was successful, and soon returned with an effectual aid of treasure. Unfortunately, however, domestic turmoil was now on the point of overthrowing those prospects of success which seemed so likely to be realized. A prince of the royal blood, named Kasiapo, aided by his impetuous brother, erected the standard of revolt against the youthful Wijaya. His untimely treachery met, however, with its merited reward, for, in the ensuing battle, he was slain, and his brother forced to fly. Flushed with recent victory, Wijayabahu marched at once against the Solleans, who, on their part, were quite prepared to meet him. By a sure but desultory warfare, and by avoiding as much as possible general engagements, the wily foreigners had well nigh worn out the patience of the ardent prince, when, at length he formed the bold and spirited resolution of besieging the capital, Pollanarua. The Solleans advanced to defend their chief stronghold, and the first decisive battle was fought under the walls of the city. The Solleans were defeated, and were driven into the town, which was well calculated to resist a siege. After a fruitless blockade of six weeks, it was at length taken by storm, and, with a barbarous policy too frequently used even by more cultivated nations, was delivered to the sword. Their chief stronghold having been thus taken, completely paralysed the unfortunate Solleans, and, with the help of a little cruelty, the authority of Wijayabahu was soon recognised over the whole country.

Having thus expelled its foreign invaders, Wijayabahu next devoted himself to the setlement of the internal policy of his kingdom. The debased state of the national faith first occupied his thoughts, and, in order to restore it to its accustomed station, he had the temples repaired, the usual ceremonies instituted, priests ordained, and every necessary provided for its renovation. Such had been the tyranny of the Solleans, however, that scarcely a high priest of note was to be met with in the island; and in order to remedy this event, the king invited them, by the most liberal promises, from the neighbouring countries.

His attention was next directed to the administration of justice, and the ordering of the national finances, but scarcely had he brought these into a flourishing state, ere an accidental circumstance had well nigh precipitated the country into its former wretched condition. Having received ambassadors from the Indian princes, and the neighbouring nations, he naturally gave precedence to the envoy of the king of Siam. At this insult the king of Sollee was fearfully enraged, and revenged it with barbarous inhumanity, by cutting off the nose and ears of the Singhalese ambassador. This was, of course, the signal for renewed hostilities between the two nations: each flew to arms,—the Solleans to invade, the Ceylonese to defend. At Mantotte the native army was just on the point of embarking, when the opposing fleet hove in sight. The landing in the face of a numerous enemy must have been a perilous enterprise. It was nevertheless accomplished; and in the battle which ensued the hitherto prosperous Wijayabahu met with a sad reverse of fortune. He retreated to Pollanarua leaving the country open in his rear, and the invading Solleans marched directly on the capital. The king was obliged to fly; Pollanarua was once more taken by the Solleans; and the noble palace of its master levelled with the ground. The invaders were not left to enjoy the fruits of their enterprise undisturbed. With an activity that did credit to his abilities, a second army was enrolled, and its command given to his son Wirabahu, a prince endowed by nature with every quality of a sovereign. Pollanarua was again invested by a Singhalese army, and was again taken. The Solleans were once more obliged to fly before the conquering natives, to seek the shore, and finally to leave the country. Not content with this success, hewever, Wijayabahu soon after invaded Sollee, and inflicted there some of those calamities which its inhabitants had inflicted on the natives of Ceylon. But the want of provisions, sickness and harassing duties, soon forced him to return and to leave his enterprise unfinished. He again directed his active mind to internal improvements: eight tanks and numerous temples were repaired under his superintendence, the canal of Minueria was restored, and once more Ceylon enjoyed a breathing time after her numerous losses and revolutions.

Wijayabahu terminated his lengthened reign (A. D. 1126,) of fifty-five years, from the time when he had been crowned in his boyhood, and ten after his return from Sollee. He was succeeded by his brother Jayabahu; his warlike son, formerly mentioned, having died before him. The appointment of Jayabahu was, however, an unfortunate event; for Wickramabahu, a younger son of the last monarch, conceiving his appointment to be unjust, attempted to dethrone him. The whole kingdom was once more thrown into a state of great commotion, in which all the members of the royal family took part, some with one, some with the other. After a reign of one year Jayabahu was dethroned, and his nephew placed on his seat. The reign of Wickramabahu seems to have been peaceful and prosperous, his only annoyance being that he was childless. This want, however, was at length supplied. "It happened (says the Mahawanso) on a certain night whilst he was enjoying rest, that he dreamed of an apparition, a divine being, magnificently apparelled, appearing before him, giving light as the sun. This being then benignantly addressed him thus: 'King, thou shalt have a son, who will be charitable, powerful, wise, learned, and the promoter of religion, as well as of public welfare.' Delighted with the intelligence, the king awoke his consort, informing her of the gracious promise, and they rejoiced greatly."

In due time this wonderful son appeared, and he was named Prackramabahu, a name greatly and justly distinguished (as we shall afterwards see) in the annals of Ceylon. Shortly afterwards Wickramabahu was superseded by his nephew, Gajabahu, retaining, however, possession of a part of the island. The reign of Gajabahu is quite uninteresting, save for the accounts introduced into it of the education of Prackramabahu; and this account is the more interesting, inasmuch as it gives us an excellent idea of the advancement of Ceylon at this period in the race of civilisation.

Nothing, perhaps, can shew more forcibly the sameness of the human character all over the globe than the fact, that the manner in which the princes of the tropical and luxuriant Ceylon were educated, was precisely similar to that by which a modern English nobleman is fitted for his duties *. Prackrama, we are informed, was first introduced to the literature of his country, or, more properly, perhaps, of his religion, by a priest of great literary at-

* We must not forget, however, that this enlightened education was given in Ceylon when Europe was confined to the *trivium* of the schools.

tainments, remarkable, as well for extent of knowledge as for profoundness of intellect. Under his tuition the young prince became a profound master of the Buddhist faith, of logic, grammar, poetry and music. Nor were more energetic exercises wanting to give strength to his body, and decision to his mind. Horsemanship, archery, and the management of elephants, were also cultivated by him with success, and, under the paternal instructions and care of his cousin, he became fit for the station which he was afterwards to fill. But he had yet to complete his education by travelling. For this purpose he set out with a dignified retinue, and, as the countries which he visited are not mentioned, we may fairly conclude that they would be the neighbouring shores of the continent, and, perhaps, Burmah.

The mind of Prackrama, however, needed not the excitement of travel to render it active and ambitious. On returning to Ceylon he was unwilling to hold the station of a subordinate, and formed the ungenerous resolution of dethroning Gajabahu and the reigning prince of Rohona. What an exemplification of the ingenious remark of Cicero does this afford us: "Verae amicitiae rarissime inveniuntur in iis qui *in honoribus reipublicae* versantur." Respecting the particulars of his enterprise we are left uninformed. It is, however, stated, that having become, by his imposing qualities, the favourite of the people, he found little difficulty in obtaining an armament. His first enterprise was against the subordinate governor of a small province called Badalattaliya. Him he defeated and slew, and next directed his march against Gajabahu, whom he obliged to fly from the capital into Saffragam. The capital was retaken afterwards by Gajabahu, and, when both parties were on the eve of a decisive struggle, the priests interposed and brought about an accommodation. By this agreement Prackrama received the sovereignty from his competitor, who voluntarily resigned it, A. D. 1153, precisely twenty-seven years subsequent to the death of Wijayabahu, making the 119th prince of the Singha race who mounted the Singhalese throne. In this great number many subordinate princes are of course included, and many whose names we have not mentioned, their reigns affording little but the name.

On the abdication of Gajabahu, Wickramabahu asserted his claim to the supremacy; a claim which Prackrama was by no means prepared to allow. Avoiding, as much as possible, a contest with his father, the young prince proceeded to reduce some other parts of the kingdom which still resisted his authority. During his absence on this expedition, Wickrama, with an ungenerous treachery, sent an army into his defenceless province, which occupied the principal fortresses. Prackrama hastened back to revenge the injury, and, by his presence, quickly changed the situation of affairs. Pihitee, the province of which Pollanarua was the capital, was quickly delivered from its enemies, and his father was obliged to recross the Mahavelli-ganga as a fugitive. Shortly before his death, he sent for his son; mutual forgiveness was exchanged between them, and the aged prince died at peace with his impetuous offspring.

We must not omit a romantic adventure related of the prince, which would, were it true, entitle him to the appellation of "Coeur de lion," more justly perhaps than its ascription to Richard of England. When travelling with a small train of attendants through an unfrequented part of the country, an enormous lion sprung forward with open jaws and lashing tail, as though maddened with rage. All the attendants of the prince fled, leaving him alone. He disdained to retreat, and, advancing, grappled with the lion to such advantage that the monarch of the forest preferred flight to the combat, and left him rejoicing in his prowess. Lions, however, being unheard of in the island, we may reasonably doubt of the truth of the story.

Having become undisputed monarch of the island, Prackrama commenced his reign by restoring Buddhism to all its ancient magnificence. For this purpose he appointed particular officers to inspect the state of the temples, and report accordingly; he spared no expense in supplying himself with valuable works for these temples, and paid much honour to the priesthood. The leaders, by whose assistance he had gained the throne, were placed in situations suitable to their merit. Guards were stationed round the coast to give notice of hostile intrusion. Canals and tanks, which had become choked, were cleared and again made beneficial. Strong fortifications were erected in convenient positions as places of refuge in case of sudden reverse. Rice fields were formed of great extent. A rampart of stone was erected round the capital, and no means were neglected to render his kingdom prosperous and powerful. Nor were these exertions vain; for we are informed that Ceylon became by them united and powerful as a nation, and its inhabitants happy and flourishing. A palace for himself and suitable habitations for the higher order of priesthood were next erected, and an extensive garden was planned, with a coronation hall in the midst. The wall encompassing Pollanarua, we are informed, was thirty-six miles in length on one side, and sixteen on the other, shewing, if this assertion be true, the enormous size of the city itself. Whilst he was thus embellishing his capital, the ancient city of Anuradhapoora was not neglected. A minister was sent there for the express purpose of investigating the state of the buildings, and of having them put into proper repair.

Whilst thus cultivating, with so much success, the arts of peace, Prackrama was suddenly interrupted by a revolt in Rohona. This revolt was instigated by Subhala, the consort of the tributary prince who had been conquered by Prackrama. The resolution to rebel having been taken, she carried on the necessary preparations with great spirit and energy, proving, by her abilities, that she was an enemy not unworthy of Prackrama himself. Large and deep moats were dug round the fortified places. The roads leading into the province were rendered impassable to elephants and cavalry by large trees, which they had felled and fixed deeply in the ground by stakes. The plains were covered by the Rohonians with brambles and thorns, and, in short, every means taken for a vigorous defence. Prackrama was not disposed to regard these things with indifference. Rackha, one of his old generals, was placed at the head of a large and well-armed force. Having marched directly against the enemy, he found them determined to defend one of the roads which they had before fortified. An obstinate battle ensued, in which the Rohonians were at last obliged to give way. Their retreat became a flight, their flight a rout, and at the same time the adjoining fort into which they attempted to throw themselves was carried in the melée. The hopes of these mountaineers were not to be overcome, however, by the loss of a single battle, and so closely was Rackha beset in the conquered fort that he was obliged to send to Prackrama for a reinforcement.

Bhutha, another of the generals and friends of Prackrama, was immediately despatched to his aid, and a junction of the two armies was, after some delay, effected. The war was then renewed " with redoubled spirit." Many battles were fought with various success, but, on the whole, so much to the disadvantage of the Rohonians, that they formed the resolution of emigrating in a body with all their goods, and, what was more thought of, with many of the relics of Buddhu. Prackrama having been informed, by some of his private emissaries, of their intention, sent strict orders to Rackha and Bhutha to leave no exertion untried to prevent its execution. In order to give them the means of obeying his command, a fresh re-inforcement was despatched under the command of Kierthy. A line of circumvallation was then drawn by the united forces round the principal strongholds of the rebels, and so well arranged were their exertions that not a man was allowed to leave the district without their permission. Straitened by the strict blockade which they endured, the Rohonians were at length forced to surrender the relics and submit. Subhala, however, the ambitious woman who had incited the rebellion, was not taken, nor does it appear that the generals of the king insisted, as they ought to have done, on her surrender. Having thus restored the kingdom once more to peace and prosperity, the king resolved to impose upon the vulgar minds of the people by a magnificent procession, as a type of his power and prosperity.

On a fortunate day appointed by the astronomers, the king appeared before his attending nobles, his courtiers holding an emblazoned canopy over his head. Immediately on his appearance instruments of music were sounded on all sides, banners waved in the air, the people shouted "like the loud bellowing of the rushing sea," Long live the king, whilst the sky was almost clouded by the smoking perfumes of all kinds. The haughty Prackrama having bowed to the multitudes around, then ascended the royal elephant, at the same time that the nobles entered into their carriages. "With great pomp, amidst the noise of the roaring of elephants, neighing and prancing of horses, rattling of carriages, beating of tom-toms, blowing of chanks and playing of music *," the procession wended its slow way along. The queen and Prackrama appeared at its head in two splendid towers placed on elephants, with golden crowns upon their heads. Next followed the principal leaders of the late rebellion walking, followed by the officers of state and grandees, whilst innumerable multitudes concluded the imposing show. Such an important ceremony was not allowed, however, to pass over without a miracle. Suddenly, in the midst of their pomp, the sky became overcast, the heavens lowered and threatened the rejoicers with an inopportune deluge. The thunder then began to roar, the lightning to flash, and a keen wind to course over the earth. Prackrama was not a man to be frightened with a tempest; the procession went on regardless of the impending rain, and now, behold the miracle! The rain descended in volumes all around, but not a drop upon a man or beast engaged in the ceremony. Whilst the neighbouring rivers and tanks were choked with water, they remained perfectly dry. "Behold" (exclaims the

* Mahawanso, ch. 73.

author of the Mahawanso) " this striking instance of the power of Buddhu."

But even this instance of divine favour could not humble the mind of Subhala; the daughter and wife of a king, she still asserted her rights to be a monarch, and scarcely had the rejoicings of Prackrama ended, ere intelligence was brought from Rohona of another insurrection. Two battles (in one of which 12,000 Rohonians fell) and a siege were the result of this temerity, and the enterprising queen was brought as a captive before her rival. Of her future fate we are uninformed; but, as her name does not occur again in the annals of her country, we may conclude that her life paid the penalty of her rebellion.

CHAPTER VIII.

Prackrama invades China—India—The war there—Sollee made tributary to Ceylon—Prackrama's enthusiasm in religion—His tanks and canals—His character and death—Wijayabahu II.—Mihindo—Kirti Nissanga—His civic reforms and character—Weerabahu—Wikramabahu—Queen Leelawatee—dethroned—re-elevated—again dethroned—Wretched state of Ceylon—Wijayabahu—Removal of the seat of government—Kalikala and his learning—Invasion of the Malays—Improvements of Kalikala—His death and character—Bosat Wijayabahu IV.—Fall of Mitta Sena—Prackramabahu III.—The Dalada taken by the Malabars and restored—The Mahawanso—Buwancko Bahu IV.—Prackramabahu V.—Ceylon invaded—Buwancko Bahu V.—Pracramabahu VI.—Buwancko VI.—Rebellion quelled—Prackramabahu VII.—Arrival of the Portuguese.

We are now entering on the most glorious part of this fortunate monarch's reign; and, here again, we have to lament the extreme scantiness of the accounts which are left us of what is, perhaps, the most brilliant part of Ceylonese history.

Subsequent to the sixteenth year of Prackrama's reign, (A. D. 1169,) and probably very shortly after that year, although we are uninformed of the precise period, he formed the resolution of revenging on the king of Cambodia * and Arramana † the injuries he had inflicted on several of the Singhalese subjects. These injuries consisted in plundering merchants, slighting the ambassador of Ceylon, and intercepting some vessels, conveying certain women of rank from that island to the continent. In the

* This country still retains its ancient appellation.

† Probably that part of the Burmese Peninsula between Arrakan and Siam.

Ratnacari and Rajawali, however, the only reason stated for this invasion is, that he slighted and dishonoured the religion of Buddhu, an offence worthy, in their eyes, of the most condign punishment. To avenge himself on this despiser of Buddhu and slighter of Ceylon, five hundred vessels and a great armament of seamen and soldiers, ammunition and provisions, were equipped in a few months. A Malabar general, named Adikaram, of great and distinguished renown, was put at the head of this expedition, and it was accordingly despatched.

Having first landed on an island called Kakha, they obtained good omens of their future success by gaining the first battle in which they engaged, the consequence of which was, the submission of that part of the island, and the taking of several prisoners. Encouraged by this success they sailed for Cambodia, and landed at a port called Koosuma, where the enemy appeared drawn up in their entrenchments in great force.

Adikaram, having drawn up his forces in line of battle, advanced against the enemy and was received with showers of arrows, which the Singhalese returned. But as the Cambodians seemed unwilling to leave their entrenchments, it was necessary for Adikaram to force them, and this he accomplished by a resolute and determined attack. Sword in hand the Singhalese advanced, disregarding the missiles of the enemy, and, after a short but severe struggle, the entrenchments were forced, the Cambodians routed, and their king slain in the confusion.

Adikaram, like a prudent general, lost no time in following up his advantages, by advancing on the capital, where the country was proclaimed tributary to the great and glorious Prackramabahu, king of Ceylon. Tribute was accordingly collected, and a viceroy appointed.

After this signal success, Prackrama turned his arms against the united kings of Pandi and Sollee, who, fearing to meet alone so formidable a prince, had prudently joined their forces. Another expedition was fitted out, and proceeded to the enemies' territories. At Madura, where a landing was first attempted, they found the shore so thickly covered with the enemy, that they were obliged to proceed up the coast to Talatchilla (probably Tellicherry): there also, however, the enemy had anticipated them, and were assembled in force. The army of Prackrama was not to be twice repulsed; numerous boats were manned with the troops, which, amidst showers of arrows and spears, advanced towards the shore, and as soon as a convenient station had been gained, the soldiers leaped out: stooping and covering themselves with their shields, they advanced in a line against their opposers, and fortunately succeeded in putting them to flight. A landing thus having been effected with so much difficulty, the invaders found the remaining part of the country was as obstinately contested as the shore had been. Five pitched battles were fought, in each of which the army of Prackrama was successful, and by which the whole province of Ramisseram came into the possession of the Singhalese. Whilst the invaders were, after these exploits, enjoying the fruits of their victories in their encampments, an army of the enemy hastily attacked them, and had well nigh rendered all their previous victories useless. But the Singhalese were now soldiers in every sense of the word, and quickly revenged the losses they had sustained, so that, in the last and most terrible conflict, the Pandians sustained a severe defeat, thousands of them were slain, and the remainder was pursued by the whole Singhalese army for a distance of sixteen miles. The consequence of these victories was, that Kulasaikera, the king of Pandi, was dethroned, and his son, Weerapandu, raised in his stead, as a tributary of Prackrama.

Having thus happily terminated his foreign wars, the attention of the king was next directed to the adornment of Buddhism. The religious edifices of Anuradhapoora were enriched with numerous offerings and additions, and Prackrama himself went there to superintend the erection of a golden spire upon the Ruanello dāgobah. Events of this kind are those upon which the Buddhist historians delight to dwell; and, accordingly, we have a particular account of how the city was ornamented, how beautiful the women were, how glittering the flags, and how noble the entire ceremony, whilst his warlike enterprises are rehearsed only by informing us of the number of the battles, and the names of the subdued countries.

Prackrama, however, did not confine himself to the embellishment of a religion already too rich and powerful. Besides erecting new, and adorning old religious edifices, he planted several immense forests of fruit trees, and turned the courses of several rivers, so that they might replenish the tanks already formed. Canals also were dug by him to conduct the waters of the tanks and lakes to a distance. The following three of this nature are particularly mentioned as extraordinary works; the Goodaiviree canal to conduct the waters of the Kara-ganga into a lake, called the sea of Prackrama, from which the water was conducted by twenty-four channels to all the neighbouring fields; the lake of Minneria he made available for useful purposes, by digging the Kalinda canal to conduct its waters to the northward; and, lastly, the Jaya-ganga canal, by which the Kalaaweve tank was rendered serviceable to the inhabitants of Anuradhapoora.

Were we to give a list of one-half of the useful buildings attributed to Prackrama, we would completely weary out our readers; dāgobahs, wihares, relic-repositories, offering-houses, caverns, priests'-houses, preaching-halls, image-halls, dancing-saloons and strangers'-houses, are but a few of the motley collection of edifices recounted with critical accuracy by the zealous Buddhists. Amongst these, however, we must remark that several halls of justice and 128 libraries are particularly enumerated. There appears little reason to doubt the truth of these details. Prackrama was by birth the sovereign of a rich, fertile, and populous country; he had, besides, rendered himself, by arms, the master of two important and extensive kingdoms, and, being of such an active, energetic disposition, it is but natural to suppose that his many years of peace were occupied almost altogether in adorning his country.

In reviewing his character there appears, as in that of most other conquerors, much to praise and much to blame. We cannot commend his evident ingratitude and injustice to Gajabahu, in the early part of his life, at the same time that we must admire the decision and promptitude of all his measures. He appears to have possessed, in an eminent degree, all the qualities of a great commander; a quick apprehension of the difficulties and advantages of his situation on every occasion; great forethought and judgment in the formation of his plans, and no less decision in their execution. He knew eminently well how to gain the affections of his people; how to oppose presumption and to reward merit. Nor was his ability displayed alone in military affairs; he appears to have been equally energetic when at peace, equally anxious to advance his own glory and that of his people. Without one spark of patriotism in his bosom he was eminently useful to his country, and it is with justice that his reign has been designated as "the most martial, enterprising and glorious, in the Singhalese history."

In the 1186th year of the Christian era, and in the thirty-third of his reign, the renowned Prackrama died, leaving his extensive dominions to his nephew, Wijayabahu the Second.

Wijaya was of a very different character from his warlike uncle. He preferred cultivating the art of poetry to that of war, and died, not in the field of battle, after a lengthened reign, but in a dispute about a shepherd's daughter, whom he desired, before he had reigned one year.

He appears, however, to have been a prince of some promise, and one who might have greatly improved the internal polity of the kingdom, and the happiness, if not the morals, of his subjects had he lived. His administration of justice is particularly lauded, as well as the gentleness and mercy of his disposition. Whatever may have been his justice in transactions foreign to himself, however, he certainly did not regard its dictates when they clashed with his own inclinations; for, when Kilekes Law, the shepherd just referred to, refused to deliver to him his beautiful daughter, Wijaya had him put to death; a step which was avenged by his own murder almost immediately after by his rival, Mihindo, who could not bear to see him carry off the prize so easily.

Kitsen Kisdaas, as Mihindo is also called, was not content with merely obtaining the prize which he sought, but also aspired, on the murder of Wijaya, to the sovereignty. This he held, however, but for five days, when Nissanga, whom Wijaya had intended for his successor, dethroned him.

Kirti Nissanga commenced his reign, A. D. 1187, and were we to believe the reports of his character, which are found engraven on tablets in various parts of the island, he must have been one of the most talented princes whom the world ever saw. Nissanga was not of the royal family of Ceylon, but of that of Kalingo *. The state of the island, during his short reign of nine years, is represented as having been most prosperous.

He is styled "the lamp which illumined the whole world;" "the protector of the earth;" the fountain of renown." We are informed that "at the festival of his coronation he was invested with a glory which filled the firmament, and overpowered all beholders." Whether these praises are the expressions of gratitude or of servile adulation, we cannot now with certainty decide; but from the many substantial acts of beneficence recorded of him, we cannot but suppose that he was a worthy successor of the great Prackramabahu. His relinquishing a part of the royal revenue to relieve the necessities of his people, and his reducing the taxes on arable land, and on dry grain, are facts which would have scarcely been feigned, had they not taken place, and they assuredly display an

* The modern *Northern Circars.*

anxiety for the welfare of his subjects worthy of commendation. Every tank in the island, whose embankment was deficient, was repaired, and a fatherly interest was exhibited by him in the welfare of his people. But perhaps no part of his administration deserves so much praise as his care to extirpate crime and banish fraud. Judges were appointed all over the island to administer justice, and with, perhaps, a questionable policy, the robbers were bribed to abstain from plundering, by the hope of greater prosperity if they left that practice off.

Amidst such accounts we may be assured that Buddhism was not forgotten. The most learned and zealous priests were highly honoured by Nissanga, and from amongst them professors of the sciences were established in the different religious universities. Not content with the reports which were brought him of the state of the different parts of the island, he made a tour of it himself, and had improvements made and fortifications erected under his own eye.

Such is the character handed down to us of Kirti Nissanga, a prince who appears to have been indefatigable in his endeavours to improve the country, and make its inhabitants happy. Unfortunately, however, his reign only extended to a period of nine years; but in that short period he appears to have done more benefit to his country than many monarchs, whom we are accustomed to praise, would have accomplished in forty.

His son, Weerabahu, was put to death by the minister of Nissanga as unworthy to succeed to so great a prince, and his brother, Wickramabahu, was raised to the throne, (A.D. 1196.) His reign continued only three months, and was so unfruitful in events, that nothing farther is recorded of him.

He was dethroned and slain by his nephew Chondakanga. This prince, who is also styled Ramedagung, we are informed "could scarcely maintain himself on the throne for nine months when the viceroy pulled out his eyes, dethroned him, and supplied his place by Queen Leelawatee." (A. D. 1197.) The "viceroy" or minister, did not adopt this bold measure without a prospect of obtaining from it some advantage for himself. Queen Leelawatee, formerly the consort of Prackrambahu, gave him her hand, and, in her name, the administration of the kingdom was virtually conducted by HIM. Leelawatee and her consort were allowed to enjoy their exaltation for three years only, at the end of which period Sahasamallewa, of the royal race, drove them by force from the throne, which he then occupied himself. Such are the short and meagre accounts left us of these transactions, and for more than 300 years, from the end of the twelfth to the middle of the sixteenth century, the history of the island is continued, with very few interruptions, in the same unsatisfactory manner.

Sahasamallewa shared, after two years of assumed grandeur, the fate of Chondakanga, being dethroned by his own minister, who elevated, in his stead, Kalianawati, the sister of Kirti Nissanga. This princess had a somewhat better fortune than her immediate predecessors, reigning in peace for six years, during which period the only events recorded of her are, that she built a temple, to which she dedicated paddy fields, gardens, servants and other riches, and several other edifices of a similar description, to which, the Mahawanso informs us, "lands, containing gardens, fields of rice, servants, servant-maids, and all *other necessaries for priests* were added."

On the demise of Kalianawati, (A. D. 1208,) an infant of three months old, named Dharmasoko, was nominated to the vacant throne, which was held, in his name, either six years or one, as we credit the Rajawali or Mahawanso respectively. He was dethroned by a Malabar, named Manikunga, who invaded Ceylon with a large force from Sollee, and held the sovereignty for seventeen days, when he was, in turn, obliged to give place to Queen Leelawatee, who was thus restored to the crown which she before lost, and which she was destined to lose again, after the lapse of another year. A foreign army, headed by Lokaiswera, was the cause of her again losing her power, which was wrested from her, however, but for nine months, when she was again restored, to be again deposed. Amidst such revolutions and disturbances no country could flourish; and we cannot be surprised that Ceylon should retrograde during this period at a rapid rate. Her foreign possessions weakened her resources; her internal administration was neglected; and, from a powerful and happy country, civilised and polished, she became the debased one which Europeans found her.

In 1216, Leelawatee was again deposed by a Malabar named Prackramapandi, who, after enjoying the supreme power for three years, was, in his turn, deposed by Māgha, an invader, who also came from the coast. All the native histories concur in representing this period as one of fearful confusion, irreligion and anarchy. The Rajawali * thus bemoans it: " And now, as there was no more virtue to be found amongst the inhabitants of the island, and as trans-

* Part iv.

gression had arisen to an enormous height, and the protecting gods had withdrawn their aid, there followed an age of irreligion, in which the precepts of Buddhu were regarded no more."

The Mahawanso * attributes the following disasters to the same cause :—" At this time, the people of Lanka, turning themselves to become wicked and superstitious, lost the care of the guardian gods of Lanka. A king of the country Kalingo, called Māgha, invaded Lanka with 24,000 brave dhamila (Malabar) soldiers, and began to destroy both the country and religion, by knocking down thousands of cupolas †, such as that of the great Ruanwelly, &c.; making the gardens and great houses belonging to priests the lodgings and possessions of dhamilas; confusing and degrading the castes, and making the noblemen bond-servants; propagating the heathen religion in the island; plundering the property of the inhabitants; tormenting the people by cutting off their limbs, such as the arms, legs, &c. So the whole island was made like a house set on fire, or like a funeral house, the dhamilas plundering it from village to village."

Vivid and powerful as these descriptions are, they must yield in horror to that of the Raja Ratnacari ‡. " After the decease of these sovereigns, the inhabitants of Ceylon became desperately wicked, insomuch that the gods withheld their protection; and the vices of wicked men prevailed to such a degree, that, *as a judgment from heaven*, the Malabar king, called Māgha nam Rajah, came from the country of Calinga, with an army of 24,000 men,

* Chap. lxxix. † The spires of the dāgobahs. ‡ Chap. ii. p. 93.

which spread devastation, and abolished religion throughout the island. They laid in ruins the beautiful Maha Sacya of Ruanwelly and many other dāgobahs, and turned the sacred dwellings of the priests, and the sacred chambers and receptacles of the figure of Buddhu, into abodes for the Malabar soldiers. The virgins and honourable women were dishonoured; and they even reduced the most dignified by birth and rank to the most menial and servile labour; seducing to infidelity the captive inhabitants, plundering the rich of all their treasure, and cutting off the hands and legs of such as did not discover the same on demand. Thus, like a house filled with fire or thieves, was the island of Ceylon at this period."

As the evils which Ceylon endured at this time are attributed to the anger of the presiding deities, so her restoration to peace and order is attributed to their gracious favour. In the midst of the destroying career of Māgha, but not till he had occupied the throne for twenty-one years, a youth of the royal family, who lay concealed in the Maya or central division of the island, arose, who, "like a burning light," burst forth into notoriety, inspiring the Singhalese with renewed hope, and filling the Malabars with dismay. His fellow-countrymen flew to the standard of Wijayabahu with alacrity; and such was the vigour of his proceedings, that in a few years the invaders were totally subdued, and the Singhalese became once more the rulers of Ceylon. The Maya and Rohona divisions of the island were entirely freed from the Malabars; but in the Pihittee, or northern one, they formed the great bulk of the inhabitants, as they do at the present day, and there Wijaya was obliged to be contented with a nominal subjection and promise of tribute.

Having removed the seat of government from Pollanarua (where it had remained for nearly 500 years, with very few interruptions, and to which town it was afterwards restored,) to Dambadiva *, the next care of Wijaya was to reinstate Buddhism as the religion of Ceylon.

During the anarchy which had prevailed subsequent to Māgha's invasion, the priests had removed the precious relics of Buddhu to an impenetrable forest, on the eastern side of Adam's Peak, where they had been till now concealed; Wijaya, with much pomp and ceremony, had them reconveyed to their proper stations, on restoring order to the kingdom. The buildings which had been partially destroyed by the Malabars were the next objects of his attention; and, besides restoring those, others were added by himself. The colleges for theological instruction were next restored to their former condition; and from some part of the continent ten learned priests were obtained, who brought with them copies of their sacred books, which had been almost totally destroyed by the invading Malabars.

Having enjoyed a long and prosperous reign of twenty-four years, Wijaya left that sceptre which he had obtained by his valour, and preserved by his virtue, to his learned son, Kalikala, also called Prackramabahu the Third, in the 1267th year of our era, and 1809th of that of Buddhu.

An interesting list is handed down to us in the Ratnacari

* Dambadiva, once a royal residence, and capital of the Maya division of the island, now an insignificant place. It stands in a very picturesque valley, which is terminated by ranges of lofty naked hills, rising perpendicularly in a variety of peaked forms, about twenty-seven miles south of Kurnagalle, and fifty-six east of Colombo. Chittie's Ceylon Gazetteer.

of the various branches of learning in which this celebrated prince was a proficient. They were the following:

1. Surtia, or oratory.
2. Smurtia—General knowledge.
3. Wyawcarana—Grammar.
4. Chandass—Poetry.
5. Nirotte—Philology.
6. Jate—Astronomy.
7. Sangshikshaw—The knowledge of affording wise counsel.
8. and 9. Religion.
10. Danurivedey—Archery.
11. Hastisilpey—Knowledge of elephants.
12. Cawmatantra—Discernment of thoughts.
13. and 14. The occult sciences.
15. Jitihawsie—Knowledge of history.
16. Neeti—Jurisprudence.
17. Tarka—Rhetoric.
18. Wydyaham—Physic.

These sciences were doubtless cultivated by the Singhalese in a very imperfect manner; but we must not forget that their very extent and number is a proof of the civilised and enlightened state of the country, and that were there not a thirst for knowledge, very few, if any of them, would have been regarded. Nor could Europe itself, in the middle of the thirteenth century, boast of much more of these sciences than their names.

Such was the fame of the learning of Kalikala, that controversies which arose between the sovereigns of India were referred to his arbitration, and many foreign princes courted his alliance. Kalikala, however, or as he is more generally designated, Prackrama, did not settle down into the uselessness of a literary king. He completed the subjugation of the refractory Malabars, and "put an end to all abuses and tyrannical oppressions."

Finding that the population of the country had seriously decreased during the long periods of oppression and anarchy, he had all the laws inflicting very heavy penalties on offenders repealed. Those, for example, which condemned the malefactor to the loss of his limbs, were softened into imprisonment. Banishment was commuted into the payment of a heavy fine, and so forth. But whilst he adopted these rather questionable means of preserving the population, he did not forget the more efficacious one of rendering his subjects happy and prosperous. This he endeavoured to effect, by means of improved roads; substantial bridges were erected in every necessary situation; lines of jungle which interrupted communication were felled; and last, though by no means least in the catalogue, a great number of princesses were brought from the continent to be married to his sons and courtiers.

In the eleventh year of this prince's reign, a large army of Malays, under Chundrachano, made their appearance to invade the island. Fortunately for Ceylon, the army which the king had been but recently employing against the Malabars was still enrolled. The king, having previously despatched a small detachment to harass them on their march, advanced with promptitude with all his forces. The two wings of his army, which consisted of his cavalry and elephants, were headed by his nephew, Weerabahu, and his brother, Buwaneko Chako, he himself leading on the centre in person. A dreadful conflict ensued, in which the Malays were so utterly destroyed, that a native historian compares their defeat to "a wood of reeds crushed and uprooted by the gust of a tempest." This being the first occasion on which we find the Malays mentioned in Ceylon, we may suppose that, at this period, or shortly before, their emigration thither commenced, forming the last great body of the eastern natives of the island,—Singhalese, Veddahs, Malabars, Moors *, and Malays. (A. D. 1278.)

The remainder of the long reign of Prackrama was devoted to internal improvement and the education of his sons. For the latter purpose he invited, from the continent, a renowned and distinguished priest, named Dharmakirti, to whom he also left the task of re-establishing the popular religion on a proper basis.

His continued and persevering endeavours to render his country more accessible and civilised merit the highest meed of praise. His minister, Dawapati, was stationed in the most uncultivated part of the country, to form an accessible road to Adam's Peak, and to repair certain temples. In the course of the former great undertaking, two bridges are particularly mentioned as wonderful structures erected by him, the one being two hundred and eighty, and the other eighty-six cubits long, *i. e.* six hundred and thirty, and one hundred and ninety-three feet respectively. The former of these, from the account given of it, was, probably, not over a river, but to connect the two opposite sides of a ravine; the last was over the Kalluganga, on the road from Adam's Peak to Bentotte. Besides these works, Dawapati, with the aid of the king's son, Wijayabahu, embellished Pollanarua by the erection

* The first arrival of these people was, most probably, as Sir Alexander Johnson affirms, about the eighth century, and we shall soon find them mingling in the politics of the island.

of several of its most elegant structures. The king, on the completion of these works, liberally rewarded and greatly honoured his minister and son, but not before he had visited their undertakings, and inspected them himself. In his reign, Siriwardhnapura, the modern Candy, and subsequently the capital, was founded in the Seven Korles.

In the midst of these energetic labours, Prackrama was interrupted by the second invasion of Chundrachano, who now came, assisted by a large force of Pandians and Solleans, but who was a second time defeated and obliged to fly with precipitation. Perhaps nothing exhibits the just estimate the Ceylonese kings formed of their duties more than their anxiety to forward learning and science. Prackrama was himself a distinguished scholar, and, amidst his other labours, did not forget the importance of literature. The several colleges which he established in various parts of the island are particularly noticed, and in these, we are informed, professors of the various sciences were invariably appointed. In his reign the Mahawanso was continued from the reign of Mahasen, by the celebrated Dharmakirti, and the Poojavalliya, another important chronicle, was compiled by Mairupada. Prackrama having now reigned for a very long period, and being advanced in years, began to think of, and provide for, his departure from this world.

He called his six sons together, and earnestly exhorted them to persevere in friendship with each other, pointing out the blessings of peace, and the miseries of dissension. He then allotted to them their various provinces which they were to hold in subordination to their elder brother, Wijayabahu the Fourth; and having thus so much benefited

Ceylon during his life, and provided for its prosperity after his death, he died, full of years and good works, in the thirty-fifth year of his reign, A. D. 1301.

Doubtless the reign of this prince has been handed down to us in the most favourable light, but "facts are stubborn things" and cannot be resisted. The double defeat of an army of Malays incontestably proves his military prowess, whilst the road to Adam's Peak, the repair of ruined edifices, the establishment of colleges, and the appointment of professors, shew, if not his ability, at least his desire for improvement; and where that desire exists in the breast of an absolute prince, the accomplishment is an easy task. Notwithstanding the excellent reigns of Prackrama and his father, however, we may reasonably doubt whether they could bring the nation back to the prosperity and happiness it enjoyed in the time of Prackramabahu the Great, preceded as they were by fifty-four years of convulsion and anarchy, and succeeded, as we shall find them, by turbulence and tumult. They were but as the golden halo with which the sun gilds the heavens, ere it finally sinks to give place to darkness; or as the mighty throes of some gigantic frame, which nothing can withstand, to be succeeded by the feebleness of dissolution and death.

Respecting the reign of his son, Bosat Wijayabahu the Fourth, there are various accounts. Mr Turnour in his "Epitome" of Ceylonese History asserts, that he was "murdered by his minister Mitta Sena, in an intrigue in which they were both engaged with the same woman." The Mahawanso, however, represents the cause of this action as having been Mitta Sena's desire for the sovereignty, not a word being related of the amour *; whilst, in the Rajawali, he is stated to have been carried off by an invading army, which landed, and advanced to the capital, under false pretences. As his reign lasted only two years, the manner of his death is not very important, inasmuch as we are sure that it was a violent one, and that the period which succeeded was one of turbulence and disquiet.

Buwaneko Bahu, hearing of the fate of his elder brother, fled to Yapahu in the Seven Korles, and there commenced active measures for seating himself on the throne and revenging Wijayabahu. Mitta Sena, or Mittra, as he is more commonly designated, next turned his attention towards securing the sovereignty to himself, and, for this purpose, was solemnly crowned at Pollanarua, whilst Buwaneko, whom he imagined dead, was remaining in his place of refuge. The aspect of affairs, however, was changed, not by the valour of the aspirant, but by the fidelity of his foreign guards. These being in the court of the usurper, demanded, on their pay day, an audience of the king, alleging that they had various grave complaints to lay before him. The king granted their request, and, on their entrance, Takurake, who was at their head, advanced towards him as though about to speak; instead of which, however, his sword was quickly unsheathed, and the next moment they beheld the head of Mittra rolling at their feet, A. D. 1304.

The fall of an usurper, especially when it occurs shortly after his elevation, is seldom lamented. Every one was anxious to hail Buwaneko First as king, and, in the gene-

* Chap. lxxxviii.

ral emulation, there was no one left to revenge Mittra's death. The throne was peaceably filled, and, in a short time after, things were proceeding just as usual. Buwaneko was a religious prince, and appears to have spent the eleven years of his reign in ceremonies and offerings. At the end of that period, and immediately subsequent to his death, an army arrived in Ceylon, sent from Pandi by Kulasaikera the king of that country, under the command of a celebrated warrior, named Areya Chakkrawarti. The youthful prince, who was then heir to the throne, was either incapable of opposing them, or unwilling to attempt it. They marched through the country, plundering wherever they came, and meeting with very little resistance. Most probably none of these particulars would have been handed down to us, were it not that, in the course of their rapine, they seized on the precious Dalada relic *, with which they retreated. On their departure Prackramabahu the Third was raised to the throne, to govern a kingdom, which he had not made the slightest effort to defend. His first care was to obtain the valuable relic which the Pandians had stolen. For this purpose he undertook an embassy to Pandi, and, either by submission, tribute, or entreaty, succeeded in again restoring the Dalada to Ceylon. It was again placed with much ceremony in Pollanarua, which Prackrama adopted also as his own residence. These are the only events recorded in the reign of Prackrama. After a reign of five years he was succeeded by Buwaneko the Second, the son of the first prince of that name, A. D. 1319. At this period, in the history of the country, the second part of Mahawanso, by

* The fabled tooth of Buddhu.

far the most credible and excellent of the native histories, ends. It is written in very elegant Pali verse, and, though abounding in tiresome repetitions, and lengthened accounts of religious ceremonies, it contains many passages of superior excellence and of vivid descriptions, whilst its reflections are, in many cases, new and beautiful. It was commenced, as we have formerly mentioned, and continued to the reign of Mahasen, by Mahanamo, and was completed to the present reign by Dharmakirti *, and forms, perhaps, the best compilation of the history of Buddhism any where to be met with.

During the succeeding period of thirty years the names alone of four kings are handed down to us, viz. Buwaneko Bahu II., Prackramabahu IV., Buwaneko III., and Wijayabahu V.; the former of these reigned twenty-four years †, so that the remaining three could only have occupied the throne for a period of four years, Buwaneko commencing to reign in 1319, and Wijayabahu dying in 1347. In that year Buwaneko Bahu the Fourth ascended the throne. The first act of his reign was to rebuild a city, called Gampola, to which he removed the seat of government. This city had been primarily founded by one of the brothers of the queen of Panduwasa, B. C. 500, but, having fallen into ruin and neglect, was restored by Buwaneko. Its extended name was Gaw Pala Ganga Sree Poorsay,—" the beautiful city near the river, *i. e.* the Mahavelle." In the

* This work has twice appeared in English. The first translation was that to be found in Upham's " Religious and Historical Works of Ceylon," 3 vols. octavo, 1833. The second by the Honourable G. Turnour, in 2 vols. quarto, 1837,—the first of which, however, only was published, that gentleman's lamented death, in 1843, preventing its completion.

† Raja Ratnacari, p. 109. The " Epitome " is here incorrect in representing the length of his reign as not being stated.

sixth year of his reign, this prince settled a religious controversy, of the particulars of which we are uninformed. He was succeeded, in the year of Budddu 1896, by Prackramabahu the Fifth, A. D. 1353, of whose long reign of eighteen years * not a single particular is stated, save that he kept his court in the city rebuilt by his predecessor. During the reign of his cousin and successor, Wickramabahu, the chief minister, Alakaiswara, erected a fort and city to the south of Kalany, and to the east of Colombo, called Jayawardhanapura, which subsequently became the seat of government, and which is well known at the present day under the name of Cotta. At this period, Alakaiswera appears to have conducted the government, Wickramabahu being merely nominally king. Ceylon was now again invaded by Areya Chakkrawarti, whom we have formerly seen carrying off the tooth relic of Buddhu. This active general, resolving to make a permanent stay, threw up fortifications at Colombo, Negombo and Chilaw, and soon succeeded in reducing the northern division of the island to subjection, fixing the seat of his government in Jaffnapatam. But besides governing the northern division, Areya reduced Alakaiswara to the necessity of paying an annual tribute. This infliction the minister bore, for some time, with patience, but soon conceiving himself able to shake off the yoke which the invader had imposed, he took the field and marched against Areya. That general, enraged at what he considered his insolence and temerity, sent for a numerous reinforcement from Pandi, which, having landed at Colombo, remained

* In these statements we rely on the authority of the Ratnacari, as more worthy of trust than any other chronicle of the period to which we have access.

there in order of battle, awaiting the troops of their general. Alakaiswara, however, always vigilant and prudent, resolved to prevent a junction, and, having advanced by forced marches to the sea-shore, gave battle to, and routed the newly arrived forces, whilst Areya and his troops were still at Matale. In the meantime, he had despatched a detachment to keep that division engaged, and now, leading on his victorious troops, flushed with recent success, against the Malabar general, gained a complete and decisive victory. Before these events were nearly concluded, however, Wickrama had died, and had been succeeded by Buwaneko Bahu the Fifth, in whose reign nothing more is recorded than the conclusion of this expedition. He died and was succeeded by Wijayabahu the Sixth, A. D. 1398. The only event recorded of the reign of this prince is, his having expelled several gangs of Malabars who were roaming through the country in search of pillage. His successor, Prackramabahu the Sixth, who ascended the throne at the age of sixteen, removed the seat of government to Cotta, and conveyed to that place the celebrated Dalada relic. In the course of his very extended reign of fifty-two years, he reduced the Malabars in the northern part of the island to complete subjection, and restored the kingdom to its regular constitutional condition. Finding the revenues of government inadequate to its expenditure, he laid a tax upon the produce of the country, by which the deficiency was changed into a surplus. Buddhism also flourished during this prince's peaceful government. Every year, we are informed, he made presents to the priests of their distinguishing yellow robes, the cloth being brought from the state of cotton on the tree, in the space of one day to be fit for use. By what means this extraordinary celerity was attained we are not informed; but the historian particularly relates, that "the cotton was plucked, cleansed, spun, wove, dyed yellow, and made into the requisite garments between sunrise and sunset." The whole number of priests' garments which he distributed during the course of his reign was about 30,000 suits. "He gave alms also beyond calculation, and was thus an encourager of his kingdom as well as of religion."

Prackrama ended his long and prosperous reign, A. D. 1462, and was succeeded by his grandson Jayabahu, also called Prackramabahu, who, after a short elevation of two years, was dethroned by Buwaneko the Sixth, a descendant of the royal family. This prince, who had held the office of viceroy in Yapahu under Prackrama, enjoyed the sovereignty for seven years. Within that period an extensive rebellion broke out in the island, to oppose which, Buwaneko sent out his brother, called, after the province which he governed, Ambulagala, at the head of an army. The prince was successful, and returned with the instigators of the revolt to his sovereign, by whom he was much honoured. However, on the death of Buwaneko, this prince, finding himself supplanted by an adopted son of the late king, who assumed the government under the title of Pandita Prackramabahu the Seventh, took up arms to assert his legal right to the throne. On advancing towards Cotta, he found the young king ready to oppose him, his forces being commanded by the two chiefs, whom the pretender had formerly conquered as rebels. A battle ensued in which the king was totally defeated, and his opponent, assuming the title of Weera Prackramabahu, ascended the throne, which he had already made slippery with the blood of his nephew. His reign, however, is represented as having been peaceful and prosperous; and as it continued for twenty years, we may suppose that no violent attempts were made to dethrone him. He had four sons and a daughter by his first wife, two of whom afterwards became sovereigns of Ceylon, and by the third of whom he became grandfather of one of the greatest men and tyrants that his country ever produced,—Raja Singha, the hero of Ceylon. He died A. D. 1505, and was succeeded by his son Dharma Prackramabahu the Ninth. During this reign, a party of Moors landed in the north to obtain pearls and elephants. Their expedition, however, partook of the nature of an invasion, and was accordingly resisted, and the party defeated. Prackrama's reign was also disturbed by the contentions of his brothers; but the event of the greatest importance during his administration was the landing of the Portuguese, the first European nation which became mixed up with the politics of Ceylon. This event occurred in the year of Prackrama's accession, A. D. 1505.

CHAPTER IX.

REMARKS ON THE HISTORY OF CEYLON, AND ITS CONDITION PRIOR TO THE INVASION OF THE PORTUGUESE.

There are few studies that have more attraction for the cultivated mind, or that more powerfully excite our curiosity, than the history of the past. The farther back the relation reaches, the more earnestly does it engage our attention, and the more influential is it over our feelings. Events and characters, seen through the vistas of a thousand years, appear like the traditions of another world, and interest every faculty of our minds in their contemplation. But as the degree of attention which they excite in us is greater, so is also our watchfulness lest we should be deceived, and our caution in receiving them, when compared with our wariness in giving credence to events of a more recent date. Every thing bordering on the extraordinary puts watchfulness on its guard; and when we fear imposition, whether groundlessly or not, we too frequently clothe ourselves with the armour of incredulity. In the preceding history, however, we trust that there is little ground for scepticism as to the truth of its details. That the native writings, in which that history was contained, should have been unknown to Europeans for 300 years, is neither so extraordinary nor unaccountable as to raise our suspicion of its truth; and the manner in which it is corroborated by every testimony that can be desired puts its veracity beyond a doubt. Whence, if it be false, arise the coincidences contained in it with the histories of the various nations of India? If Ceylon were not at an exceedingly remote period civilised and refined, whence came the vast ruins of Anuradhapoora, and the massive embankments of the various tanks? If that civilisation were not handed down to a more modern period, whence came the ruins of Pollanarua and Dambadiva, of Kandy and Cotta? But the fact is too indisputable to be for a moment seriously questioned. It would, we imagine, be an anomaly in the history of the universe, a thing unprecedented in the annals of the human race, were a history of a nation to be feigned for upwards of 2000 years, and that romance laboriously substantiated by names and numbers and dates. Nor is this all. Were such the case in the history of Ceylon, upwards of ten historians, at least, writing at different periods and in different languages, must have combined in the imposture, and that for no other reason than to impose upon the public.

But it may be again objected, that, allowing the facts to be true, we draw from them unwarranted conclusions, and that Ceylon never reached the height of civilisation which we have claimed for her. The conclusions, it must be remembered, however, are not solely ours: they are those drawn by every one who has studied the subject with attention, or even superficially regarded all the circumstances of the case.

"From the native chronicles, we find" (writes Major

Forbes *,) "that the ancestors of a people whom Britons long regarded as savages, and for some time treated as slaves, existed as a numerous and comparatively civilised nation at a period antecedent to the discovery of Great Britain and its semi-barbarous inhabitants."

"There is another point" (remarks Mr Upham †) "we can dwell on with pleasure, (besides the influence of Buddhism,) namely, the rapid and remarkable progress of the Singhalese in every branch of national improvement, which seems to have followed the benign influence of Buddhism, as compared with the state in which it found them. They scarcely appear, in these narrations, to have entered on the career of civilisation, ere we find them, under Panduwasa and his successors, founding cities, building temples, and, above all, forming immense lakes for facilitating the operations of agriculture—the true riches of a state. These extraordinary excavations rivalled the most remarkable labours of antiquity, *and were hardly surpassed by the kindred wonders of Egypt.* The remains of these national monuments demonstrate *an amount of population and a state of prosperity infinitely superior to what exists at present*, or has for a long period existed, in Ceylon, and therefore should recommend some consideration of the mode of government and civil administration, which so essentially contributed to the aggrandisement and prosperity of this beautiful island.

"Not less striking than these lakes are the vast mounds, temples and mausoleums which are generally adjacent to their borders, and the remains of which, at the present day, attest the former splendour of the state."

* Eleven Years in Ceylon, vol. i. chap. 1.

† Sacred and Historical Books of Çeylon, Introduction, page 32.

Mr Turnour *, also, speaking of the state of Ceylon in the twelfth century, when it was much degenerated indeed from the Lanka of former days, remarks; "Taken altogether, the view thus presented of the internal government of Ceylon during the twelfth century is such as may well excite the curiosity of the antiquary, encouraged as he must be by the certainty that the pursuit will be rewarded by the discovery of important historical facts, characteristic of the principles of Asiatic government."

An inspection of the ruins of the ancient works alone led Mr Bertolacci † to make the following remarks: "In this work (the formation and embankment of one of the tanks) we find, then, incontestable signs of an immense population and an extensive agriculture." Again, "This gives us the idea of a very populous country, and of a flourishing nation." And, again, "We must therefore say, that the further back we go towards the remotest antiquity, we find this island rising in the ideas it impresses upon our mind, respecting its civilisation and prosperity.

But, perhaps, nothing will more incontestably prove to us the early refinement of the natives of Ceylon than the fact, that, in the refutation of the supposed ancient civilisation of the Hindus, by Mr Mill in his history of British India, almost every argument adduced by him is directly contradicted by the history of Ceylon. In speaking of the annals, or rather traditions, of the Hindus, he states ‡, "It is a most suspicious circumstance, in the pretended records of a nation, when we find positive statements, for a

* Introduction to his "Translations of Inscriptions."

† Introduction to "A View of the Agricultural, Commercial, and Financial Interests of Ceylon."

‡ Vol. i. book ii. chap. 1, page 96.

regular and immense series of years in the remote abyss of time, but are entirely deserted by them when we descend to the ages more nearly approaching our own." Such is precisely the reverse of the history which we have just related. There, the transactions recorded three and four thousand years ago are few, fabulous, and at a wide distance of time from each other, whilst those of more recent date are probable, connected and exact. There, the blanks are found in antiquity, the circumstantial relations in more modern times."

Again, in giving us the test of the purity of a religion, and its influence, he writes *, "There is no circumstance connected with a religious system more worthy of attention than its morality; than the ideas which it inculcates respecting merit and demerit, purity and impurity, innocence and guilt. If those qualities which render a man amiable, respectable and useful, as a human being; if wisdom, beneficence, self-command, are celebrated as the chief recommendation to the favour of the Almighty; if the production of happiness is steadily and consistently represented as the most acceptable worship of the Creator, no other proof is requisite, that they who framed, and they who understand this religion, have arrived at high and refined notions of an all-perfect being. But where, with no more attention to morality than the exigencies and laws of human nature force upon the attention of the rudest tribes, the sacred duties are made to consist in frivolous observances, then, we may be assured, the religious ideas of the people are barbarous."

This, it will be perceived, proves at once the barbarous

* Vol. i. book ii. chap. vi. p. 263.

ideas of religion possessed by the Hindus, and "the high and refined notions" of the Buddhists. On the debasing influence of a debasing religion, Mr Mill comments, in various parts of his elaborate work, with truth and precision; and surely we may, with equal justice, expatiate on the elevating effects of a religion so pure, so simple, and so moral as that of Buddhism. In regarding its moral precepts, its blameless ceremonies, its refined tenets of faith, and its simple exposition of duty, we are compelled to admire and reverence it, and its professors.

Another criterion which Mr Mill propounds, by which we may judge of the advancement of a nation, is the condition of the female sex. His words are *, "The condition of the women is one of the most remarkable circumstances in the manners of nations, and one of the most decisive criterions of the stage of society at which they have arrived. Among rude people, the women are generally degraded; among civilised, they are exalted." Professor Millar also proposes the same opinions, which he philosophically treats with admirable good sense and judgment, in his "Inquiry into the Distinction of Ranks †." Perhaps there is not a single point to which we could more triumphantly have pointed, in confirmation of our views, than the notices the preceding history affords us of the respect paid by the Ceylonese to their women ‡. Amongst the Hindus, they were

* Vol. i. book ii. chap. vii. p. 293. † Chap. i.

‡ What may be said of them in other Ceylonese works is of no importance. If the reader thinks otherwise, then he must conclude the Romans to have been barbarians in the time of Trajan. What is woman? says Plinius Secundus in his series of questions. Mark the answer; "The desire of man, a companionable wild beast, a sociable (συγκοιμωμενη) lioness, a dragon to be guarded, a clothed viper, a voluntary war, πολυτιλης πολεμος, a daily

incapable of inheriting the smallest possession; amongst the inhabitants of Ceylon they could govern, and succeed to the sovereignty of their country. Surely no fact could more indubitably prove the estimation in which they were held. Not only could they succeed to the government, however, but (as we have seen in the case of Queen Leelawatee) on being deposed by foreign invasion, or domestic treason, they were, on the restoration of tranquillity, again exalted to their former dignity. In the history, too, of this queen, we perceive the jealousy of the Ceylonese for their rights, when they would not allow her consort to assume the title of king. Nor were they excluded from any other honourable office, to which they could with propriety aspire. The dignity next to the king was that of the priesthood; and there also, not only were females admitted, but even highly honoured. If the sovereignty and priesthood, then, were not denied them, may we not assert, that no other right to which they could pretend would be debarred them?

In speaking of the tanks of India, the same author endeavours to shew that they afford proofs rather of the barbarism of the natives than of their civilisation since—" It is only in a small number of instances, where the whole power of an extensive government, *and that almost always Mahommedan*, had been applied to the works of irrigation, that they are found on a considerable scale, or in any but the rudest state. In a country in which, without artificial

hurt, the means of procreation, a wicked animal, *a necessary evil.*" The Hindus or Hottentots could not, surely, be much more complimentary.

Τι εστι γυνη; Ανδρος επιθυμιον, συνεστιωμενον θηριον, συγκοιμωμενη λεαινα, συντηρουμενη δρακαινα, ἱματισμενη εχιδνα, αυθαιρετος μαχη, πολυτελης πολεμος, καθημερινη ζημια, ανθρωποποιον ὑπουργημα, ζωον πονηρον, αναγκαιον κακον. From the Opuscula Mythologica of Gale, p. 636.

watering, the crops would always be lost, the ingenuity of sinking a hole in the ground, to reserve a supply of water, need not be considered as great *." The most superficial reader must perceive that there is not a single depreciatory remark in the foregoing sentence, which could, by any possibility, be applied to the tanks of Ceylon. 1. These are, or rather were, so numerous, that scarcely a situation in which they would be useful could be found in which they were not constructed at a later or earlier period. 2. The Mahommedan power in this island was never the ruling one, and, therefore, never the projector of improvement. 3. So different were the tanks of Ceylon from "holes sunk in the ground," that we have seen them in a former extract, compared to the wondrous monuments of Egypt, "by which," we are there told, "they were hardly surpassed." To multiply authorities on this head would be utterly useless. We have only to refer the reader to every one who has described the island, in proof of the immensity, utility, and vastness of the undertakings,—to Knox, Valentine, Baldaeus, Marshall, Ribeiro, Cordiner, Percival, Forbes, and a host of others.

So convincing are the proofs of the early civilisation of the Ceylonese, that there is scarcely a point or feature in their manners, character and history, at those remote periods, and even till comparatively modern times, which does not directly contradict the supposition of their barbarity. In proof of this, as we have just observed, if we but apply the characteristics of the Hindus, which are adduced in

* Of the difference between "sinking a hole" and forming a tank, Mr Mill seems to have been profoundly ignorant; but this, it will be perceived, makes little alteration in the value of his argument.

support of their continued want of refinement, for a series of ages, to the Ceylonese, we shall find them all directly contradicted by the plainest evidence. We have already shewn that this remark holds good with regard to their "annals," their "religion," their "treatment of females," and their "agricultural operations;" and, were we to multiply instances, it would but weary, uselessly, the patience of the reader. We shall, therefore, adduce but two remarkable contrasts in addition, between the pretensions of the Hindus and Ceylonese to refinement. These are their respective literatures, and their respective systems of education. In proof of his opinion, that the ancient Hindus should not be considered as refined or civilised, Mr Mill * adduces their taste for the marvellous and poetic in their literature. Such, he observes, is the characteristic of all rude nations: nor will he allow that elegant fable, or heroic poetry is any conclusive proof of the advancement of the nation that produces them. "All rude nations," he asserts, "even those to whom the use of letters has long been familiar, neglect history, and are gratified with the productions only of mythologists and poets." Whether this assertion be true or false, we are not now about to investigate; but as it is the foundation on which he rests his proof of the barbarity of the Hindus, we will, for the present, allow it to pass unquestioned. The Hindus resemble, in many respects, perhaps, more than any other nation, the inhabitants of the island, whose history we are endeavouring to compile; and, therefore, if we can shew that the arguments adduced to prove the barbarism of the former are futile when applied to the latter, we have gone

* Vol. i. book ii. chap. ix.

far towards establishing the truth of our impressions. Mr Mill proceeds in his argument thus: "It is allowed, on all hands, that no historical composition whatever appears to have existed in the literature of the Hindus; they had not reached that point of intellectual maturity, at which the value of a record of the past for the guidance of the future begins to be understood. 'The Hindoos,' says that zealous and industrious Sanscrit scholar, Mr Wilford, 'have no ancient civil history.'" The Ceylonese have. Poetry was certainly cultivated amongst them with assiduity and success, nor was mythology forgotten; but not the less successfully did they cultivate history. We have already made numerous extracts from their historians; and, allowing for the concomitants of eastern style, unnecessary amplification and superfluity of imagery, we may, with justice, pronounce them admirable and excellent works. But not only have the Ceylonese histories of their country, but also others of a more confined and particular nature; such as a history of dāgobahs *, a history of their holiest relic †, the tooth of Buddhu, and histories of various particulars and districts. If, then, the possession of continued histories be a proof that a nation has arrived at a particular point of intellectual maturity much above that of those which possess poetry alone, we must rank Ceylon high in the scale of civilisation, compared with that of other eastern nations. Nor was it by the possession of histories alone that Ceylon exemplifies itself as thus improved. Treatises on various subjects are continually mentioned, (as, for instance, that on medicine by Bujas, A. D. 339,) and on subjects

* The Thupawanso. † The Dathadatu-wanso.

too of the highest utility. But a much superior mark of refinement exists in the patronage continually afforded by the princes to their learned men. Throughout all the bright part of Ceylonese history, names are handed down to us rendered eminent by their literary character, and influential by the favour thence bestowed upon them by the kings. Numerous poems and philosophical treatises exist in the island, and tradition assures us that to the writers of these were appointed revenues and power by their sovereigns in consideration of their merit. At the present moment we have before us a poem of a very peculiar construction *, to which is appended a commentary by the author, in which he informs us that his liberal patron, the king, granted him, for its composition, the command and revenues of a district containing a number of villages. The philosophical works mentioned in the historical ones are for the most part on cosmography, astronomy, medicine, chemistry and mathematics. In recording these facts let it not be supposed that we wish to represent the Ceylonese as a highly intellectual or philosophical race, far from it. The greater number of their philosophical works are meagre and rude; but the fact of the encouragement of these higher studies proves a certain degree of refinement, and a considerable advance in the scale of civilisation.

In refuting the claims of the Hindus to civilisation, the historian of "British India †" particularly remarks their defective plans of instruction. Were we to judge of the diffusion of education in the glorious days of Ceylonese

* It resembles a monkish riddle, and was doubtless written at a late period.

† *Ut supra*, chap. ix.

history, by that which Europeans found on arriving here, we would be led into much error. That the country had been gradually declining from before the eighth century is a fact abundantly testified by its history. Of the causes of this decline we shall have to speak hereafter; but the fact has been noted by all who have attended to the subject. Yet we are not left utterly in the dark respecting the diffusion of education in the earlier periods of the history. Were there no other fact handed down to us on this subject, the simple one of the rank which the instructor held would be sufficient to establish their attention to this important point, the gannoonaney or instructor being the next in order of rank, honour, and presidency, to the terroonaney or high-priest. In a country where the system of castes, though contrary to the spirit of its religion, prevailed, a large mass of the lower orders must invariably have been precluded from the blessings of instruction; but the frequent mention of schools and colleges may assure us, that the middle and higher classes had every opportunity afforded them of obtaining, comparatively, an excellent education. Even at the present day it is rare, indeed, to see a Ceylonese, even of the poorest class, who cannot read and write his own language. Can the most civilised nations of Europe make the same boast?

But the fact to which we would particularly direct attention is, the excellent manner in which the initiatory course of the priesthood was conducted. Colleges, containing from 100 to 200 students each, were established in various parts of the island. The candidate for the priestly office was first obliged to attach himself to one of the higher order of priests, by whom he should be instructed in the fundamental principles of religion. Having lived with him a sufficient length of time, he might, if the terroonaney considered him properly qualified, adopt the yellow robes, and be considered one of the lower orders; but he could not be admitted to the more advanced and honoured rank without spending a certain period at one of these colleges *; there he was engaged in studying, not theology alone, but also science and mathematics from the professors appointed for the purpose. On the termination of his course an examination was held, and, if qualified, the candidate was duly ordained by the head of the faith.

We have before seen the excellent education given to the youthful heirs to the throne. They were instructed in all the sciences of which the learned men of the island had any knowledge, and, in many cases, when the fame of some foreign *savant* had reached Ceylon, the monarch used all his influence to obtain him as the tutor of his sons. Even the immolation of Kumara Das on the pile of his friend Kálidas, romantic as the incident doubtless is, shews his devotion to his friend, and the respect and love which literary excellence alone could excite in the refined breast of a Ceylonese monarch.

Events and institutions, such as we have described, are not those for which we would look, or which we would expect to find amongst a people so degraded as the Chinese or Hindus; and when we have established the claim of Ceylon to a somewhat higher civilisation than these attained, we have done all that we aspire to.

* At present, in this waning period of Buddhism there are but two colleges, both at Kandy; and it may be readily conceived that much irregularity exists in their course of study and probation.

But as we have touched on so many of the *facts of civilisation* *, in reference to this nation, we cannot omit to notice, however imperfectly, the state of the military art amongst them. With many, we are aware, it is a favourite custom to decide the claims of various nations, as far as advancement is concerned, by this criterion alone, without making the slightest allowances for the dissimilar circumstances of different nations. Yet so influential are these circumstances, that, perhaps, no science could be erected as the standard more liable to mislead. One race of people, for instance, dwells in the midst of barbarous and warlike tribes, ever ready to disturb and harass them. *There* one of two states of society must prevail, if the people remain free; either they are a nation of warriors, or a nation of homeless vagrants and nomades. Another people, we will suppose, inhabit a country, unconnected with, and severed from every other, either by means of the sea or by ranges of inaccessible mountains. These may be subject, indeed, to occasional invasions and partial conquests, but, if we suppose this nation contented with its own dominions, should we look for as perfect a military system amongst them, as we would expect on the other supposition? Certainly not. The one lives in perpetual solitude and quiet, the other in eternal war. The one may, indeed, be occasionally overrun, but the other, were it not always on the watch, would be perpetually so. Which of these, in a modified sense, is most similar to the island in question the reader will at once perceive. But we would, by no means, be

* For this phrase we are indebted, I believe, to the elegant Monsieur Guizot, in his History of Civilisation in Europe.

understood to believe, that war was, as a science, unknown to the Ceylonese. In this respect, as in every other, a comparison with the other nations of Asia will, we imagine, establish, instead of refuting our assertion. We must first, however, distinguish between the different classes of the inhabitants of the island. Every one, at all conversant with Ceylon, must be aware of the great difference in physical force and mental energy between the Singhalese of the maritime and the Singhalese of the interior provinces. The former a weak, pusillanimous and unwarlike race, the latter a nation of *men*, hardy, brave, and passionately attached to their native hills. The former ready to acknowledge any masters, the latter possessing all the love of liberty and detestation of bondage natural to mountaineers.

These inhabitants were justly contented with the island in which they dwelt. The population, although it must have been at one time immense, appears never to have been incommoded by want, and emigration was of course unthought of. Nor do they appear to have ever been desirous of foreign conquests, as, in the cases in which we have described their having obtained such, their sole object seems to have been revenge. Under these circumstances, the only use of war amongst them was to defend their liberty and possessions. This we surely must allow them to have done with no ordinary success, when we reflect that for 2300 years they preserved upon the throne descendants of their royal house, with scarcely an interruption. How many times, within this period, has every country and island in Europe been overrun and conquered?

Nor do we find, in the history of Ceylon, a single battle, as in Persia, China and Hindustan, deciding the fate of the kingdom. On the contrary, lengthened and well-contested warfare is everywhere mentioned as the result of powerful invasions, and that, too, when these invasions followed each other with frightful rapidity. But whatever may have been the fate of the first few battles, Malabars, Bengalees, natives of the Circars, Cambodians, Moors and Malays, were all finally repulsed, and Ceylonese valour invariably prevailed in the end over foreign impetuosity, until the tactics and thunder of a far distant nation overcame, but did not subdue, their bravery and love of liberty. In the reigns of Dutu-Gaimono and Prackramabahu the Great, we have ample evidence that they wanted only leaders of valour and genius at their head to render them both warriors and conquerors. That foreign conquest, however, was not more frequently attempted, may be wondered at, when we reflect on the indifference with which a monarch, and especially an absolute one, wastes the lives of his subjects on the most trifling occasions,

——ὅσις ἐν τοῖς κέρδεσι
μόνον δέδορκε, τὴν τέχνην δ᾽ ἔφυ τυφλός ;*

for that this sentiment of Sophocles was precisely their character, is proved by the trivial occasions on which they undertook the erection of the most stupendous works. To expect amongst the effeminate nations of Asia the tactics, military abilities, and effective discipline of European forces would be as unreasonable as to expect in Otaheite the civility and polish of Paris. The two races are totally different; the one possessed of great

* Οἰδ. Τυρ. 388-9.

physical force, innured to hardships and accustomed to danger; the other of much weaker frames, leading sedentary, listless lives, and quite unused to active exertion. The one, with the example of Greece and Rome to urge them on to plunder and devastation; the other, with the example of their forefathers alone, only anxious to preserve what they already possessed. For these reasons, then, we think the state of the military art in Ceylon, during its glorious days, rather favours than opposes our views. It only now remains for us to shew the causes and extent of the degradation of the island from the eighth to the fifteenth century.

In considering this subject, we must remember that events are much more circumstantially related, generally, at least, in the latter than in the preceding era, and, therefore, we can only guess at the extent of the change, by the degree of inferiority exhibited between the events of the two periods. Perhaps nothing more clearly proves the existence of such a decline than the inferiority of the structures of later times, both in magnificence and excellence, when compared with those of the preceding period. Thus the ruins of Anuradhapoora surpass, in every respect, those of Pollanarua, whilst the latter, in like manner, are far more imposing than those of Cotta and Dambadiva. The embankments of the tanks, when they are such as to raise our admiration, or to excite our astonishment, were likewise the productions of *the great dynasty*, as the predecessors of Mahasen are very appropriately styled. Indeed, from a consideration of these works, we might almost doubt whether they could have been erected with the rude tools and implements of later ages, knowing, as we do, that other nations have forgotten how to manufacture, or use, the implements commonly employed by their ancestors *. In the early ages of Ceylonese history all their most celebrated and most excellent works were produced, whilst those of later times are almost invariably weak imitations of more ancient authors. Besides these marks of a falling state, however, others more unequivocal are not wanting. The universal consent of the native histories would in itself establish the fact, and so well known was it, that the dynasty preceding Mahasen, as we have before hinted, (A. D. 300,) is distinguished by a different title from that which succeeded him; the one being styled the Maha, or great, the other the Sooloo, or inferior, race †.

The causes of this decline are neither difficult to discover, nor complicated in themselves. Before that period but one considerable invasion had been experienced, and the erection of religious edifices so completely employed the attention of the monarchs as to keep them continually active and engaged. After that period, the irruptions of the Malabars and Bengalees became so frequent and for-

* But perhaps, in all such cases, the following remark of Voltaire will assist us in accounting for this wonder: "Il y a dans l'homme un instinct de méchanique que nous voyons produire tous les jours de très grands effets, dans les hommes fort grossiers. On voit des machines inventées par les habitans des montagnes du Tirol et des Vosges, qui etonnent les savans." Essai sur les Mœurs et l'Esprit des Nations. Intro. p. 32.

† Almost every writer who has examined, with attention, the present condition of Ceylon, has been convinced of its former grandeur and present debasement. An elaborate dissertation on the subject is therefore unnecessary, and it will be surely sufficient to refer the sceptic to the following works: Turnour's Introduction to his Translation of the Mahawanso.—Davy's History of Ceylon.—Preface to Boyd's Embassy to Kandy, by Mr Campbell.—Bertolacci's "Ceylon."—Major Forbes' Eleven Years in Ceylon, &c. &c. in all of which this evident decline is acknowledged and described.

midable, as to waste away, in continued warfare, the inhabitants of the island; and that to such an extent, that the whole of the northern part became almost completely depopulated. The consequence was, that a race of Malabars gradually settled in this unoccupied province, and thus Ceylon became the scene of a constant struggle between the original but diminished aborigines and the recent invaders. To such an extent did this continual rivalry extend, that, in almost every case, after a foreign war, we might say with Livy *, "paci externae confestim continuatur discordia domi."

This fact alone, we imagine, would be sufficient to check the improvement, and materially deteriorate any state of society; but, in connection with this, we must not forget the establishment of castes, and the effects of that establishment. The advantages experienced, by a recently founded nation, from this institution, are, probably, numerous and influential. Were such not the case, we can scarcely suppose that the custom would have been so universally adopted over the east as it has been †. But if it be useful in a rising state, it becomes one of the greatest clogs on the advancement, and one of the heaviest encumbrances in the policy of a nation, already settled and established, thoroughly preventing, as it has ever done,

* Lib. ii. chap. 54.

† It seems to have even extended into Europe at an early period; as for instance, to Attica (Diod. Sic. lib. ii. p. 32, 33,) and Crete (Aris. Polit. vii. c. 10.) It seems also to have pervaded the whole of the south of Asia. In Persia, we may gather from the Teudavesta, that castes originally existed. *Vide* Duperron's, i. 141. And it is well known that it has been always prevalent among the Hindus, and a part of the Chinese. Indeed, from the expressions of Herodotus, Strabo and Diodorus Siculus, we would be led to suppose that it originally pervaded all Asia.

improvement and advancement beyond a certain point. Such a system, elevating one class and depressing eternally the other, must have kept the ideas of the last for ever subdued, and entirely prevented those aspirations after superiority and influence, which form the greatest incentive to active exertion. Let us but suppose, for instance, that the great mass of the working people in England were suddenly to be deprived of all desire to obtain any thing but a mere livelihood of the plainest and coarsest kind,—what an utter stagnation of business would this create, and how lifelessly inert would it make them. But let us suppose, again, that such a principle had been in force for some centuries, and what a mass of talent would have been lost to the country, what an amount of improvement would never have been thought of, and what an amount of genius would have been born "to blush unseen, and waste its *power* on the desert air." In such a state of society what could prevent England, or any other country under heaven, from gradually retracing its steps to barbarism and poverty? But not only would so much talent and genius have been useless, but their valour also would be utterly destroyed. Why should those fight who had nothing to preserve but their lives; why should the poor exert themselves, strenuously, for the advantage of a country to which they owed nothing but their birth, and how debased would that nation become, the great body of whose inhabitants had no other object in life, than to obtain present gratification at any sacrifice or expense?—*ὥσπερ γαρ τελεωθεν βελτιστον των ζωων ανθρωπος εστι, ουτω και χωρισθεν νομου, και δικης, χειριστον παντων* *.

* Aris. Polit.

One of the most surprising events in Ceylonese history is certainly the introduction of this institution of castes, totally opposed as it is to the spirit of its religion. We have already expressed our conviction, that it was introduced by Wijeya and his followers, on the foundation of his dynasty as the sovereigns of Ceylon. Once introduced, however, it is easily perceived that the most powerful motives would combine to preserve it in force, and hand it down from generation to generation. The kings and royal family, seeing themselves thus separated by an insurmountable barrier from the rest of the people, would naturally preserve the institution which thus distinguished them; whilst the priests, second only by the same arrangement, to the sovereign, would have an equally powerful motive to enforce its observance, and continue the institution. ῶ φύσις ἐν ἀνθρώποισιν ὡς μέγ' εἶ κακὸν *. This evil, then, the system of castes, operating at first for the advancement, but afterwards for the retardation of the nation's improvement, combined with the growth of a hostile power in the very heart of the kingdom, could not but gradually undermine the prosperity, and sap the foundation of the grandeur of the state, at the same time that the greater frequency of external invasion was tending to dissolve the whole civil and political fabric. Combined with these causes, another would operate, more secretly and insidiously, but not less certainly, to bring about the same result. We have already mentioned the wild race of the Veddahs, inhabiting the barren and forest districts, who were a nation totally distinct from the Singhalese proper, and were, in their manners and customs, still more

* Ευριπ. Ορεστης. 126.

different than in their origin. These, leading the wild life of the hunter, with few wants and fewer enjoyments, were quite ready to take up arms in favour of any party who would pay them, utterly regardless of the consequences. Hence that fertility of rebellions, and those innumerable tumults, which too frequently interrupted the deep quiet of contentment and prosperity, and changed the country from being " as the garden of Eden," to " a desolate wilderness." Too often was it the case, that the patriot of Ceylon might adopt the words of the " father of Rome," and say, " tanta perturbatio et confusio est rerum, ut perculsa et prostrata, fœdissimo bello, jacent omnia *."

Can we wonder, then, that, with these powerful causes in operation, Ceylon should have gradually declined; its population decreased; its arts and manufactures be forgotten; its monuments of primeval grandeur be neglected; its inhabitants debased; its agriculture neglected; and its whole social system deranged; reduced from the state of a flourishing, prosperous, powerful and comparatively civilised people, to the state of degradation and comparative barbarism in which it was found by Europeans?

* Fam. Epist. l. iv. sit. 4.

CHAPTER X.

Jurisprudence of Ceylon under its native sovereigns—Rights of persons—Rights of things—Private injuries and actions—Crimes and punishments.

THE system of jurisprudence prevalent in different countries, and amongst different nations, are naturally based on, and influenced by the prevalent systems of religion. But however the minor points of the laws of various nations may differ, the great principles of equity must ever remain the same. The savage, who finds himself despoiled by a stronger neighbour, condemns the deed as vehemently as the most enlightened philosopher, at the same time that he is quite ready to act similarly towards those weaker than himself. However, then, the punishments awarded by various nations for similar offences may differ, the fundamental principles of right and wrong will agree, whilst the minor points of equity will vary only according to the genius of the people, and to the state of barbarism or refinement in which they exist. An investigation of the principles of Ceylonese jurisprudence will, we imagine, give us no reason to alter the opinion we have frequently expressed respecting its early improvement. Various customs, which shock the feelings of Europeans, may be found amongst them; but if we are inclined, on this account, to set them down as barbarous, we must, if we act consistently, conceive the Romans, and, indeed, every nation of antiquity, to have been also barbarous.

Ceylonese jurisprudence was most probably moulded

and modelled by the introducer of civilisation, Wijeya, whom we have formerly concluded to have instituted the system of castes; and it would seem probable, from the complexion of the subsequent history, that he had, with that system, introduced the outlines of equity, to be filled up by subsequent reformers. The simple moral code of Buddhism, we can have little doubt, would have been that which at first regulated their conduct and decided their contentions. In time, however, more complicated offences would arise; crimes of nicer shades of turpitude would gradually occur, and possibly certain actions might be doubtfully classed as crimes by some, which, by others, might be considered perhaps indifferent, or possibly virtuous. For these cases more refined distinctions would be necessary; and the simple prohibition of robbery, for instance, would be obliged to be widely extended to all the cases of varying fraud to which relationship or right might give occasion. In this manner, innovations, unimportant, perhaps, at first, but gradually stretching on to more startling additions, would be continually occurring, until the genius or perseverance of some master-mind had examined and remodelled the whole. In this way a code would be gradually formed, which would doubtless be the universal guide, until the additions of presumption or necessity rendered a second purgation as necessary as the first.

It does not seem probable, that, in the reformation and establishment of Buddhism by Mihindo, in the reign of Tisso, (B. C. 306,) the system of laws would have been forgotten; and we may be certain, that succeeding princes would remodel the system to suit their superior knowledge or presumptuous vanity. Nor can we easily conceive, that, in the reign of Walagambahu, (when the discourses of Gautama were first transmitted to writing in Ceylon, B. C. 89,) the laws were totally neglected, as continual references, and the close connexion of the two, would continually suggest the subject to their minds. Mahanama, the king of the island, and a voluminous writer in the beginning of the fifth century, it is probable compiled a code of laws, as well as added commentaries to those of Buddhu. We have a certain and distinct intimation, however, in the history of the reign of Dapulo the Third, (A. D. 797,) of his having compiled a distinct code of laws, which he had transmitted to posterity with the greatest care. But although these are the only cases in which the composition of codes of laws seem to be explicitly referred to, yet the frequent commendation of the various sovereigns in the native histories, for their just administration *of the laws* on the one hand, and the frequent condemnation of those who administered them unjustly on the other, leave no manner of doubt but that they were kept constantly in view, and generally promulgated.

The duties of the sovereign appear to have been imperfectly understood and badly defined by the legislators of Ceylon *. They seemed to depend altogether on the influence of their religion in restraining him from injustice, and inciting him to virtue. Human nature, however, unfortunately requires the dread of punishment in this world,

* Notwithstanding this defect in Ceylonese jurisprudence, we may justly apply the praise which Machiavel gives to the government of France to that of Ceylon: "That which constituted the government there," says he, "determined that the kings should dispose, as they pleased, of the armies and treasures, but that all the rest should be subject solely to the laws." —Discors I. 16.

as well as the hope of reward in another, in order to render it, in any succession of men, just or equitable. One may be so impressed with the conviction of his duty as to need no other restraint in order to keep him in the path of equity; but the history of the world assures us, that to hope for such a principle producing similar results for any length of time on different individuals is both foolish and dangerous. Bad and despotic as the government of Ceylon might have been, the Ceylonese seem never to have attained that depth of debasement, or that servility of soul, which would oblige them to obey every command, however unjust, and to comply with every irregular desire of their monarch's mind. This fact we have frequently seen exemplified in the antecedent history; and, to the honour of Buddhism, it must be recorded, that its priests were generally found the most instrumental in bringing about reconciliations, and that they frequently acted as "the messengers of peace." Nor must it be disguised, on the other hand, that in those instances in which we find them obtaining an ascendancy over their sovereign, they too frequently directed his attention more to the embellishment of their religion than to the due administration of justice, whilst in their histories they universally applaud those who promoted their ends without any regard to their civil administration or judicial conduct.

The government of the provinces seems to have been but a transcript of that of the capital. A vassal or subking ruled with almost absolute sway, being dependent on him alone from whom he derived his authority. Unlike other eastern despotisms, the inhabitants in every district seem to have had the privilege of petitioning their sovereign when they conceived his deputy acted without justice or moderation. Nor could these appeals be easily neglected by the king, as the council which ratified his decrees had the first consideration of them; and, unless he were lost to all sense of shame or rectitude, he would be obliged to give to them an account of the transaction, with the reasons for his conduct, before the final settlement of the question.

The ceremonies accompanying the inauguration of the monarch were few, but imposing. An assembly of all the dignitaries of Church and State having been made, the royal canopy (or mandappa) was brought forth richly ornamented, amidst much reverence. Beneath this the monarch's throne was placed, and, on his having occupied it, "a royal virgin, adorned with costly ornaments, and holding a sea chank full of the purest river water," approached him. Then, elevating the chank above the king's head, she poured upon it the libation, addressing him at the same time, thus,—"Your majesty is hereby anointed to rule over this whole assembly of Rohatries; may it therefore please your majesty to perform the duties of a sovereign, and to exercise your sway, with benignity and justice." A silver and golden chank of water were then successively poured upon his head; and having received the crown, he became henceforward "the king of kings, *and* emperor of Lanka."

I. *Persons.* If "the distinction of ranks and *persons* be the firmest basis of a mixed and limited government *," we must give the highest degree of praise to that system which for ever divides one class from the other, and

* Gibbon's Decline and Fall of the Roman Empire, vol. v. p. 348.

places an insurmountable barrier between the two. Revolutions and tumults may, in any other state of society, confound the one with the other; but under the system of castes, such an intermixture is impossible, whilst a mighty western empire may assure us, that the greatest degree of liberty may consist with perfect equality.

The different dispositions of different men are represented in Singhalese laws, as the cause of the first introduction of the system of castes, and the policy of early legislators was unquestionably the cause of its continuance. Besides this distinction, however, another more unjust and degrading appears to have existed from the earliest times, —that which separated the free from those in bondage.

The slaves were of four kinds.

1. Those who came into the world in this state, or slaves by birth.

2. Those sold into slavery in infancy by their inhuman parents *.

3. Those doomed to slavery by the king; women who by gross misconduct had lost caste; captives taken in war, and those brought by the traffickers in human flesh, and sold as slaves.

4. Those who have voluntarily bartered their liberty for a sum of money †.

The first class, slaves by birth, included all the offspring of the female slaves, whether their fathers were bond or free; and, in like manner, the offspring of free

* This unnatural traffic was also permitted by Roman law. *Vide* Institutes of Justinian, lib. 1, tit. 9, patria potestas; also the Pandects and Code.

† This and the following distinctions are taken from two papers on "Kandian Laws," published in the Ceylon Miscellany by Mr Armour.

women were invariably free. The distinctions by which they preserved the freedom of those born free, in their connection with the more debased class, were nice and curious. Thus, if a freeman, drawn by the strong arm of love, lives for any length of time with a female slave, the owner of the latter has a right to his services for that period, however long it may be, whilst he, on his part, is at perfect liberty to depart whenever he pleases, under the compulsion, however, of leaving all the goods acquired in the interval with his dusky *innamorata*.

The controul of the father in Ceylon was not nearly so absolute and irresponsible as that of the sterner Roman. In the former case the woman, being more reverenced and better treated, had a voice in the disposal of her children, to which she was not entitled in the latter, whilst the son or daughter on their part were released from the parental authority on reaching the age of discretion. So authoritative were the distinctions between the different castes, that the slightest intermixture of blood between them was considered as highly criminal. As the infidelity of the woman, however, has ever been considered as a greater crime, and worthy of more condign punishment than the similar dereliction of the man, so, in the jurisprudence of Ceylon, the most severe punishment which laws could inflict were imposed on those females who had intercourse with the lower castes of the opposite sex. In such cases the connections of the contaminated woman were at full liberty to put her to death, or, in case punishment were not inflicted, she was taken by the king and numbered amongst his female slaves for the rest of her life. When the castes were equal, however, the turpitude of the crime was greatly decreased, if not wholly removed; and indeed certain occasions are specified, on which, for benefits conferred, the wife might be lent for a proportionate space of time to the obliging party.

Even in the management of slaves the restrictions of caste could not be neglected by the master. Although he had the liberty of inflicting any punishment short of maiming or death, yet he could not compel the female to receive the addresses of a man of inferior rank, whether bond or free.

The excessive fertility and the rapid growth of vegetables in tropical countries seems to bear some analogy to the rapid development of the bodily strength in individuals. In Europe, chilled by the cold, but strengthening temperature, the human frame scarcely attains its full growth until the age of twenty or twenty-one; nor does the mind seem to attain to its full vigour short of the same period. But in the more genial and luxurious climate of Ceylon, both mind and body reach maturity much sooner, and, accordingly, the age of discretion was fixed at sixteen years, before which period no engagements entered into were legal, and no promises binding. At that period the youth became a man; and, although previously under the absolute controul of his parents, was now perfectly free, and might remain or depart as suited his own inclinations. If we compare such regulations with those of ancient Rome, we cannot but yield superiority to the former. There, "neither age, nor rank, nor the consular office, nor the honours of a triumph, could exempt the most illustrious citizen from the bonds of filial subjection *."

* Gibbon. Within a certain limitation, however, as, in the exercise of his legal duties, the son was independent. "In publicis locis atque numeribus, atque actionibus patrum, jura cum filiorum qui in magistratu sunt, potesta-

In the marriages and divorces, as appointed by the laws of Ceylon, we shall find much to censure. The consent of the parents or lawful guardians of the female seems to have been in every case necessary. Two forms of marriage are particularly distinguished from each other, both in their respective privileges and rights. In the one case, that styled a marriage in Deega, the wife was supposed to leave her parents' home and proceed to the house of her husband; in the other, or the marriage in Beena, the bridegroom is supposed to be admitted into the residence of the bride. The privileges of the husband, and his authority over his wife, were materially influenced by these circumstances, inasmuch as in the latter case, the unfortunate swain might be lawfully expelled from the house of his bride, on exciting the ire or jealousy of her parents; whereas in the latter, no divorce could take place without his consent.

The ceremonies of the marriage rite varied under different circumstances. The more ostentatious kind required five separate meetings of friends and relations, at each of which different customs were complied with. Astrologers were consulted, and the horoscope of the bride and bridegroom examined to select a propitious day, and a kind of unction was administered by way of legalising the union. These ceremonies, as we have said, however, were not universally observed. In some cases, mere union for a single night, with the consent of the parents, was sufficient to ratify the covenant. Breaches of the marriage-contract were equally condemned by the laws of Buddhism, whether committed by the husband or

tibus collata interquiescere paululum et connivere," &c. Aul. Gellius. Noc. Att. ii. 2.

wife. In the latter case, the husband was obliged formally to divorce his wife, and disinherit her children, if he wished her and them to be excluded from all share of his property on his death, even though he were evidently not the father of the offspring. His own will *, however, was in every case sufficient to dissolve the marriage-contract, but, in that case, he forfeited all claim to his wife's property, which remained intact. In case of a divorce, however, he was obliged to support his pregnant wife till the time of her delivery, and the child till old enough to be separated from its mother.

Marriages between relations in nearer degrees of affinity than that of cousins were deemed penal, and punished by law.

In most of these institutions we perceive openings for licentiousness but too apparent, less, however, by far, than those allowed on the Continent, and in the other parts of tropical Asia. But the most disgusting feature remains to be yet exhibited, in that polyandry, no less than polygamy, was allowed, with no other restrictions than the riches of the man, and the will of the woman †.

II. *Things*. By what rights or tenures property was held in Ceylon previous to its conquest by Wijeya we are

* The same authority was delegated to the Roman husband, but with a more debasing addition, inasmuch as he could condemn his wife to slavery, on the slightest transgression, by selling her. The only point in which early Roman jurisprudence appears to have excelled that of Ceylon was in polygamy as well as polyandry being strictly prohibited. In many cases, however, the system of Ceylon is evidently more in accordance with reason good sense and justice.

† Polyandry was not unknown even in Greece. Polybius (in a fragment of his twelfth Book,) states that it was an old and common occurrence in Sparta. Fragm. Vatican. tom. ii. p. 384.

totally ignorant, but we may reasonably conclude that his followers, like those of William the Norman in England, were amply provided for out of the confiscated lands.

In the later periods of Ceylonese history, property was divided into two distinct kinds, designated *addrawyawat*, or incorporeal, and *drawyawat*, corporeal or substantial. The first of these comprehended all rights of inheritance, titles, privileges, immunities, rank, reputation, caste, &c. In the second class we may note four divisions, under which all their substantial property may be included; 1. Things immoveable; 2. Things moveable; 3. Things inanimate; 4. Beings sentient or animate. These, if lawfully procured by descent, purchase, labour, or as free gifts, were the sole property of the possessor, of which no other man, however great or high, could deprive him.

The right of the king extended to all forests and wildernesses unoccupied by man; all the mines of precious stones or metals, and the produce of the pearl banks. He was not at liberty to dispose of the sacred relics, as these belonged to the whole country, and could not be legally claimed by any individual. This important regulation extended likewise to the various ponds and tanks, aqueducts and water-courses, temples and dāgobahs.

The laws relating to the property of those who died intestate seem to have been just and equitable. In the case of the married man his goods descended to his nearest relation in preference to his wife, whilst property, received from an adopted father or mother, descended to their heirs-at-law. In the case of the childless father, however, who had adopted an infant and reared it as his own, the widow received half his goods, whilst the adopted son or daughter might legally claim the other. Heir-looms, such as weapons of war, gold trinkets, frontlets, or honorary gifts, descended not to the widow, on her husband's dying intestate, but to the rightful heir of his ancestral property.

The right of inheritance possessed by the eldest son was unknown in Ceylon, and on the death of the father the property descended, unless otherwise disposed of, in the more equitable manner of an equal division amongst all. On entering the priesthood, however, the pious son forfeited all claim to his rights of inheritance, as he could not legally beget children to whom it might afterwards descend; but in the event of his not entering on that profession till his father's death, the land previously acquired remained his own.

We have formerly asserted that the most severe laws prohibited the slightest intermixture between the castes, and in the disposition of the property in such a case we have a remarkable instance of its severity. "If," says the stern edict of intolerance, "If a daughter *degrades herself* by becoming the wife of a man of any tribe or caste inferior to her own, she thereby forfeits all right to inherit property of any kind from her parents or other relations, and if *her degradation* happened subsequent to the demise of her parents, she then forfeits the landed property she may have inherited from her ancestors, which will forthwith pass from her to her legitimate children, or in default of those, to her brothers and sisters."

Of the remarkable strictness with which such inflictions were imposed, we had a striking instance in the preceding history, in which Sali Koornoraya, the son of the renowned Dutu-Gaimono, was deprived of his right of succession by his own father, for having contracted an alliance with a beautiful female of a low caste.

III. *Private Injuries and Actions.* On this branch of Ceylonese judicature we need not dwell, every information on this subject being easily procurable from the various works which describe the island and its inhabitants. In making promises they ratified them in a manner peculiar to themselves. Thus, by the transfer of a small stone to the person receiving the promise, the engagement was legalised; and on its breach by the promiser, the possessor of the stone might legally sue the faithless granter, and would find his claim supported by law. On this subject, one who knew them well, and described them truly, has the following remark: "When one proffers something as a gift to another, although it be a thing that he is willing to have, and would be glad to receive, yet he will say, 'Eeppa queinda,'—No, I thank you, how can I be so chargeable to you? And at the same time, while the words are in his mouth, he reaches forth his hand to receive it *."

In the receipt and use of another's property, as, for instance, corn, the owner expected to receive, either at the harvest or before the year's end, the quantity he had lent, together with half as much in addition, or at the rate of fifty *per cent.* But were payment delayed beyond the end of the first year, the interest then increased to double its former amount, so that instead of fifty he was obliged to pay at the rate of 100 *per cent.* Beyond this, however, it could not go, whatever period of time might elapse between the original loan and the payment of the principal. In such cases a harsh provision entitled the lender to seize on any property which the creditor might possess, so that he had even

* Knox "Historical Relation," &c. part. iii. c. ix.

power to sell his wife, his children, or himself, "provided," said the law, with decent carefulness, "provided she had come with him to fetch the debt, *otherwise* she is perfectly clear from such violence."

For the decision of cases in which injuries were alleged by some to have been inflicted by others, which they, on their side, denied, various measures were resorted to; the chief of which were, swearing before their gods in their temples, and, on more particular occasions, a trial similar to the fiery ordeal of ancient times. In this latter case burning oil decided the judgment, which, having been applied to the hands and wrists of those attesting their innocence, the gods were left to elucidate the truth by delivering the innocent from marks or pain.

"They have an odd usage among them to recover their debts, which is this: they will sometimes go to the house of their debtor, with the leaves of *neiingala*, a certain plant which is rank poison, and threaten him that they will eat that poison and destroy themselves, unless he will pay him what he owes. The debtor is much afraid of this, and, rather than the other should poison himself, will sometimes sell a child to pay the debt; not that the one is tender of the life of the other, but out of care of himself: for if the person dies of the poison, the other, for whose sake the man poisoned himself, must pay a ransom for his life. By this means, also, they will sometimes threaten to revenge themselves of those with whom they have any contest, and do it too. And, upon the same intent, they will also jump down some steep place, or hang, or make away with themselves, that so they might bring their adversary to great damage *."

* Knox, *ut supra*.

IV. *Crimes and Punishments.* Their crimes were seldom heinous, but their punishments were frequently barbarous. The frightful system of retaliation was practised in its fullest extent, "an eye for an eye, and a tooth for a tooth" were literally obeyed. More pernicious crimes, however, such as murder, treason, sacrilege, highway robbery, and theft, received more condign punishment. In these cases death was invariably inflicted, and, in the later ages of the native government, in its most horrible forms. Malefactors were impaled by huge stakes thrust, with barbarous cruelty, through their bodies; and, under some of the later sovereigns, burying the body in the earth, but leaving the head exposed to be shattered by blows, was inhumanly practised. These were scenes unknown in the early history, where we invariably find the punishment of death inflicted by the comparatively lenient method of beheading, but in every age a disregard of human life was but too apparent, and their punishments were too frequently disproportioned to the offence.

On the whole, however, taking into consideration the influences continually at work, we regard the laws of Ceylon as a triumphant proof of its early civilisation, and flourishing prosperity; and, after an impartial scrutiny we shall find that the indications of barbarism, wherever met, are the introductions of late and comparatively modern periods.

CHAPTER XI.

KNOWLEDGE POSSESSED OF CEYLON IN EUROPE BEFORE THE ARRIVAL OF THE PORTUGUESE IN 1505—AND THE INTRODUCTION AND DECLINE OF CHRISTIANITY.

I. Whether Ceylon is the country known to the ancients under the name of *Taprobane* or not, is a question frequently disputed between the maintainers and opposers of that opinion. It has been asserted that Sumatra, and not Ceylon, is the island referred to, and that, as the latter does not extend to the south of the equator, it cannot be the Taprobane of the Greeks and Romans *. In the former part of this work we have assumed that it is, and we shall now endeavour to maintain that opinion. Before bringing forward any evidences of its truth, however, we shall endeavour to answer the arguments advanced against it. We are told that Ptolemy † describes Ceylon as stretching from north to south fifteen degrees, two of which he supposes to be to the south of the equator, whilst all ancient writers agree in attributing to Taprobane a much greater size than that of the modern Ceylon. Such are

* Such is the principal argument brought forward in a late number of Blackwood's Magazine against the supposition.—See Mag. for Nov. 1843. art. Ceylon. † Ptol. Lib. vii. chap. 4. D'Anville Ant. de l'India, p. 142.

the chief objections to the commonly received opinion, and in them, on consideration, we will find but little to make us doubt its truth.

That Ceylon was formerly much larger than it is at the present day is an opinion maintained, not by the Greeks and Romans merely, but by the inhabitants themselves. We have already seen that various subsidences of the land are related, by which whole provinces have been covered, and its size materially reduced. Nor is it any extraordinary circumstance that an island, imperfectly known, should have been represented as seven degrees to the south of its real position. Instances are every day occurring in which mistakes of a much more erroneous nature and serious character are being exposed and rectified. But if part of Ptolemy's description is thus adverse to what we maintain, the rest is not less in our favour, inasmuch as he declares it to have stretched from Cape Comorin to the south, and to have been at no great distance from the Continent. An objection founded on so unimportant an error, then, is one which cannot overturn an opinion supported by so great an amount of evidence. There is scarcely a remarkable feature about the island which we do not find displayed in one or other of the accounts of Taprobane left us by the ancients.

Thus, Dionysius *, the geographer, one of the earliest who refers to the island, mentions it as distinguished for its elephants, whilst Ptolemy gives it the appellation of Σαλικη, and calls its inhabitants Σάλαι, a name evidently derived from the Arabic Seylan or Silendib. But the identity of Taprobane with Ceylon is plainly established

* Μητερα Ταπροβανην Ασιηγενῶν ελεφαντῶν. V. 593.

by the evidence of Pliny *, who tells us that Onesicritus celebrated it for its elephants, and Eratosthenes for its pearls. If, then, we adopt the supposition that the ancient Taprobane is not the modern Ceylon, we must suppose the former to be merely a creature of the imagination, supposed to exist by these laborious geographers merely for the sake of adding a new name to their nomenclature, as there is certainly no other island in Asia to which the descriptions referred to can be attributed with nearly so great a degree of probability as to Ceylon.

It seems, indeed, almost superfluous to give a formal proof of that which has been acknowledged by the greatest poet, and two of the greatest historians, of whom England can boast. We refer to Milton †, Gibbon ‡, and Robertson §.

We have already stated that the knowledge of Taprobane or Ceylon possessed by the ancients was both scanty

* Onesicritus classis ejus præfectus, elephantos ibi majores bellicosioresque, quam in India gigni scripsit; Megasthenes flumine dividi, incolasque Palæogonos appellari, auri margaritarumque grandium fertiliores quam Indos. Hist. Nat. lib. vi. c. 22. The mention of the river in the last paragraph is, though apparently an unimportant particular, one which, in reality, goes far to support our opinion, inasmuch as the Mahavelli-ganga was, for a long period, the boundary between the territory of the native princes, and that of the Malabars, so that Ceylon (or Taprobane) was both naturally and politically *divided by a river.*

† Embassies from regions far remote,
* * * * * *
From India and the Golden Chersonese,
And utmost Indian Isle Taprobane.

Par. Lost.

‡ Dec. and Fall of the Rom. Emp. vol. iii. p. 175, note of the 8th vol. edit., and iv. p. 142 of the edit. in 12 vols.

§ Disquisition on Ancient India, p. 28, Oc. Edit.

and incorrect. Nor did the much disputed embassy mentioned by Pliny either give certainty to their opinions, or circumstantiality to their information. We shall briefly notice the principal facts of this embassy, adding the remarks of one writer who opposes, and of another who maintains, the credibility of the facts contained in it. A freedman of Annius Plocamus, the farmer of the customs in the Red Sea, in the reign of Claudius, having been blown by a violent tempest from the coast of Arabia, was driven, at the end of fifteen days, upon that of Taprobane. The king of the country treated him with respect and kindness, nor did he depart till he had spent six months upon the island. During this period inquiries were naturally made respecting the country from which he had come, its resources, its extent, its population and its sovereign. The Roman did not fail to impress the listening foreigners with a favourable impression of his native country, extolling its vastness, its power, its riches and its commerce; and so powerfully did he excite the admiration of the king, that, on his departure, he was attended by four ambassadors to the Roman monarch. Of the account given by these attendants of the freedman we can find very little, indeed, that can, with any degree of consistency, be applied to Ceylon. In the palace of their king alone, they said, there were 200,000 inhabitants, whilst the wisdom of their political administration could only be surpassed by the splendour of their magnificence both of power and of riches.

We may reasonably doubt, however, whether any storm would drive their ill-constructed vessels, for fifteen days continuously, at the rate of one hundred and forty miles a day, and we may be positively certain that in no country under heaven was the force of public opinion ever a sufficient punishment for the grossest crimes. Under these circumstances, then, we consider the account of this embassy perfectly useless, as far as our investigation of the Romans' knowledge of Ceylon is concerned, nor can we bring ourselves to imagine that so exclusive and proud a king, as that of Ceylon usually was, would send a deputation to a prince with whom he had never had the slightest connection *.

* M. Latronne in a paper read before the French "Institute," and published in 1815, writes thus. After relating the facts of the case he continues,—"Mais les absurdités qu'ils (les ambassadeurs) débitèrent, sur leur île, preuvent clairement qu'ils n' y avoient jamais été (en Ceilan.) Comment expliquer autrement leur admiration pour la grande ourse et les pléiades, que, disoient-ils, ils ne voyoient pas chez eux, quand il est certain que l'une se voit trente degrés au-delà de Ceilan et que les autres s'élèvent au zénith de cette île? Que dire encore de leur surprise de ce que les ombres étoient tournées vers le pôle arctique, quand le même phénomène a lieu à Ceilan pendant sept ou huit mois de l'année; et de cette autre circonstance, que la lune ne se montre dans la Taprobane que de la huitième à la seizième heure, ou bien encore de ce que de leur pays on voyoit les monts 'Emodes; et enfin d'autres détails qui, sans être d'une absurdité aussi choquante, sont ou ridicules ou fabuleux? Il est à peu près impossible qu'on n'ait pas été dupé à Rome de quelque supercherie: l'affranchi d'Annius Plocamus aura voulu tirer parti de son naufrage; ayant emmené avec lui quelques naturels du lieu où il avoit débarqué, il les aura investis du caractere d'ambassadeurs et les aura fait venir de Taprobane, d'où il étoit bien sûr qu'aucune ambassade réelle ne viendroit lui donner un démenti."—Mémoires de l'Académie Royale des Inscriptions et Belles Lettres, Tome x. p. 228.

Captain Wilford endeavours to reconcile these "*absurdités*" by accusing Pliny of misrepresentation, and by explaining Hindu customs:· "The account given by the son of Rachias, (one of the ambassadors) has nothing very extraordinary in it, when the whole is considered in a proper light; and it shews the carelessness of the Greeks and Romans, in inquiries of that nature. The regard the Hindus have for the seven Rishis, or the seven stars of the Great Bear, and which they saw so much above the horizon, made them often

Of the embassies related by Arminanus Marcelinus * to Julian the Apostate, he tells us, some were sent by the Ceylonese, (absque Divis et Serendivis,) but as he professes to give little information respecting the island, we need not detain the reader by examining its probability or unlikelihood.

Perhaps the best accounts the ancients had of Ceylon were those of Diodorus Siculus and Strabo. The former mentions † that its inhabitants were distinguished by their extreme longevity, and by their freedom from disease.

look up to them, as well as to the Pleiades. From this circumstance, the Romans *foolishly conceived* they never saw them before. They also often mentioned the star Canopus, for which the Hindus entertain the highest respect.

With respect to the moon's course, there is the bright half and the dark half; which, in India, constitutes what is called the day and night of the Pitris. The day is reckoned from the first quarter to the last; and this is called the bright half or the day of the Pitris; the dark half is from the last to the first quarter of the next moon; and this constitutes their night. When Pliny says, that, in their country, the moon was seen only from the eighth to the sixteenth, *he was mistaken ; he should have said* that the bright half, or day of the Pitris, began on the eighth, and lasted sixteen days, including the eighth; and then began the dark half, or night of the Pitris; and, from these expressions misunderstood, the Romans concluded that the moon was not to be seen in their country during the dark half." Essay on Anugangam, &c. Asiat. Res. ix. 42.

Captain Wilford seems to have forgotten that the ambassadors were, most probably, not Hindus but Buddhists, and that no one could be a better judge of *what he ought to say* than Pliny himself.

* Inde nationibus indicis certatim cum domis optimates mittentibus ante tempus, absque Divis et Serendivis, (xxii. 7.) See a critique on this embassy in the "Mémoires" before mentioned, p. 230. That author justly ridicules "*ces relations presque de bon voisinage*" implied in the phrase *ante tempus*, in the above paragraph.

† *Πολυχρονιους δ᾽ ειναι τους ανθρωπους καθ υπερβολην, ὡς αν αχρι των πεντηκοντα και ἑκατον ετων ζωντας*, &c. Diod. Sic. vol. ii. p. 163.

The climate he also mentions as delightfully temperate, being neither rendered oppressive by excessive heat, nor unpleasant by cold. Besides these facts, however, much that was fabulous and imaginary was recorded by the same writer. Strabo * informs us that Ceylon, in his time, supplied the market of India with ivory, tortoise-shells and various manufactured articles of excellence and beauty; nor are the elephants forgotten, as, in common with Dionysius, he praises the breed, and mentions their extraordinary size. "But" (says an acute author †) "cinnamon is not enumerated amongst the other articles, though it could hardly have been omitted, if the country which he mentions, under the name of Taprobane, were the same as the modern Ceylon, and if that island were, in his time, as famed for the growth of that species of aromatic as it has since been." The second part of this supposition, it will be perceived, answers the first, as far as the doubt respecting the identity of Taprobane and Ceylon is concerned.

There is little doubt, however, notwithstanding the imperfect nature of their knowledge of Ceylon, that several of its productions and manufactures found their way into the houses of the Roman nobles. In the first century after the Christian era, a regular commercial intercourse had been established between the southern Europeans and the coasts of India and Ceylon. Pliny ‡ and Strabo § inform us, with some inaccuracies, of the manner in which this trade was conducted. Every year, we are told, a fleet of upwards of 100 vessels proceeded from the Red

* L. ii. p. 70, and again, 690.

† Philalethes in a History of Ceylon, prefixed to Knox's "Historical Relation."

‡ Hist. Nat. l. 6.

§ Strabo, lib. 17.

Sea to the coasts of Malabar and Ceylon. We may reasonably doubt, however, whether the slight and rude barks of that remote period could "traverse the ocean in forty days," as Gibbon * has recorded, especially when we reflect, that they were sailing at a period when the Indian ocean is much agitated by furious storms. Instead of *crossing* the Indian sea, it seems more probable, that, in accordance with the usual practice, even to a much later period, they would keep along the shore, in which case the "traversing of the ocean," in less than three or four months, is extremely improbable. Under this supposition, we may reasonably suppose that they would avail themselves of one monsoon in going, and of the opposite in returning. "The objects of oriental traffic were splendid and trifling; silk, a pound of which was esteemed not inferior in value to a pound of gold; precious stones, among which the pearl claimed the first rank after the diamond; and a variety of aromatics, that were consumed in religious worship and the pomp of funerals †."

It would seem, also, from the concurrence of Roman and Indian testimony, that besides this trade to the west, which was carried on till the invasion of the Mahommedans, another, of at least equal extent, connected Ceylon with the east. This we may gather as well from the accounts of the west, as from the imperfect chronicles of the east. We know that several of the articles traded in by Ceylon at that early period must have been thence derived, and that, had a regular trade not been established, the annual traffic in them could not have been continued.

* Dec. and Fall, &c. vol. i. p. 65. † Gibbon, *ut supra*.

Captain Wilford, in speaking of this traffic, particularly with China, proceeds thus:

"The predeliction of the Chinese for the people of India and Ceylon was very natural. Thus we see, that the people of that island (Ceylon) traded to China, at the very beginning of our era, and by land. There can be no doubt that they went first by sea to the country of Maghada, or the Gangetic provinces, where their legislator, Buddha, was born, and his religion flourished in the utmost splendour. There they joined in a body with the caravans of that country, and went to China, through what Ptolemy and the author of the Periplus call the great route from Palibothra to China. It was in consequence of this commercial intercourse, that the religion of Buddha was introduced into that vast empire, in the year 65 A.C.; and from that era we may date the constant and regular intercourse between Maghada (Ceylon) and China, till the extirpation of the religion of Buddha, and the invasion of the Mussulmans." *

The influence which Ceylon must have acquired in the first centuries, as well by its power as by its commerce, is curiously confirmed in the writings of St Ambrose. A Thebean, he informs us, named Scolasticus, visited the island in the fourth century, and described to him both it and Malabar. He veraciously describes the islanders as living chiefly upon milk, rice and fruits, which the country produced in abundance. The king of the island he represents as being the chief of the kings of India, whom the others obeyed as viceroys. He was detained for six years by one of these tributary Malabar sovereigns; but on his

* Essay on Anugangam, &c. by Capt. Wilford, Asiat. Res. vol. ix. p. 41.

confiner rebelling against his superior, (τὸν μέγαν βασιλέα, τὸν ἐν τῇ Ταβροβάνῃ νήσῳ καθεζόμενον,) he regained his liberty.

The account of the extensive trade of Ceylon at this early period is also confirmed by Cosmas, surnamed Indicopleustes, who travelled through India and that island during the sixth century, in the reign of Justinian. Having afterwards retired to a monastery, he there devoted himself to piety and literature; and, amidst other works, left us one, styled *Christian Topography*, in which he describes Ceylon. "He supposes it to lie at an equal distance from the Persian Gulf on the west, and the country of the Sinæ on the east; and asserts that it had become, in consequence of this commodious situation, a great staple of trade; that into it were imported the silk of the Sinæ, and the precious spices of the eastern countries, which were conveyed thence to all parts of India, to Persia and to the Arabian Gulf." * Cosmas calls it Sielediba † doubtless a corruption of the Arabic Selendib.

As the Mohammedans became the most influential people shortly after this period, so from them we obtain the next account of Ceylon. In the discourse ‡ of Abu Zeid al Hasan, prefixed to the account of the voyages of two Arabian merchants, who visited it in the ninth century, we find a somewhat particular account of Ceylon. In this work we find the first attempt at a sketch of the Singhalese, and a description of the face of the country. The next information obtained in the west of this famous island,

* Robertson's "Disquisition on Ancient India," p. 31.

† Cosmas apud Montfaucon Collect. Patrum, lib. xii. p. 336.

‡ This work was translated by the Abbé Renaudot, A. D. 1718, and the original manuscript was afterwards found by M. De Guignes.

is to be found in the travels of Marco Polo, the celebrated Venetian traveller of the thirteenth century, whose relations were for so long a period treated with incredulity. We shall give his relation in his own words. He states, that at the period of his visit, (A. D. 1244,) it was about "two thousand four hundred miles in circumference, but in ancient times it was still larger, its circumference then measuring full three thousand six hundred miles." "Both men and women go nearly in a state of nudity, only wrapping a cloth round their loins. They have no grain besides rice and samé, of which latter they make oil. Their food is milk, rice and flesh, and they drink wine drawn from trees." "The island produces more beautiful and valuable rubies than are found in any other part of the world, and likewise sapphires, topazes, amethysts, garnets, and many other precious and costly stones." "In this island there is a very high mountain, so rocky and precipitous, that the ascent to the top is impracticable, as it is said, excepting by the assistance of iron chains employed for that purpose. By means of these, some persons attain the summit, where the tomb of Adam, our first parent, is reported to be found. Such is the account given by the Saracens."

The successors of Marco Polo from the fourteenth to the seventeenth centuries give us much valuable information respecting the island. To particularise the account of each would probably be as useless, as it certainly would be tedious, and we shall therefore content ourselves with merely pointing out the chronological order of their visits, and the additional information which each account conveys.

The first that we shall mention is that of Ludovico Barthema of Bologna, whose journey is to be found in the first volume of Ramuseo's collection. The date at which he visited the island is not stated, but it was, most probably, in the latter part of the fourteenth or beginning of the fifteenth century. He mentions that the inhabitants were dependent for rice upon the southern provinces of India, their own country not yielding sufficient for their consumption. The inhabitants he states to have been by no means warlike, and that although they had spears and swords, little blood was shed in their contests, from their cowardice *. From the account of Nicolo De Conte, a Venetian, who in the year 1444 related his adventures, by way of penance, to the famous *Poggio Florentino*, we obtain a particular account of the Talipot tree. He describes it as one that does not bear fruit, whose leaves are eight yards (braccie) long and as many broad, but so thin, that when folded up, it may, without inconvenience, be carried in the hand: that it was used for writing, and, when extended, as a defence against the rain. He also mentions its precious stones and pearls; describing, too, with much minuteness, the cinnamon, its appearance and preparation for use.

The next traveller in chronological order, Jerome de Santo Stephano, also alludes to the cinnamon. He spent but one day on the island in company with his friend and countryman, Jerome Adorno, and wrote the account of his wanderings at Tripoly, in Syria, A. D. 1499. The cinnamon he particularises as a kind of laurel, and cele-

* "Gli habitanti suoi non sono multo bellicosi."—"Hanno alcune lancie e spade, lequali lancie sono di canna, e con quelle combattono fra loro, ma non se ne amazzano troppo di essi, *perche sono vili.* Itiner. di Lud. Barthema. Ramusio, vol. i. fol. 162-3.

brates, like his two predecessors, the precious stones and pearls.

Andrew Corsalie, a native of Florence, has left us two letters, in which he mentions Ceylon, the first written in 1515, and the other two years later. Its elephants he states to have been a great source of its wealth, and asserts that they were paid for by the merchants according to their weight, at a certain rate *per* hand.

Edward Barbosa, a Portuguese, who visited Ceylon in 1516, gives a somewhat particular account of its inhabitants, but seems to have been much more conversant with the Malabars and Mussulmen than with the native Singhalese. He tells us that it was called, amongst the Indians, Tennaserim or the "Land of Delights."

A particular account of the pearl fishery is to be found in the curious travels of Cesare di Fredericia, who set out in 1563. He describes the whole process of diving and picking with great minuteness and fidelity, and gives an admirable account of the small island of Manaar, and of the channel separating it from Ceylon. After detailing the political concerns of the island, he proceeds to mention the cinnamon. Of this, together with pepper, ginger, beetle and areka nuts, he tells us great quantities were produced, and is, perhaps, the earliest writer who notices the value of the *coir* for cordage, procured from the husk of the cocoa nut. The Portuguese were at this period engaged in hostilities with the natives, and were obliged, in consequence, to remain shut up in their forts; but our author, being anxious to obtain a correct knowledge of the preparation of the cinnamon, ventured into a plantation about three miles distant from the fort. It was then April, when, as he asserts, trees "*vanno in amore*," and when the cinnamon is fit for gathering, and, in consequence, he had a full opportunity of witnessing its growth, appearance and preparation.

From this period the accounts of Ceylon became correct and numerous, as the fullest opportunity was afforded to the Portuguese of describing its productions, appearance and inhabitants. It would, therefore, be a useless and unprofitable task to notice here the succeeding writers, as we shall have frequent occasion to refer to their respective works in the course of the history *.

II. Perhaps no event has more powerfully contributed to distinguish the civilisation of the West from that of the East, than the introduction and extension in the former of the Christian religion. When Christianity has been for fifteen centuries the religion of India, it will then, and not till then, be fair to contrast and compare the advancement of Asia with that of Europe. It does not appear, however, that India was prevented from receiving the gospel either by the want of teachers or of effort. On the contrary, at a very early period, it appears to have received missionaries and labourers from the west. It would be much beyond the design of the present work to discuss the disputed point of the mission of St Thomas, or that of the bishop of Shireburn sent by Alfred of England, especially as they had no immediate connection with Ceylon. We shall content ourselves with referring inquirers to the writings of Jerome †, Fabricius and Assemann ‡,

* In this account we have received much assistance from a MS. of the Hon. Fred. North, first English governor of Ceylon, kindly lent us by the Rev. J. G. Macvicar.

† Ad Marcellum, Epist. 148. ‡ Biblioth. Orient. tom. iv. p. 391-451.

for the first point, and to the History of the Anglo Saxons by Mr Turnour for the other. However these disputed points may be settled, there can be little doubt that the gospel of the New Testament had found its way to India in the second century. We have it on unquestionable authority that the venerable Pantænus * of Alexandria visited India in the year 189, and that Frumentius, the Abyssinian missionary, preached on the coasts of Malabar shortly after. We may conclude, therefore, that from the early period just mentioned Christianity spread over India, and, most probably, shortly afterwards reached Ceylon. At the Council of Nice, A. D. 325, the Indian church was then of such importance that a primate from it was in attendance, a fact incontestably proving its extent and rapid growth. The first direct intimation of its existence in Ceylon is to be found in the Travels of Cosmas Indicopleustes, before referred to. He informs us that there were many Christian churches established there in the sixth century, as well as in most of the Indian cities which he visited; churches doubtless supplied by, and subject to, the Nestorian primate †. In the ninth century, also, the two Mohammedans formerly mentioned state that they found in Ceylon many Christians, Manicheans, Jews, and Musselmen. The king, they inform us, encouraged their various meetings, and many learned Hindus frequented them. Nor do we want the evidence of history on the subject. Ferishta, in his general history of Hindustan, writes thus, "Formerly, before the rise of Islam, a company of Jews

* Eusebius, Hist. Eccles. Book v. c. 10. Jerome, Catal. Scriptor. Eccles. c. 36. † On the subject of the Nestorian heresy, *vide* Mosheim, 8vo. Edit. vol. i. 133-145. Milner, Cent. v. chap. xii. near the end. Gibbon, vol. vi. c. xlvii. p. 60

and Christians came by sea into the Malabar country, and settled as merchants or pishcaras. They continued to live there until the rise of the Musselman religion *." Perhaps the strongest indirect proof we possess of the early propagation of the gospel in India is to be found in the introduction of the facts of Christianity into the fables of Hinduism.

In the histories of Sālivāhana and Vicramāditya, confused and confounded with each other as they are, we perceive many points of our Saviour's life introduced, under circumstances plainly shewing that the coincidence is more than accidental. We shall, therefore, disregarding the various other traditions about the same personages, point out that which plainly evidences the introduction of the facts related in the New Testament into these annals of Hinduism. Sālivāhana, the prophet of Western India, is represented as having been born about five years before our era, and as having lived for eighty-four years. His birth is said to have been foretold for a thousand years †, as well as the object of his mission—the removal of sin and misery from the world. Again, we are informed ‡ that he was born of a virgin; that his mother's honour was for some time suspected, but that the suspicion was removed by choirs of angels who sang praises to the heavenly messenger. Scarcely a point of the sacred history is omitted in some or other of the accounts handed down to us of this extraordinary prophet. The enmity of the king, the dispute with the doctors, and his subsequent miracles, are all regularly chronicled, although mixed, of course, with the interferences of gods and goddesses peculiar to the

* Asiat. Reg. Miscell. p. 151.

† The Vicrama-Charitra of Northern India. ‡ The Vansavali do.

genius of Hinduism. We might notice several other legends of the same kind current in the east of India * and in Cashmere †, in which other points of sacred history are amalgamated with fable, and related in a loose and unconnected manner; but the instance of Sālivāhana is sufficient for our purpose ‡. It proves that Christianity was early introduced into India, but that it, before long, became corrupt and degenerate, probably from the want of copies of the sacred volume. The mixture of its events with those of the legends of Hinduism exhibits its extensive diffusion, and gross corruption. From these facts we may conclude that, from about the fourth to the eighth century, the light of revelation burned in Ceylon, but that, from that period, it gradually waned, and was completely extinguished before the arrival of the Portuguese, until revived by the zealous efforts of Francis de Zavier. We shall now find it occupying a conspicuous place in Ceylonese history, either as the excuse for intolerance and bigotry, or as the peaceful harbinger of civilisation and prosperity.

* *E. g.* Those relating to Vicramaditya, *vid.* Vicrama-charitra, Sinhāsana Divādrinsati, and Vetāla-pancha-vins'ati.

† Those relating to Arrjya. *Vid.* Hist. of Cashmere, &c.

‡ The curious reader will obtain much information on these, as well as other subjects connected with India, in the essays of Captain Wilford, to be found in the ninth and tenth vols. of the Asiat. Res., from which we have liberally drawn in the preceding accounts.

CHAPTER XII.

CONTINUATION OF THE HISTORY OF CEYLON FROM THE ARRIVAL OF THE PORTUGUESE, (A. D. 1505,) IN THE REIGN OF PRACKRAMABAHU IX., TO THE ESTABLISHMENT OF SINGHA IST'S POWER, (A. D. 1581.)

Discoveries of the Portuguese— Arrival of Almeida in Ceylon — Native account of his landing—His treaty with Prackrama—Contentions—Second treaty—Death of Prackrama—Noble conduct of Sakala—Depredations of the Portuguese—They are besieged—Distress and relief—They quit Ceylon—Their return—The Moors attack Colombo—Impolicy of the Ceylonese — Wijayabahu — Buwaneko Bahu VII.—His alliance with the Portuguese—Dunnai opposes him—The war—Death of Buwaneko—Dunnai and the Portuguese—Don Juan—Dunnai's Policy—War—The Portuguese and Don Juan worsted—Rajah Singha—He defeats Don Juan—The Portuguese obtain succours from Goa—Are again worsted—Siege of Colombo proposed by Singha—An insurrection prevents it—Cruelty of Singha—He besieges Colombo—Insurrection of Don Juan—Singha defeated—His death and character.

The impulse which the extraordinary discoveries of the Spanish and Portuguese, both in the eastern and western hemispheres, gave to the spirit of enterprise and commerce, was felt in the remotest regions of the world. Columbus and Vasco de Gama opened, at the end of the fifteenth century, new regions of hitherto unknown lands, which promised to give to their respective patrons a degree of power and influence unheard of in the annals of nations. Perhaps no brighter prospects have ever opened upon a nation than those which the Portuguese acquired on the discovery of India. Nor has it frequently been the lot of any to obtain such a commander as Albuquerque, in an enterprise of such extent and importance. Looking at the glorious prospect which then opened upon Portugal, we may, indeed, wonder that the power of bigotry, and the influence of rapacity, could have been of weight enough, however predominant, to overthrow such bright beginnings. The vast continent of India lay before them, the rich and beautiful Ceylon was directly in their path, and the whole east appeared as a genius ready to bow before that of Lusitania. Yet such has been the course of events: Portugal, blinded by avarice, and foolish by bigotry, acquired, but to hand over to others, territories wrested from the feeble inhabitants of Asia, which might have rendered her what England has since become, the mother of India, and the mistress of the ocean *. The history of the events which prepared the way for her decline is every where the same; and Ceylon was but a sample of other countries, in which the same consequences followed causes of a similar nature.

We have already explained that on the arrival of Almeida, Ceylon was divided into three distinct principalities, of which Dharma Prackramabahu the Ninth, who then resided at Cotta, was king of the larger and more important one, the other two being the territory of the Malabars in the north, and the wild Veddahs on the north and east. Europeans have frequently been misled into the idea that the island was divided into a vast number of

* Γης και θαλασσης σκηπτρα και μοναρχιαν Λαβοντες.—Cassandra.

petty kingdoms, each independent of the other. Such, however, was not the case. Sub-kings, or, as we should call them, lieutenants, subject to the Emperor of Cotta, were appointed in many places, who frequently endeavoured to play upon western visitors, by representing themselves as independent princes.

The Portuguese, on their first landing in India, under Vasco de Gama, A. D. 1496, were extremely active in obtaining settlements and commencing a profitable trade. In 1505, Francisco D'Almeida, then governor of Goa, their principal possession on the Malabar coast, sent his son Lorenzo in pursuit of some Moorish vessels which had been observed in the direction of the Maldives. The wind proving adverse to an easterly passage, D'Almeida was, unfortunately for Ceylon, driven on its shores. His vessels were anchored in Colombo, and the report of his arrival soon reached the palace. It may be interesting to Europeans to hear the account of this event given by one of the native historians:—"And now it occurred in the Christian year 1522 *, in the month of April, that a ship from Portugal, in Dambadiva †, arrived and anchored in Colombo. Whilst lying in the harbour, information was thus sent to the king of that event, by the inhabitants of the place: 'There are now in our harbour of Colombo a race of men, exceeding white and beautiful. They wear boots and hats of iron, and they are always in motion.'"

* We cannot consider it very extraordinary that Buddhists should have mistaken the year of an era which they were unaccustomed to use.

† This name has two different significations in Buddhist geography. In its more confined and local sense it signifies a district of the modern Bengal, but, when generally applied, as in this case, the whole earth—*cognita aut incognita.*

Of the diet of the Portuguese they gave the following account: "They eat *budhu gal* (a sort of white stone) and they drink blood *: if they get a fish they will give two or three ride in gold or silver for it; and they have guns which make a noise like thunder, when it breaks upon Jugandere Parivata, and even louder; and a ball shot from one of them, after flying some leagues, will break a castle of marble, or even of iron." This, with an infinity of similar news, they conveyed to the king †.

Prackrama immediately on the receipt of this intelligence called a council of all his generals and ministers, to decide the question, whether war or peace was preferable. After some discussion, the politic measure was adopted of sending one of the most experienced of their number in disguise to Colombo, who might there reconnoitre and inform them of his opinion. Chachra, the lieutenant, who had been sent, returned with the advice that an embassy, which the Portuguese might be secretly incited to send, should be received and heard, but that, for his part, he conceived it both impolitic and unwise to commence warlike operations, thus suddenly and unprovoked. By the exertions of the native chieftain of the district an embassy was accordingly despatched, which the Singhalese monarch received with kindness and respect. Presents were mutually given and received, and a treaty of peace at once concluded. By this treaty, we are informed by European historians ‡, it was stipulated, that the Singhalese monarch should pay an annual tribute of 250,000 lbs. of cinnamon, whilst the king of Portugal

* Bread and port wine. † Rajawali, part iv. p. 277. ‡ Ribeiro and Valentyn.

should, on his part, defend Ceylon from all enemies. A pillar is also said to have been erected in commemoration of the conquest of the island! But if such a treaty ever existed, why was so immense and valuable a quantity of this precious spice allowed to remain, for twelve years at least, without even being asked for? or why should the Portuguese have re-embarked without enforcing the payment of a part? " The treaty itself must have been an invention of the Portuguese commander, or some qualified evasion of his demands by the Singhalese monarch, who probably never intended to execute, and certainly could not have fulfilled such a contract *."

Thirteen years after this event another Portuguese commander arrived with nineteen sail in Colombo †. Lopez Suaar Alvarengo, in accordance with the commands which he had received from Emmanuel of Portugal, immediately on landing proceeded to erect a fort. This proceeding was vigorously, but ineffectually opposed by the Ceylonese. Their untrained bands of infantry were far from being capable of making an impression on the disciplined troops of the Europeans, flushed as they were with continual success and habituated to victory. The fort, consisting at first of clay and stone, was quickly finished, and the Portuguese soon became the aggressors. On the first opposition of the Ceylonese, Alvarengo attacked them with such ardour and success, that his

* Forbes' Ceylon, vol. ii. chap. xi.

† That the trade of Ceylon, even at this debased period, was considerable, is evident from the number of vessels which Alvarengo found in the harbour of Colombo: there were—" plusieurs navires de Bengale, de Perse, de la Mer Rouge et d'autres lieux, lequels venoient là pour y charger de la Canelle et des Elephans."—Ribeiro, c. v.

prowess was not less dreadful to the natives than his fire-arms and artillery. The latter were forced to sue for peace, and the Portuguese commander despatched four ambassadors to Cotta, on which occasion their historians again assert that an annual tribute of cinnamon, elephants and precious stones, was once more promised by the Emperor of Ceylon. Yet the amount of the cinnamon, which they hand down to us as having been mentioned on this occasion, (120,000 lbs.) is not half as great as that recorded in the former case.

The dissensions of the Ceylonese combined with the superior knowledge of the Europeans to lay their island prostrate before the foreigners. On the death of Prackramabahu in 1527, civil war and bloodshed reigned throughout the island. Sakala Rajah, a brother of the deceased monarch, was, by a majority of the people, called to the vacant throne. Sakala, however, with rare moderation and strength of mind, was not to be blinded by the prospect of power and eminence, which he foresaw would involve his country in tumults and dissensions. Having come down to Cotta, from the capital of his own province, Odegampola, he there assembled and addressed the ministers and people, assuring them that, although his selfish nature might comply with their request, his love for Ceylon restrained him, and that whilst another lived who had a better title to the throne than himself, *that* other, and not he, should be their king. He then produced before them a youthful brother of their late sovereign, (who seems to have been born of the same mother, which most probably Sakala was not,) and him he had proclaimed Emperor of Ceylon, under the title of Wijayabahu the Seventh. After this noble conduct, worthy of the best days of Greece or Rome, Sakala retired to honour and obscurity at Odegampola, where, in the jurisdiction of his province, he lived in peace and died in happiness.

In the meantime, however, events of considerable importance had been transacting at Colombo. The Portuguese having at length erected substantial and permanent fortifications, commenced a series of violence, rapacity and injustice, which too frequently followed the footsteps of their power. The Ceylonese had not yet learned to suffer without attempting to redress, nor were they disposed to endure, without retaliation, injuries thus unwarrantably heaped upon them. Every European who came in their way was seized and put to death, conduct which at length roused the Portuguese commander, Lopez de Bretto, to take active measures in order to ensure safety to his followers. Having suddenly attacked a marauding party of the natives, they took to flight, but soon returned with a considerable reinforcement to the charge; and, in a short time, an army of 20,000 men sat down before Colombo, to form the irregular, unformidable siege of Asiatics. For five months the fort was strictly invested, and the want of provisions began to make the insolent Portuguese fear a worse enemy than the injured Ceylonese. At length an opportunity afforded itself of sending to Cochin. A messenger was accordingly despatched to the viceroy of the place, informing him of the perilous state of the garrison in Colombo. A reinforcement, which the European historians assure us consisted of but a single galley *, soon made its appearance, and revived

* We have, in a former instance, exhibited the *penchant* of Ribeiro for magnifying the prowess of his countrymen, and we can scarcely help ima-

the drooping spirits of the soldiers. An unexpected sortie was shortly after made by Bretto, at the head of three thousand Portuguese, when the native army was at once put to flight, and their camp and works taken. A treaty was once more concluded in consequence, and the energetic Bretto, warned by past transactions, became more careful of the behaviour of his followers, and their treatment of the Ceylonese. He was not long destined, however, either to exhibit improvement or revenge.

The court of Lisbon, fearing that the too extended limits of its eastern empire might become at length the cause of its overthrow, and feeling embarrassed by the support of so many garrisons, and such continual war, resolved to maintain their stations on the coast, and to leave Ceylon to its native dissensions. Orders were accordingly despatched by Emmanuel, the king of Portugal, A. D. 1524, in which the destruction of the fort of Colombo and the evacuation of Ceylon were enjoined. These orders seem to have been but very partially obeyed by Ferdinand Gomes de Lerne, who at that time commanded there, and accordingly seventeen of his countrymen were left upon the island. These had the good fortune to meet with countenance and protection from the reigning sovereign of Ceylon, whom we shall find, with generous ignorance, assisting them against their enemies. The Moors were at this time highly incensed against the avaricious Portuguese. Before the arrival of the latter they had the whole traffic of the east in their hands, from

gining that the present is an instance of a similar kind. Unfortunately not a word of the transaction appears in the native chronicles, shewing that the whole affair was by no means considered as important by the native historians at least.

which they derived vast profit; but now when that traffic had found a new channel, and was conveyed by a foreign nation, they found themselves excluded from the profit which they had formerly enjoyed. Hearing that but a small detachment had been left upon the island, they resolved to attempt its destruction, and thus once more become the carriers of Ceylon. A chieftain was accordingly despatched with a force of 500 men to destroy the small garrison of Colombo; but finding himself opposed by the natives, whom he naturally imagined would have been his warmest friends, he was obliged to abandon the enterprise without having performed any thing of importance.

From this period we may date the fall of Ceylon. Instead of vigorously uniting to expel the invaders, each of the opposing parties in the native quarrels was ready to accept of their aid, and thus more firmly rooted them upon the island.

Although placed upon the throne by a man eminent for virtue and rectitude, Wijayabahu the Seventh soon gave evidence of his injustice and immorality. Having had three children by a former wife before his accession to the regal power, he endeavoured to procure their exclusion from the throne in favour of the issue of a later marriage. This the three princes, who were now of age sufficient to understand their rights, determined to oppose, and, finding their father resolved to prosecute his design at every hazard, they fled into different parts of the interior, resolving to defend their privileges with the sword. Sakala, having remonstrated with Wijayabahu, and finding him deaf to reason, vigorously assisted them, and in a short time an army was assembled, and the three princes advanced on Cotta, (A. D. 1533.) The king was obliged to sue for peace, and, at the same time, resolved to strengthen his situation by an alliance with the Portuguese. He was shortly afterwards murdered by a hired assassin, on which his eldest son, Buwaneko Bahu * the Seventh ascended the throne. The old king was not allowed to depart thus, however, without a generous, but unsuccessful attempt having been made to revenge his death. A number of his adherents, having assembled an army for this purpose, commenced operations by reducing some inconsiderable villages in the interior; whilst Buwaneko was not less active on his part. His youngest brother, Maya Dunnai, was immediately despatched to quell the insurrection, and after a short but severe campaign succeeded in restoring peace. On his return, Buwaneko, with politic prudence, appointed him and his other brother to important lieutenancies in opposite parts of the country. Having resolved on adopting his grandson, Dharmapala, as his successor, and finding his design opposed by his brothers, he determined to court the assistance of the Portuguese. Maya Dunnai, whom we have just seen crushing a rebellion, was the first who openly resisted. He was at that time the tributary prince of a district, of which a town, called Sitawak †, was the capital, situated thirty miles to the east

* In Valentyn's History he is styled Dharma Prackramabahu, and in Ribeiro's Aboe Negabo Pandar.

† Sittawakka, once a royal residence, and a place of considerable importance, is now merely a name. No traces of what it once was are now to be seen by the traveller passing along the road, and for a considerable time none were supposed to exist. Lately, some remains of buildings have been discovered. In June 1819, when travelling this way the third time, I was conducted by the natives to an old fort, concealed by wood, situated on a tongue of elevated ground, formed by the confluence of a small deep stream with the river. I went in a boat, and ascended from the river by a short

of Colombo, and, foreseeing the consequence of his disobedience, he strenuously exerted himself to put his district in a posture of defence. Forts were accordingly erected, the defences of the city were repaired, and energetic means adopted to resist effectually. Buwaneko came assisted by an ally too powerful for the rebel chief to withstand, and accordingly the combined forces of the Portuguese and Ceylonese entered Sitawak in triumph after a short resistance. Dunnai had escaped, and, flying to his brother Bandara, he endeavoured to rouse him also against the common foe. Bandara, however, was afraid or unable openly to oppose his sovereign, and contented himself with vague promises and unfulfilled assurances.

In the mean time Buwaneko was adopting a measure of the utmost importance, from its effects on the future prospects of Ceylon. Finding that assistance could not

flight of hewn-stone steps, and after walking about a hundred yards, came to the building, which I found to be nearly square, formed of three walls, one within the other. The walls were of kabook, as the stone is called by the natives; and in this instance, as in most others, appeared to be clay, strongly impregnated with red oxide of iron, to which, probably, it owes its property of hardening by exposure to the atmosphere. The outer wall was between eight and ten feet high, and six and eight wide. It was widest at its angles, where it communicated with the inclosure by steps. Between this wall and the next, the distance might be twenty-four or thirty feet; the space was overgrown with bushes. Here I observed a deep well, carefully made, and its sides lined with masonry. The second wall, only a very few feet from the inner, seemed intended for its defence. The inner inclosure was probably roofed, and was the donjon keep of the fortress. There were no marks of its having been divided into different compartments, and, indeed, it was hardly large enough to admit of it. The natives, who call this ruin Kotua, (a fort,) have a tradition, which is probably correct, that it was built and occupied by the Portuguese, when the neighbourhood was the arena of bloody contention between these bold invaders and the princes of Sittawakka. Davy's Ceylon, part ii. ch. 2.

be procured from his countrymen in the prosecution of his project, he obtained that of his most insidious enemies—the Portuguese, and thereby, as a native historian expresses it, "brought ruin on his country, and contempt on his religion *." A statue of his youthful grandson, together with a golden crown, were prepared by his orders, and these he purposed to have sent to Europe, in order that the effigy of the prince might be solemnly crowned by John the Third, then king of Portugal. An ambassador, Salappo Arachy, was accordingly appointed, and having embarked with the important statue and crown at Colombo, arrived in safety at the capital of the desired land. The king of Portugal, doubtless regarding the event as the harbinger of a new empire, acceded to his request, and accordingly the unconscious statue, under the name of Don Juan, was decorated with the crown by his own hands, and amidst much ceremony, in the Great Hall of the palace of Lisbon, A. D. 1541.

Dunnai had, in the meanwhile, become thoroughly disgusted with the dilatory proceedings of his brother, and having obtained an auxiliary force from the Continent, headed by an eminent follower of Mahomet, resolved once more to advance against the successful emperor. Bandara, seeing him at the head of such a body of troops, willingly joined him, and, after an absence of three years, Dunnai advanced with the combined forces against Sitawak. That city was quickly taken, and, animated by their success, the lands adjoining Cotta were ravaged by the advancing brothers. Buwaneko was not idle, however, but, having again obtained an auxiliary band of Europeans, confidently advanced against the rebels. The battle took

* Rajawali, part iv. p. 287.

place at a mountain pass called Gooruwila, and, for a short time, it was doubtful whether his wonted success would once more smile upon the king. His native forces were repulsed by the resolute followers of Dunnai, and it was not till the guns of the Portuguese opened their murderous discharge upon them, that they turned and fled. Sitawak was once more invested and punished for the faults of its ruler, and, having left it a pile of smoking ruins, Buwaneko returned in triumph to Cotta. He was not long allowed to enjoy his prosperity; for, in the year succeeding that in which the effigy of his son had been crowned by the Portuguese sovereign, he was shot by a gentleman of that nation whilst visiting the ancient town of Kallany on the river of the same name. This event is represented by the European historians as having been accidental, as it most probably was; since we cannot readily conceive what object the Portuguese could have had in removing a monarch so subservient to their wishes. The native historians seem to be undecided on the subject: thus the author of the Rajawali having informed us, that he was proceeding against his brother once more, and had halted at a house on the bank of the river, proceeds thus: "Now the king being in this house with the doors open, and walking backwards and forwards, looking up and down the river, a Portuguese loaded his musket, and shot the king in the head, of which he immediately died. Hereupon various conjectures were rumoured respecting the cause of this event; some ascribed it to treachery, and others said, that having been foolish enough to make a league with the Portuguese, and to deliver his grandson into their protection, that this judgment fell upon him from heaven *."

* Part iv. p. 290.

The death of Buwaneko, as we may readily conceive, was but the signal for tumult and disorder. The Portuguese, who had been for a long period the real governors of Cotta, became now its occupiers, and thus obtained the supremacy over the greater part of the country on the western coast. In the interior, every petty prince endeavoured to render himself absolute by renouncing all correspondence with the seat of government, and thus anarchy, confusion and bloodshed, desolated the whole country. At this crisis, all eyes were turned upon the rival of Buwaneko, and Maya Dunnai seemed not disposed to resign the contention on the death of his brother. Advancing again upon Sitawak, he had the city quickly put into a posture of defence, and every thing prepared for resistance. The Portuguese were not disposed to allow his usurpation of the government to continue unopposed. An army, composed of their own troops, with a large band of auxiliary natives, was accordingly despatched against him, in the confident expectation of submission or defeat. Dunnai, however, was gradually becoming more expert in warfare, whilst his troops were acquiring discipline and courage. The forces sent against him were unable to perform any service of importance, and were at length obliged to retreat with precipitation to Colombo. Succours were accordingly implored from Goa, and a large reinforcement headed by Don John Arriko, and accompanied by a zealous priest, named Alphonso Perera, despatched to Ceylon. The youthful prince *, whose statue had formerly been crowned by the sovereign of Portugal, was now elevated to the throne, and the rite

* We have formerly noticed that he was called Don Juan by the Portuguese, but amongst the natives he was known under the title of Dharmapala.

of baptism solemnly administered to him and to several of the nobles. The king and his European allies now turned their attention to the prince, who had for so long a time kept the country in continual warfare. With a much larger force of Portuguese than had ever before marched through Ceylon, they advanced against Dunnai, and Sitawak, the devoted city, fell once more into their hands, and was once more consumed. But a new adversary was gradually reaching manhood, who proved a more formidable opponent of Don Juan and his allies than Dunnai had been of his grandfather Buwaneko. This was the fourth son of the rebellious prince, known at first as Tikiry Bandawra, but subsequently as Rajah Singha,—the lion king.

The state of the coast was now gradually changing, and a revolution, most important in its effects, imperceptibly advancing. The arrival of the Portuguese, and their indiscriminate commerce with the natives, gave the first great blow to the system of castes, whilst new principles, unheard of ideas, and a new religion, were working slowly, but surely, upon the mass of the population. "From this time forward," says a native historian, "the women of the principal people of Cotta, and also the women of the low castes, such as barbers, fishers, humawas and challias, *for the sake of Portuguese gold* began to turn Christians, and to live with the Portuguese, whilst the priests of Buddhu, who till now had remained in Cotta, were forced to repair to Sitawak and Candy."

Dunnai appears to have acted with great prudence in all his proceedings. Perceiving that Don Juan would unquestionably be his determined enemy, both from education and religion, he endeavoured so to ally himself with his father, Weedeya Rajah*, as to separate him from the Portuguese. For this purpose, a marriage between his daughter and Weedeya was proposed and agreed to, whilst negotiations were entered into, having for their object a perfect union. In this, however, he was disappointed: his new son-in-law determined on supporting the pretensions of his son Don Juan; and, with the barbarous policy of a savage, he procured a rupture by the indecent usage of his lately acquired bride. Dunnai, fired at the insult, sent his already renowned son, Singha, at the head of a powerful army, to revenge his wrongs; and so well were the measures of that prince taken, that Weedeya was not only defeated with considerable loss, but was prevented, for a series of years, from joining the Portuguese. From Candy, the baffled prince was driven into the inaccessible forests of the south-east; and there, in degradation and misery, paid the penalty of his late crime.

At length the court of Cotta was roused to attempt a diversion in his favour, and accordingly a combined army of natives and Portuguese, headed by the youthful Don Juan, advanced to his assistance. Marching to the northward, and passing Negombo, they suddenly changed the direction of their route, and advanced by one of the passes leading to the southward, where they were met by the refugee, Weedeya. The indefatigable Dunnai, however, was not to be surprised. The combined forces found an army prepared to resist them advantageously posted on one of the mountain passes. The battle was commenced by the intrepid followers of the son of Dunnai, who impetuously charged their enemies in front. A dreadful

* Weedeya had married a daughter of Buwaneko, and was thus *his* son-in-law, and Don Juan's father.

carnage ensued; and one of the best-contested battles ever fought in Ceylon attested the growing prowess of the mountaineers. The combined army was worsted, and, having lost the best of their officers and men, retreated with speed to Colombo, where, in the security of their well-built fortress, they defied the irregular attacks of the Ceylonese. It would be as unprofitable as tedious to relate every event of this protracted warfare; let it suffice, therefore, to say, that in an unsuccessful attempt to enlist the Malabars in his service, Weedeya was massacred; and that, not long after, his opponent, Maya Dunnai, left his crown and dominion to his able son, Rajah Singha.

The Portuguese, on hearing of his death, despatched a great force to take possession of Sitawak, and punish his rebellious sons. Rajah Singha heard of the expedition, but disdained to meet an enemy in person whom he had formerly vanquished. One of his generals was accordingly despatched against them, but was unable to maintain his ground, and was forced to retreat. Singha now learned that he was premature in despising so powerful an enemy, and was obliged to make every effort to repel him with effect. Having assembled the remains of the last army, and having mustered every available soldier, he quickly had his forces in a condition to meet the enemy. No less expert in stratagem than in open warfare, he had a well-concealed ambuscade planted in the rear of the enemy, who were leisurely advancing upon Candy. He was too well aware of the dreadful effects of the European artillery, to allow his forces to maintain a distant combat; and accordingly, animating his troops by frequent exhortations, and riding from rank to rank, he hurried them on with impatient fury, at the first attack. Scarcely had the battle joined in front, ere the forces of Don Juan perceived another enemy to be encountered in the rear; and whilst consternation at this unexpected attack kept them for a few moments irresolute, the soldiers of Singha were already upon them, and the battle was to be decided sword in hand. Thousands of the auxiliaries of the Portuguese quickly covered the ground with their lifeless carcasses, whilst the impetuous valour of Singha left no room for evolution or tactics. " The king," (Rajah Singha,) says the native annalist, " mounted on his horse, flew from one side to another; the battle, with its incessant thunder, resembled the bellowings of innumerable fire-works, whilst the smoke, like the vapours of January, obscured the combat. The blood was flowing like water on the field of Moolleriawe." Unable to retreat, and too weak effectually to oppose, the Portuguese were cut down man by man at their guns, until the death of 1700 of their comrades had satiated the revenge, or prevented the further success of Singha. Such is the account of the Ceylonese historian, and the prudent silence of Ribeiro * rather confirms than contradicts it.

This signal success of the usurper struck consternation and dismay into the breasts of the Portuguese. Succours were earnestly implored from Goa; and, in the meantime, they shut themselves up in Colombo, where, protected by the strength of the fort, they defied their enemies. Their application was not neglected, and, on the arrival of the auxiliary forces, energetic measures were again adopted.

* He passes it prudently over by telling us, in the words of his French translator, that " les Portugais souffroient aussi beaucoup de cette guerre." The general accuracy of the native annals is fully proved by their very rare attempts at exaggeration.

Admonished by dear-bought experience, that their enemies were not to be despised, they now adopted more cautious measures, and advanced more circumspectly. Batteries and fortifications were erected on the river Kallany, and both banks of the river were lined with troops, as they slowly advanced. Rajah Singha regarded their preparations in silence and without dismay. Two pieces of ordnance, part of the number captured in the various engagements, were planted by his orders in a concealed situation on the bank of the river, and whilst the flotilla of the Portuguese was warily approaching, a well-directed fire was opened on it immediately on its becoming visible. This so shattered their boats, and thinned their crews, that the Portuguese were once more forced to retreat before their enemies. Even this, however, was no easy task. On reaching a pass which they had left a detachment to defend, they found their indefatigable enemy ready to receive them; and it was not till they had cut their way through their foes, that the Portuguese, having lost a great number of men, slain and taken prisoners, were enabled once more to reach their city of refuge.

Singha, in his turn, became now the aggressor, and, advancing to Colombo, he made every preparation for a siege. His own countrymen, however, prevented his design; for no sooner had his arrangements been completed than an insurrection broke out near Candy. Ravaged and desolated as it was, Ceylon could not afford two armies to its prince, and he was obliged once more to retrace his steps. Is it any wonder, then, that, chagrined and enraged by such disappointments, he should have become treacherous and cruel?

His wonted success attended him here, and the lion

king left his new rival a wanderer in the forests of Jaffnapatam.

News of this event having reached Colombo, Don Juan embarked for Monaar, in order to make a diversion in his favour, but, on reaching his ally, this new enemy of Singha expired.

We now come to one of the blackest instances of treachery to be found in history. Suspecting that a young prince of the royal family, (variously designated as Wijaya Sundera Bandawra *, and Fimala Lamantia †,) was about raising a rebellion against him, Singha sent to him an amicable message, requesting that he would come to him, and assuring him that he should receive the government of a certain province. The unfortunate man complied; and we must either believe him to have been cast into a pit on the road, the bottom of which had been needlessly armed by sharp stakes, or fixed in the ground up to his shoulders, and then despatched with clubs, as we give credit to the native or European accounts respectively. This iniquity brought its own punishment. His sons, but especially Kanapo Bandawra, fled to Colombo, and we shall soon find him amply revenging his father's death, by his opposition to the tyrant. On arriving at Colombo this prince assumed the name and character of a Christian, and was baptised under the title of Don John, after the Duke of Austria, brother of Philip of Castille and Portugal. For this change in his religion we can surely find reasons enough, without impiously prying into the designs of the Almighty ‡.

* Rajawali, p. 308. † Valentyn and Philalethes.

‡ Dieu, dont les voyes sont toujours justes, admirables et *impenetrables!* se servit de l'etat malheureux où le Roy de Candy (Kanapo) se voyoit reduit, pour le gagner. Ribeiro, c. v.

The character of Rajah Singha the First seems to have been an extraordinary mixture of greatness, cruelty and ability. At the advanced age of 100 years he retained all the vigour and energy of his youth, maintaining his rights with the same impetuosity and success, and indefatigably persevering to accomplish the schemes of early manhood. He appears doubly illustrious from the great number and force of his enemies, all of whom, whether Europeans or Ceylonese, Christians or heathens, he withstood with a firmness, and repelled with a degree of success, to which we can find few equals in the history of nations.

Finding the royal family almost to a man opposed to him, he put to death all whom he could apprehend, thereby rendering the others more certainly his enemies.

The siege of Colombo, upon which he had long resolved, was at length attempted, and would, most probably, have been successful but for the opposition of his own countrymen. Having made every preparation he at length sat down before it, doubtless expecting to quit his situation only on the reduction of the fort. The Portuguese were now thoroughly alarmed. All hope of sustenance from the surrounding country was, by this measure, eradicated, and nothing but the removal of Singha from their walls appeared likely to save them. It was now that his former treachery recoiled upon himself. Kanapo, the son of the prince so barbarously murdered by him, and who had been baptised under the name of Don John, was now made use of by his enemies. Having sailed to the north and thence having made his way to Candy, he put himself at the head of the malcontents, whom hatred of Singha's cruelty, or jealousy of his greatness, had prepared to unite against him. His stealthy advance at length became a regular march, and his march a triumph, so that in a short time Sitawak itself was threatened with a siege. This Singha was unable to prevent but by advancing against him with his whole army, and accordingly the siege of Colombo was once more raised, after it had continued for nine months *.

On the advance of Singha it would appear that Don John slowly retreated towards the south and east, and that many fruitless years were spent in harassing marches and partial engagements. In the mean time Candy was occupied by the Portuguese, and a new prince, Don Philip, a royal convert, elevated to the throne. In this Don John considered himself slighted, and became from that moment the bitterest enemy of his allies. Advancing to Candy, however, he dissembled his rage, until a favourable opportunity occurring, Don Philip was removed by poison, and the Portuguese disarmed.

Scarcely had this tragedy been concluded ere Singha was once more advancing upon his foe, and Don John was again forced to put himself into a posture of defence. Ceylonese, Portuguese, and Dutch annalists all concur in ascribing to this indefatigable old man the enormous age of 120 years, and we may surely be allowed to pity him, tyrant as he was, called at such an age to acquire once more that crown for which he had so frequently fought before with such valour and resolution. The battle occurred at the pass of Kadduganava, where the troops of Singha, though advantageously posted, were unable to

* Ce siege a été un des plus considerables que les Portugais ayent soûtenu dans les Indes. Ribeiro, Addition of French Translater to the fifth chapter.

withstand the impetuosity of Don John's attack. Flying detachments, and a field strewn with corpses, were the only sights that met the old man's eye at the close of the day, whilst he himself, wounded in the foot, perceived that the end of his power and life would be cotemporaneous. "Alas!" was his sorrowful exclamation, "have I conquered for an hundred years to be overcome at last by this upstart prince. My might is decreased, my end is at hand." He lingered but for a few days, and left his own foe to renew the contest of his life with the enemies of his country, (A. D. 1592.)

Rajah Singha evidently shines most conspicuously as a warrior, and in this character alone does he merit commendation. It is curious to observe, in the history of nations, with how slow a progress improved manners and arts make their way into an inferior state of society. This truth we find variously exemplified in the history of almost every nation; and it is in a very few cases, indeed, that we find men of distinction and influence who rise above prejudice, and are willing to act themselves, and to cause others to act, so as to elevate their countries out of the degradation in which they find them. A blind adherence to old customs, and a violent suspicion of every thing new, are the characteristics of the many; but Singha was one of the few; he saw the evils under which his country laboured; he also saw the causes of these evils, and perceiving that a want of discipline and an inferiority of arms rendered his countrymen unable to cope with their enemies, he used every means to introduce the one and reform the other. His first essays in war were rude and unimportant but successful. When the Portuguese came into the field, however, he found himself totally unable to oppose them, and was at first constantly defeated. Perceiving the causes of these defeats, he immediately changed the mode of his warfare and, instead of trusting all to the issue of a single struggle, he engaged them in petty skirmishes, long marches, and wasting delays. This much he learned from his father, but his own ability gradually turned the aspect of events. His whole energy was next directed to obtain fire-arms and cannon, without which he perceived at once the futility of his attempts. These a few sucessful combats gradually yielded him, until, in the greatest of his conflicts near Candy, he became master of their whole park of artillery, and, with this, Colombo would most probably have been taken had not the consequence of his own treachery and cruelty prevented it. Had he been born under more favourable auspices there can be little doubt but that he would have become one of the most able generals, or one of the greatest monsters that have ever been inflicted on humanity.

It only remains for us to state that he was by religion not a Buddhist, but a Brahmin, and that on every occasion he shewed his enmity to the former, and love of the latter, by debasing the one and exalting the professors of the other. This fact has probably caused the Buddhist and Christian historians to combine in representing his character as black and as iniquitous as possible.

CHAPTER XIII.

A. D. 1592 TO 1634.

Don John and De Souza—Don John's Stratagem—Defeat of De Souza—Donna Catharina—Defeat of Azevedo—Assassins hired to kill Don John—The Dutch land under Spilbergen—Spilbergen honoured at Candy—His treaty with Don John—De Weerd arrives—His proceedings, vulgarity and death—Don John's death and character—Senerat obtains Donna Catharina and the crown—Boschhouder—His embassy to Europe—His death—Death of Don Juan—Successes of Constantine de Saa—Defeated by Prince Singha—Death of Senerat—Singha II.

Don Juan, who had been, during all this war, an imbecile tool in the hands of the Portuguese, now saw himself, says the historian of that nation, the undisputed sovereign of Ceylon *. He had, indeed, the *name*, but the more warlike Don John had the *power*. Seeing himself now delivered from the only one of his nation whose ability or ambition could oppose his projects, Don John resolved to render himself independent. With this view he caused a proclamation of his accession to the throne, under the name of Wimala Dharma, to be made, and used every outward means to ingratiate himself with the natives, whom, inwardly, we are told, he hated and despised. Free from the trammels of religious restraint, he knew no other

* "He lived," says Ribeiro, "like a good Christian: he was mild, pious, affable and charitable"—an exceedingly convenient character for the Portuguese at that time.

law than his own will, and had no other object to pursue than the dictates of his own ambition.

The Portuguese were not disposed to view his usurpation with indifference, and yet had not the power to oppose it with effect. Whilst in this perplexity, one of their commanders, Pedro Lopéz de Souza, in sailing from Malacca to Goa, touched at Colombo. To him they represented the situation of events, and prayed him to return quickly to their assistance with a competent body of troops. He was not inattentive to their wishes, and, on reaching Goa, represented to the viceroy the necessity for active measures. Distinguished by the nobility of his birth and having the reputation of great abilities, the viceroy and council resolved to appoint him to the command of the army which they had collected for the service. He unwillingly accepted the situation, and, having landed at Manaar, proceeded with expedition against the enemy. He did not leave Goa, however, without having obtained an important concession from the council. This was that Donna Catharina, daughter of Don Philip, and lineal heir of the crown *, should be given in marriage to one of his nephews, and thus secure his most energetic exertions for the conquest of the island. This, after much opposition, was agreed to, but with the proviso that the marriage should not be consummated till the reduction of Ceylon.

Thus impelled by honour and ambition, De Souza lost no time in advancing against the enemy. Having met with Catharina at Manaar, he placed her, with much ceremony, at the head of the army, and, by her presence and favour, acquired great influence over the minds of the na-

* By the terms of the agreement under which she was delivered to the Portuguese she could not marry but with their consent.

tives. Advancing towards Negombo, a native chief came with 20,000 men to attend the standard of his queen, and aid her arms. De Souza was, of course, delighted at this acquisition, and already saw himself uncle of the king of the island.

Don John, in the meanwhile, lost no time in preparing for his enemies, and advanced with confidence to meet them. The report of the great accession brought to his rival's army by the native chieftain filled him for a moment with dismay; but he was not unequal to the crisis. Seating himself at once, a letter was indited to the chief whose defection he so much deplored, in which the warmest expressions of regard, and the tenderest professions of confidence, were displayed. "Now," said he, "am I encamped two leagues from Wellane, and expect, with impatience, the fulfillment of your promise; nor do I doubt you; finish then the measure so happily begun, and, with the life of your Portuguese general, finish this unhappy war." The letter was immediately given into the hands of a confidential servant, with instructions to advance to the lines of the Portuguese with apparent confidence, but, on being observed, to fly into the woods, and having been taken, to appear especially anxious to conceal the letter which he carried. These instructions were fulfilled to the letter, and, with well-dissembled anxiety, the treacherous Singhalese appeared to desire above all things the retention of the writing with himself. In the presence of De Souza, the farce was continued, and was only ended by force. On hearing the contents the general became absolutely furious with rage. Stamping in the violence of his passion, he called the chieftain before him, and, having delivered the fatal scroll into his hand, allowed him to peruse it. The chief, undaunted by his ferocity, calmly went over the document at length, and as, with conscious innocence, he raised his eyes to his general's face, the poniard of De Souza was plunged into his breast. His precipitancy was the cause of his ruin. Hearing of the transaction, the Ceylonese forces on every side dispersed, and many thousands of them swelled the ranks of his opponent's army. Undaunted by his loss, however, he advanced by the only practicable mountain pass in his route, determining at once to end the war by the capture of Candy. With unsuspicious confidence the Portuguese had now reached the centre of the pass, when suddenly, from every side, the shrill chank and dissonant tom-tom sounded. Before, behind, on the right hand and on the left, their enemies leaped forth, and clouds of arrows and balls and spears descended upon them. It was a moment of fearful carnage; nothing was to be done by bravery, nothing by genius, nothing by flight. Every man was cut down in the place where he stood, and of that powerful army not a living being was saved but Donna Catharina.

With the eyes of the whole army upon him, we should have supposed the lust of Don John would have been ashamed to exhibit itself, and that he would have deferred its gratification to the retirement of privacy. Such, however, his enemies assure us *, was not the case, and that in consequence, she was at once compelled, by this public disgrace, to accept of him as her husband. With *her*, Don John obtained a firm hold over the minds of his countrymen, and a firm seat on the throne of Ceylon †. So

* Ribeiro, chap. viii., broadly and unblushingly asserts it.

† The Dutch historians give us a long and curious account of the wars of Don John and De Souza, asserting that the latter entered Candy, placed

completely was the power of the Portuguese crippled by this signal overthrow, that for four years they remained inactively shut up in Colombo, unable either to revenge their loss or to attempt it. Don John during this period acted with prudence and perseverance. Towers were erected under his own superintendence at the various mountain passes, whilst several towers of the interior were put into a posture of defence. Over the battlements of these fortifications the Ceylonese had the proud pleasure of beholding the Portuguese standards waving in subjection to their own, whilst those of that nation whom the sovereign had taken prisoners were forced to assist in the erection of the buildings.

At length the Portuguese at Goa had another squadron equipped, and a force of Europeans and auxiliaries embarked, which was considered amply sufficient for the reduction of the island. Don Jerôme de Azevedo was placed at the head of this new expedition, and, with the most sanguine expectations of success, sailed for Ceylon. The level maritime districts on the western coast were quickly reduced, and every thing promised fair for success. At length the pass of Wellane, that pass which had proved so fatal to the army of Souza, was approached, and there the indefatigable Don John was again posted to receive them. Azevedo, however, approached with more caution than his predecessor, and took care, before entering the

Catharina on the throne, and obliged John to take refuge in the woods, whence, if we believe them, he occasionally issued, notwithstanding a large price having been put upon his head, to enjoy the recreation of setting Candy on fire, and watching those who extinguished it. The whole account, we need scarcely add, appears to be evidently fabulous. It may be seen in Philalethes' Hist. of Ceylon.

defile, to dislodge the ambuscades. Thus frustrated in his stratagem, Don John perceived that he must now depend on a regular battle, and accordingly drew out his army into regular lines in an advantageous situation. The Portuguese advanced with confidence, and attacked them with fury, fully relying on their superior discipline and arms. But what was wanting in his army was more than compensated by the abilities of Don John. His presence was everywhere felt, and, with a persevering courage, rare in eastern warfare, the battle was, for a long time, equally maintained on both sides. The Europeans fought with fury; instigated by honour and despair they appeared determined to conquer or die. The Ceylonese, on the other hand, withstood their charge with calmness, confiding in their numbers and the abilities of their general. For a long time the fickle goddess, victory, appeared to waver in her choice, and to alight now on the standards of Portugal, and now on those of Ceylon. At length numbers, perseverance, patriotism, and resolution conquered, and, at a great price, the Ceylonese remained masters of the field. Azevedo, who had conspicuously displayed his own talents and bravery in the battle, did not forget the duties of a general in the retreat. With a harassing enemy around them, his little band marched painfully along, and five tedious days were spent in the retreat to Colombo. There they were safe, and Don John was contented. A revolted chief having been about this time taken by the Portuguese, he was put to death, notwithstanding the most solemn assurances given him to the contrary. This execution was the signal for fearful cruelty on the part of Don John, and numbers of the Portuguese arrived soon after in Colombo horribly mutilated.

Perceiving that force could not accomplish their ends, the rulers of Colombo now tried treachery. Five assassins were hired by Azevedo himself to despatch his rival, but at the fatal Wellane they were themselves slain, the sovereign having had notice of their intention. Foiled both in open force and secret stratagem, the Portuguese desisted from the combat, and allowed their future enemies, the Dutch, to make advances, in peace, to the ruler of Ceylon.

Such was the situation of events, when the Dutch or Hollanders began to look upon the island with a wistful eye. They had now an extensive East Indian trade, and the importance of Ceylon for its protection was every day becoming more apparent. Accordingly, in the year 1601, Admiral Spilbergen, one of their bravest naval commanders, was despatched with three vessels to open a communication with the natives. On the 29th March 1602, he anchored in the mouth of a river a little to the south of Batticaloa, and immediately commenced a correspondence with the native governor of that town, who, as usual, endeavoured to make himself appear an independent sovereign. After some unimportant altercations with that prince, the Dutch admiral found out the truth, and on the 15th of June despatched a messenger to Candy. Don John received him with cordiality, loaded him with presents, and gave him a letter written with his own hand to the admiral. On returning to his countrymen and informing them of the gracious reception which he had met with, Spilbergen at once determined to proceed to the emperor in person, having got orders, on sailing, from the Prince of Orange and the Governor of the Dutch East India Company, to conclude an offensive and defensive alliance with the natives. On the 6th of July he accordingly set out, and was treated during the whole journey with peculiar marks of honour and respect. When he had advanced within a short distance of the capital, the sovereign sent his private palanquin for his conveyance, together with a number of elephants for his attendants.

The same evening he was nobly entertained by Don John in person, who cunningly dispensed with the unmeaning ceremonies usually practised on such occasions by the Singhalese court. He himself walked with the admiral for a few turns up and down the spacious hall of his palace, conversing (probably in Portuguese) on the causes and objects of his visit. At length, remembering that his guest was probably wearied with the journey, he allowed him to depart, requesting his attendance, however, on the ensuing morning.

Nothing could exceed the familiarity and kindness of Don John to his new guest. Horses were daily in attendance, feasts were continually given in the accustomed European style, and he was allowed free entrance into every public building. The king himself delighted in his conversation, and eagerly inquired after European intelligence. His religion, his nation, his friends, his circumstances, and his position, were all demanded of Spilbergen by the curious potentate; but it was in listening to the accounts of European wars and revolutions that Don John experienced the highest gratification. Every particular was demanded, and again and again would the inquisitive prince listen to the details.

In the midst of his favour, however, Spilbergen did not forget the interests of his country. Permission for the Dutch to build a fort on the sea-shore was demanded and granted, and a free trade in cinnamon and pepper also yielded. Thus successful in his mission, the admiral departed for his squadron, with which he sailed from Batticaloa on the 2d September, and, almost immediately after, having fallen in with three Portuguese vessels, he captured them and presented them to the king.

Scarcely had the vessels of Spilbergen left the coast of Ceylon, ere another Dutch expedition arrived, but with less ultimate success. Sibald de Weerd having landed near Batticaloa proceeded at once to the capital, and was there received by the king in the most friendly and amicable manner. He was soon obliged to sail for Achen, however, and with him he conveyed the Ceylonese ambassador, who was ultimately the cause of his death and misfortunes. Having previously entered into a treaty with Don John, De Weerd now highly offended him, by releasing four Portuguese vessels which he had lately captured. On returning to his former station on the coast, that prince hastened to meet him, in order to prevent the intended release. It was done, however, before he arrived, and he was consequently greatly enraged at this apparent breach of faith. The ambassador, before mentioned, inflamed his anger, and cautioned him against the treachery of his new allies. On these accounts, when requested by the admiral to visit his vessel, the king refused, and would not even advance to the sea-shore in his company. De Weerd, heated with wine, pressed his demands with indecent urgency, but was answered that the king could not longer delay, but must at once return to the empress, who was now left alone by the departure of her brother for one of the provinces. The coarse Dutchman replied that she certainly would not be long without having some one to supply his place *, and, furthermore, that he himself had no intention of proceeding to attack Galle, according to his promise, until his wishes were complied with. "Bind that dog," said the king, and immediately departed. A struggle ensued and De Weerd was killed, with the greater number of his attendants. Don John immediately proceeded to Candy, sending to the second officer of the expedition the following short but pithy note in Portuguese,—"He who drinks wine is good for nothing. God has executed justice. If you desire peace, let there be peace; if war, war †."

Such are the principal events recorded of the reign of Don John, or Wimala Dharma, one of the few princes of Ceylon who penetrated into the designs of the Portuguese, and used every means to counteract them. The remainder of his life was extended and peaceable; his enemies seeming to have no hopes of success but in his death. At length, in the twelfth year after the demise of Singha, this occurred, (A. D. 1604 ‡.)

In a consideration of his character, we shall find much to commend, but more to condemn. That he was talented and persevering, resolute and determined, an able general and a good soldier; that he knew how to seize every opportunity, and that he had the power of quickly discerning the intentions of others, his history clearly proves; whilst

* "Het eerst deel van zyn antwoord was een taal, die hy niet erger van een openbare snol en bordeel-hoer kon gevoerd hebben en die hy nogtans van de Keizerin gebruikte,"—was his insulting expression.

† "Que behem venho naon he bon. Deos ha faze justicia. Si quisieres pas, pas; se quires guerra, guerra."—Valentyn.

‡ In this date, and in the length of Don John's reign, we are obliged to differ from Mr Turnour, but with the concurrence of the Ceylonese, Dutch, and Portuguese historians. *Vide* Rajawali, Valentyn, Ribeiro, and Baldæus.

it no less certainly stamps him as selfish, cruel, and tyrannical. He hated the Portuguese with a mortal hatred, not because they were the enemies of his country, but because they had thwarted his own schemes. He exerted all his power and force against them, not from patriotism, but from revenge. He favoured Buddhism, and restored its forgotten rites, not from a conviction of its truth, but from a hatred of Christianity; and one of his first questions to Admiral Spilbergen was, whether his god was the god of the Portuguese, and whether his religion was that which they professed? Such was the character of his reign, the last flickering of Ceylonese power, with the exception of one twinkle more, inferior in greatness, and insignificant in result *.

The death of Don John, as we would naturally expect, gave rise to much contention amongst the Ceylonese nobles. Of these, however, two were pre-eminent, both in rank and influence, and each of them aimed at obtaining the hand of the queen as their surety for the crown. Don John had left, by Catharine, two sons, Wijayapala and Kumara Singha, neither of whom was, as yet, equal to asserting and maintaining his rights. To obtain the guardianship of these was then the second object of rivalry between the two princes just alluded to. The more politic and fortunate of the two, Senerat Rajah †, brother of the late king, was successful in the latter point, and

* Ribeiro will scarcely allow him any virtue since he wanted Catholicism, but his French translator is more just; he asserts, and truly, that he was "grand capitaine, habile politique," &c. Addition au Chap. Huit.

Baldæus characterises him as "a valiant and great captain." Chap. vii.

† The Dutch style him Cenmuvleraat; the Rajawali, Surat and Senerat; Ribeiro, Cam-Apati-maha-d'Aschix.

soon ended the contest by the murder of his rival, the prince of Uva. This murder greatly displeased the queen, who, although still in the prime of life, was willing to dispose of herself as her nobles should resolve. The success of Senerat, however, ended the question; and such was the insinuating blandness of his manner, notwithstanding his having just relinquished the priestly robes, that very shortly after, Donna Catharina willingly gave him her heart and hand, and, with them, the more glittering gift of the sovereignty.

The peace concluded shortly afterwards in 1609, between Holland and Spain, did not prevent the inhabitants of the former from continuing and prosecuting their designs on Ceylon. In 1612, Marcellus de Boschhouder arrived at Candy, where a treaty was once more entered into between the Dutch and the Ceylonese monarch. In this treaty, an offensive and defensive alliance against the Portuguese was agreed upon by the two powers, whilst the Dutch obtained permission to erect a fort at Cottiar, near Trincomalee and an exclusive right to the trade of Ceylon. So ardent was Senerat in his desire of amity with the Hollanders, that he retained Boschhouder in his service, making him his own admiral, and conferring on him several dignified titles. The Portuguese were not inclined to regard this interference of the Dutch with indifference or neglect. But that which they most disliked was the small fort of Cottiar, in which a company of soldiers had been left by Boschhouder. This they resolved to attack, and accordingly, during the same year, 1000 Portuguese and 3000 Indians, under the command of Simon Correa, proceeded from their possessions silently to invade it. It was quickly taken, and, with barbarous inhumanity, every one of its occupants was murdered. Senerat nobly resolved to revenge the injury which his allies had sustained, and accordingly, before the perpetrators of the massacre had reached their own territory, a body of 5000 men fell upon and overcame them.

These proceedings gave rise to immense preparations on both sides. Fifty thousand men were collected by the Ceylonese monarch, whilst almost every available soldier of the Portuguese was called into the field. From such beginnings we would naturally expect important results. Such, however, was not the case; for either mutual fear or mutual cowardice withheld them, and their mighty preparations ended without any result.

"Laborat mons, nascitur ridiculus mus."

At this period, (1613,) Senerat lost his most influential hold over the affections of his subjects by the death of Donna Catharina. Her eldest son by Don John had shortly before died, not without suspicions having been entertained against the king, who had also, by her, a son and heir. So much did this circumstance prey upon her mind, that she shortly after yielded up her soul into the hands of that Being, in whose existence she had lately ceased to believe. Her conduct in this respect is said to have produced the sharpest reproaches of conscience on her deathbed, an account which, though probable, is rendered doubtful by its frequent occurrence in Ceylonese history, if we believe the historians of Portugal.

In the same year also, Boschhouder ingratiated himself still more with the Ceylonese monarch, by the reduction of a rebellious native chief, who, relying on the assistance of the Portuguese, had treated his sovereign's commands with indifference and contempt.

Senerat, who was still determined on expelling the Portuguese, adopted the unprecedented policy of sending his favourite, Boschhouder, to Europe, there to demand succours which were not to be found in India. In 1615 he departed on his mission; and having been disappointed in obtaining either promises or assistance at Mazulipatam, he sailed at length to Holland. There he appeared before the Prince of Orange and the Directors of the Dutch East India Company, in the extraordinary character of plenipotentiary of Senerat, king of Ceylon. Boschhouder's long residence in Candy, and the habits to which he was there accustomed, totally unfitted him for communication with the plain plodding merchants of the Hague. His affectation of superiority displeased them, whilst they were no less disgusted with his supercilious behaviour, and finding that nothing could be done in his native land, for "who is a prophet in his own country?" he proceeded to Denmark and there entered into a treaty on behalf of Senerat with Christian IV., king of that country. By him he was provided with a ship and yacht, in which he once more left Europe for Ceylon (A. D. 1619.) The Danish East India Company was not indisposed to follow up the adventure, and accordingly despatched after him five other vessels under the command of Gule Gedde, one of their noblemen.

During the passage, however, Boschhouder died, and with him died all the fond expectations of the Danes. On arriving at Ceylon and informing Senerat of the death of his ambassador, Gedde found the king indisposed to ratify the treaty, and was obliged to return to Denmark without having performed the slightest achievement to remunerate his masters.

The Portuguese were, of course, delighted at the event, and seeing themselves now apparently undisputed masters of the maritime provinces, they eagerly erected the forts of Trincomalee and Batticaloa as a defence to the eastern coast.

A short time previous to this transaction, Don Juan, the nominal sovereign, who had remained for so long a time in the hands of the Portuguese, died, and by his will left the kingdom to that nation: "Hence," says their historian, with an air of pleased success, "hence arose the rightful claims of the king of Portugal to the whole island of Ceylon," a claim which he assures us was recognised by all the native chiefs except the contumacious *king of Candy* (Senerat) *. This king, however, was too influential to be despised, and too powerful to be conquered.

In 1630, Constantine de Saa, who had been for seven years the commander of the Portuguese, seeing that the king was resolved on hostilities, and was making every preparation, put himself as quickly as possible into a posture of defence. Every soldier whom he could press into his service, whether European or Indian, was engaged, and, with an overwhelming force, he advanced into the interior. Wellane was first besieged, and, after a brave defence, was taken, thus opening up the road to Candy. Constantine lost no time in availing himself of these ad-

* It is amusing to hear him asserting that his countrymen were delighted, "de se voir maitres d'une isle si puissante, dont la possession leur convenoit tres-fort." We shall soon find them unable to penetrate twenty miles into this island of which they were "*maitres*."

vantages, nor was Senerat in a condition to oppose him. The latter was in consequence obliged to fly to Uva, where he sought a retreat, not in the bravery of his troops, but in the ruggedness of the country. Here he was pursued by Constantine, who found, after much exertion, that little could be done against a flying enemy assisted by the inhabitants and accustomed to the country *. He was in consequence obliged to retreat, but urged on by the commands of the viceroy of Goa, and by the impatience of his own officers, he again advanced at the head of 1500 Portuguese and 20,000 auxiliaries. After burning the chief town of the province, which Senerat's son, Singha †, had just left with his army, Constantine took up a favourable position on an opposite hill, where he re-

* During the progress of this expedition, Senerat sent out a part of his troops under the command of one of his generals to the north, there to make a diversion in his favour. Of this general, Ribeiro gives the following character: " Ce Modiliar (commander) étoit un des plus braves et des plus honnêtes hommes du monde. Il étoit aussi tres-bon Chrétien, et de plus si modeste, qu'il ne parloit ni de se famille, ni de ces ancêtres, chose autant plus extraordinaire, *qu'il n'y a point de maison un peu considerable en ce pais-là, qui ne se croye descendue de quelque divinité.*" His portrait is that of an enemy, so that we need not fear partiality.

† The following anecdote of this youthful warrior is handed down to us in the " Account of Ceylon," by Davy. " On the day that the fort of Gannoroowé," (one built by Simon Correa,) " was taken, Rajah Singha, who exposed himself very much, had a narrow escape of his life: a Kaffer aimed at him and sent a bullet through his cap; the prince returned the fire with effect. For very many years the cap was kept as a court-curiosity, and the gun which the prince used may be in existence even now; for it was in the late king's armoury. It was left-handed, as the prince was; there was this inscription on it: 'This is the gun with which Rajah Singha killed the Kaffer who fired at him at Gattambe,'" (another name of the place.)

solved to refresh his army for a few days before accomplishing the final reduction of the country.

He was not long allowed, however, to remain in security. On a sudden the whole of the neighbouring plains and eminences were covered with his enemies, who seemed to multiply without end, as detachment after detachment occupied their allotted situations. Fortunately for the wearied aggressors the night was too near to admit of an immediate conflict, and both armies now prepared for the conflict on the morrow, which should, in all probability, decide the fate of Ceylon. The Portuguese passed the night in the duties of religion, whilst Constantine went from rank to rank exhorting them to remember their former valour, and the weighty consequences which hung on the combat of the morrow. "Before this," said he, "you have battled for glory; now you must fight for your lives." Whilst such was the aspect of the Portuguese camp, their enemies appeared to rest assured in the confidence of victory; and, like the Saxons, before the battle of Hastings, of old, spent the night in singing and recreations.

On the morrow the first unfavourable omen appeared on the side of the Portuguese, in the defection of a great number of their native auxiliaries. The battle then began with equal fury on both sides. The Europeans, hemmed in by their enemies, fought with desperation, and made a fearful slaughter of the Ceylonese, whilst Singha, then but seventeen years of age, confident of ultimate success, sent fresh troops every hour to occupy the place of the slain. In this manner, without rest or cessation, the dreadful combat continued during the whole day, nor did the contending parties relax their exertions till interrupted by the darkness of the night. Even that, however, was unpropitious to the brave Portuguese. The heavens seemed to conspire against them *, torrents of rain prevented repose, and, worse than all their other misfortunes, rendered their fire-arms useless. With generous affection they would have had their general retire with a suitable guard, and, having cut his way through the forces of the enemy, thus give him a chance of saving his life. The brave Constantine refused it, and told them that to die with his companions was the only glory to which he would aspire. The fate of his gallant band was now sealed, and, on the morrow, Constantine de Saa e Noronha, and every one of his fellow soldiers, met with that death for which the two preceding days must, in some degree, have prepared them.

Such was the result of this fatal expedition, and from that moment we may date the downfal of Portuguese power in Ceylon. The army of Senerat did not lose any time in attempting the reduction of Colombo on this success. Assault after assault was fiercely made and bravely repulsed, not however without the utmost exertions of the garrison. On a particular occasion every thing seemed lost, and it was only by the resolute valour of the citizens and slaves that the fort was preserved, so nearly were the Portuguese to being expelled, even by the unassisted endeavours of the untrained natives. Their brethren in Goa and Cochin did not behold the struggle with unconcern; but unfortunately the succours which were despatched were long delayed by adverse winds and violent storms.

Senerat did not long enjoy the fruit of the successes

* Botelho (m. 5.) assures us that this rain was miraculous, and that their enemies did not receive a drop.

of his son. In 1634, after a prosperous reign of thirty years, old age, affliction at the loss of Donna Catharina, and disease, brought him to the grave; before which, however, he did not forget to leave his son, Singha the Second, the fairest portion of his territories *, assigning to the remaining son of Don John an insignificant province, of which Singha soon deprived him. Senerat seems to have been a prince of some political ability. He certainly had penetration enough to discern the true interests of his kingdom; and, had he been more of a warrior, might have succeeded in expelling the Portuguese.

* Botelho (m. 3.) informs us that he had three sons by Donna Catharina; most authors mention but two.

CHAPTER XIV.

A. D. 1634 TO 1658.

Singha defeats Diego de Mela—His treaty with the Dutch—Batticaloa and Trincomalee taken by the Dutch—Negombo taken—Galle taken—Negombo retaken by the Portuguese—Coster murdered—Negombo again taken by the Dutch—Siege of Colombo—Sufferings of the Portuguese—Colombo surrendered to the Dutch.

On the death of his father, Singha was not long in asserting his right to the sovereignty of the entire island, nor did he long delay in maintaining his assumption by force of arms. Wijayapala was willing, but unable, to retain his territories, and was, in consequence, obliged to fly to the Portuguese, with whom he ever after remained, despised and slighted from the imbecility of his mind. They, hoping that civil war and the evils of a disputed succession would ensure their success in again invading the interior, boldly advanced under the command of Diego de Melo, their governor, with 700 Europeans *, and an auxiliary force of 28,000 Indians. The former exploit of Singha's boyhood might have taught them his resolution and military abilities, but with that infatuated

* Valentyn asserts that there were 2300 whites and half castes, with 6000 Indians. His account of the expedition is, however, very inaccurate, according to Ribeiro and Botelho.

blindness which made them ever despise the Ceylonese, they rashly advanced to the pass of Wellane, which had been, on two former occasions, so fatal to their forces. Here they were met by Singha, who, with well-feigned apprehension, sent an embassy to their leader, demanding of him whether his religion taught him to advance into the territories of one who was then at peace with him, and solemnly invoking the curse of that God whom he professed to adore on the party which He considered culpable. Rendered still more impetuous by this extraordinary embassy, the Portuguese rashly advanced into the very heart of the pass, without taking the slightest precaution. They were not long left, however, to boast of their fancied superiority. They were speedily surrounded and attacked on every side ; showers of arrows and spears poured forth from unseen combatants, and even the darkness of the night neither assisted nor screened them. They defended themselves gallantly for a night and a day, but, badly supported by their auxiliaries, (as they constantly were, according to their historians,) and being few in number, they could make no impression upon their enemies. Thirty-three Europeans only escaped the carnage, and these were taken prisoners. Such was the first essay of Singha, and his succeeding measures were not less successful.

Perceiving his own inability to drive the Portuguese from the island, and the continual wars in which he would be engaged if they remained, Singha resolved to send an embassy to the Dutch, requesting their assistance to expel them from his dominions. His ambassadors were received at Batavia (September 1636) with every demonstration of respect, and plenipotentiaries were despatched to treat at Candy with the Ceylonese monarch *. A treaty was accordingly entered into, by which the Dutch agreed to send him troops for this purpose, the whole expenses of the expedition being borne by Singha, while it was stipulated that the fortified places should be delivered into his own hands. Accordingly, in 1639, Batticaloa was vigorously attacked, and soon taken by Admiral Westerwold, who commanded a force of 500 men and six pieces of cannon. Trincomalee was next invested, and, from the paucity of men, and the want of ammunition, was reduced in a very few days. In conformity with the directions of Singha, both these forts were entirely demolished, and not a vestige left on the eastern coast of a regular fortification.

In 1640 the war was renewed with redoubled ardour. Twelve Dutch vessels appeared suddenly before Colombo; but, either intimidated by the aspect of the defences, or wishing to reduce all the other strongholds first, they immediately proceeded to Negombo, a fortress about nine leagues to the north, where they disembarked upwards of 2000 men, and quickly took it by assault, the Portuguese having been unable to throw in succours as they desired. Philip Lucassan, the commander of the Dutch, acted with becoming energy and resolution. All his efforts were at first directed towards fortifying Negombo in a regular and suitable manner, and for this purpose fascines and pallisades were advantageously planted, earthen mounds thrown up, and a deep and wide ditch excavated. These preparations being completed,

* The letters of Singha and the commands of the Dutch are given in full by Baldæus, chap. xix.

300 men, six cannons, and abundance of powder and ammunition were left in it, whilst he, with 2000 soldiers, advanced upon Colombo. This, however, was merely a feint, for, without the slightest delay, they passed on to Galle before any reinforcement could reach the place, and, after a resolute defence of eighteen days, it also was carried by assault *.

The arrival of Jean de Silva Tellez, however, as viceroy of Goa, and the active measures which he adopted in favour of Ceylon, quickly changed the posture of affairs. D'Philippe Mascarenhas was at once despatched with an auxiliary force of 400 men, and with a supply of warlike stores, to drive the Dutch from their lately acquired territories. He was a young and ardent commander, unenured, indeed, to war, but more than supplying in valour and abilities what he wanted in experience. His first enterprise against Negombo was perfectly successful, and after a short cannonading the place was conditionally surrendered. At Galle, however, he was not equally successful, whilst, at the same time, his exertions were so

* Ribeiro relates a beautiful instance of heroic female devotion which occurred in this assault. The governor, Ferreira de Bretto, had been but lately married to a wife who passionately loved him: on the night of the assault she was by his side on the batteries, animating him by her presence, and assuring him by her courage. At length, after receiving five wounds, a blow of a musquet levelled him to the earth, and the soldier who gave it was just about to despatch him, when his youthful and lovely wife threw herself between them, and called upon him, as a man and a Christian, to spare his life, entreating that, if he was determined to refuse her, he should first slay herself. An officer of the invaders saw the action, re-assured the gallant lady, and having attended the wounded commander with great kindness, had him and his spouse safely embarked for Batavia.

vigorous and important that the governor of that fortress, Jacobson Coster, thought it necessary to proceed to Candy, there to demand succours from the King. The progress of events was not unmarked by Singha, and he, seeing that the expulsion of the Portuguese would be but a change, and not an extinction of his enemies, was more liberal in promises than in performances. The hasty Dutchman, forgetful of the fate of De Weerd, exclaimed loudly against this conduct, and, having openly accused several of the king's ministers by name, was murdered by his Ceylonese guides on their return.

In the meantime, domestic strife and civil war combined with the wars of the Europeans to uproot the very foundations of civilisation. A war broke out between Singha and his brother, the Prince of Uva, relative to some Portuguese prisoners, which, after raging with fury for a short time, ended in the expulsion of the latter, and his defection to the Portuguese. By them he was sent to Goa, where, having embraced Christianity, he lived an exemplary life, and " passed from this life to a better in 1654."

In 1642, notwithstanding the treaty concluded between the king of Portugal and the States General of Holland, the war continued with unabated fury in Ceylon. In January thirteen Dutch vessels, containing a force of 3500 men, appeared before Colombo, but after an extraordinary exhibition of themselves for thirty-five days, they departed, as they had come, without effecting the slightest enterprise. Singha, however, was still acting upon the defensive, and, with prudent foresight, had established a chain of forts round his dominions, from the garrisons of which he obtained continual advices of the movements of his enemies *.

During the year 1643 several petty engagements were fought in the neighbourhood of Galle, which were too insignificant to merit a detailed recital. The following year, however, the campaign was vigorously renewed on both sides, somewhat to the advantage of the Dutch, who, under the command of Carron, once more became masters of Negombo, which they again applied themselves to fortify by the erection of four earthen bastions at each corner of the square which formed the fort. On each of these, eight pieces of cannon, from eight to twelve pounders, were mounted, whilst walls and fascines formed the connecting lines between the extremities. From this period till 1646 nothing of importance was attempted on either side, and in that year an armistice was concluded between the two powers, which continued in force till 1654, during all which period, however, a desultory warfare was carried on between Singha and the Portuguese. These he now found were but one portion of his enemies, for the rapacity of the Dutch soon unveiled their intentions; and, accordingly, he maintained an irregular struggle with both, like a noble lion, who, finding himself attacked by two tigers at once, keps them both at bay.

The final scene of the long continued tragedy was at length closed in 1658, by the siege and capture of Colombo. It was blockaded both by sea and land, no provisions or reinforcements could be thrown into it, and, in consequence, the garrison suffered severely from hunger. The operations of the Dutch were planned with skill, and exe-

* Whether these were the Portuguese, or Dutch, or both, he seems not very well to have known.

cuted with judgment, so that between hunger, want, and showers of balls and shells, no hope was left to the unfortunate Portuguese. At length, reduced to the utmost extremity *, they capitulated, only requiring that they should be allowed to depart without molestation to their brethren in Jaffnapatam. This was granted, and on the 10th of May they yielded the fortress and their arms into the hands of their enemies, who were, in time, to deliver it to another and a stronger foe. In Jaffna and Manaar they did not long find a refuge, the Dutch, perceiving that a revolution in the affections of Singha might be the means of reinstating them in their territories, advanced at once against this last stronghold †, and they were soon after (June 21. 1658,) taken prisoners of war, in which condition the Portuguese historian complains bitterly of the injuries which they and their female relations endured from the passions of the Dutch. Such was the end of their reign in Ceylon, a reign characterised throughout by the vilest rapacity, and the most blinded fanaticism. In the whole of their proceedings " we may look in vain for any traits of sound judgment, or common justice in their conduct towards the natives of the island."

Nor is this a solitary opinion. " The improvements made in the cultivation of Ceylon by the Portuguese were by no means considerable. That people, when they first

* The following horrible instance of maternal barbarity exhibits a revolting proof of the sufferings which they endured : " Il arriva même q'une femme qui étoit demeurée dans la ville, et qui nourrissoit son petit enfant, voyant qu'elle n'avoit plus de lait, et qu'elle alloit mourir, lui coupa la gorge, et le mangea." Ribeiro, chap. xxi. p. 336.

† For a particular and tedious account of the operations of the Dutch up to this period the reader may consult the first forty-five chapters of Baldæus. Churchill's Voyages, vol. iii. pp. 667 to 800.

took possession of it, were rather warriors than merchants. Their continual wars with the natives contributed to keep up the same spirit, and their principal attention seems to have been directed to the fortification of a few stations on the coast, and the erection of some military ports to awe the natives. But the Portuguese appear never to have properly discovered the advantages to be derived from this island, either in a commercial or military point of view. Their dominions extended all around it; and no station could be pointed out more commodious for a depôt either of merchandise or military stores. These advantages were overlooked by the Court of Lisbon; and those individuals who were sent to command at Ceylon were more anxious to gratify their pride by conquest, and their avarice by extortion, than to pursue any plan of permanent advantage either to the mother country or to the colony. The Portuguese, therefore, by their own misconduct, were deprived of this valuable island, before they were aware of the benefits to be derived from it *."

* Percival's Ceylon, chap. i. p. 12.

The following is the list of Portuguese commanders, as given by Ribeiro at the conclusion of his interesting work: "Pedro Lopés de Souza. Jerôme de Azevedo. François de Menezes. Manuël Mascarenhas-Homen. Nunho-Alvarés Perreira. Constantin de Sâ y Noronha. George d'Albuquerque. Constantin de Sâ y Noronha for the second time. D. George d'Almeida. Diego de Mello. Antoine Mascarenhas. Philippe Mascarenhas. Manuël Mascarenhas-Homen. François de Mello de Castro. Antoine de Souza-Coutinho, under whom we lost Colombo. At Jaffna and Manaar we had also Antoine d'Amaral y Menezes, the sixteenth and last of our Captains-general."

CHAPTER XV.

A. D. 1658 TO 1786.

Obsequiousness of the Dutch to the Ceylonese monarchs—Their embassies and presents—The French make a descent on the coast—Embassy of M. de Lanerolle—Death and character of Singha II.—Wimala Dharma Suria—Kundisala—Embassy of the Dutch—Sri Wijaya Singha—Kirtisree Singha—War with the Dutch—The Dutch take and evacuate Candy—Rajadhi Singha—Vuist's barbarity—The Dutch governors—Excellent administration of Van Goens—Van Imhoff and Falck—Rapacity and avarice of the Dutch governors in general—Exceptions.

THE history of the Dutch in Ceylon is comparatively uninteresting. Being more merchants than warriors, they endeavoured to take advantage of their present position, rather than to make that position secure. Singha was not long in perceiving that they had no intention to fulfil the treaty which had been concluded between them. The fortified places were still retained, and not the slightest prospect held out of an ultimate surrender. Justly enraged at this glaring breach of faith, and perceiving the character of his new enemies, Singha gave strict orders to his maritime subjects to lay waste the entire districts in which they dwelt, and thereby to destroy all hope in the Dutch of commercial gains. The wily Hollanders, however, anticipated him, and before his orders could be, to any extent, executed, they had taken possession of the districts around their strongholds. The natives were not less displeased at this measure than the Europeans; and the ill-feeling to which it gave rise amongst them had well-nigh cost the king his throne and life. In 1664, they rose in rebellion against him, and he, being then at a village about fourteen miles south of Candy, was unable to prevent their occupation of the capital. His infant son was proclaimed emperor by the insurgents, and Singha himself was obliged to fly to the mountains. Their measures, however, were planned without ability, and executed without vigour. A sudden panic seized them on the refusal of the youthful prince to become their leader; Singha once more appeared at the head of his forces, and the insignificant struggle terminated ingloriously in the barbarous murder of several of the nobility, and, above all, of his own son *. This wanton cruelty would almost make us believe, that the second Singha had inherited the vices of the first with his name.

The object of the Dutch being, as we have observed, to gain by their commercial intercourse with the island, they kept themselves as much as possible on good terms with the natives. They despatched numerous embassies to the Candian court with pledges of their sincerity in desiring peace, but the suspicions of Singha were not to be lulled either by professions or assurances. He received

* "Just at the instant of the rebellion," (says Knox,) "a fearful blazing star was right over our heads; and one thing I very much wondered at, which was, that whereas, before this rebellion, the tail stood away toward the westward, from which side the rebellion sprung, the very night after (for I well observed it) the tail was turned and stood away toward the eastward, and by degrees it diminished quite away." Knox was taken prisoner at Cottiar in 1659, and remained in the island for nearly twenty years. His Admirable "Historical Relation, &c." is the fruit of that incarceration. Valentyn, vol. v. p. 196, *et seq.*

their ambassadors, indeed, but without the slightest intention of making any formal alliance, and, in many cases, he even detained their ministers, without the shadow of an excuse for doing so. The conduct of the Dutch was base and obsequious; unrepelled by repeated neglect they still persevered in their endeavours, and, on one occasion, their unfortunate ambassador resolved to regain his liberty or die in the attempt. He came into the palace armed, and bowing obsequiously, as in leave taking, to the naked walls, departed for Colombo, (A. D. 1670.) Singha, with strange caprice, did not resent this liberty, but, on the contrary, aided him on the journey *. The conduct of the Dutch and the disposition of the king, are admirably described in the following paragraph by the quaint, but faithful Knox.

"The Dutch, knowing his proud spirit, make their advantage of it by flattering him with their ambassadors, telling him that they are his Majesty's humble subjects and servants; and that it is out of loyalty to him that they build forts, and keep watches round about his country, to prevent foreign nations and enemies from coming; and that, as they are thus employed in his Majesty's service, so it is for sustenance, which they want, that occasioned their coming up into his Majesty's country. And thus by flattering him, and ascribing to him high and honourable titles, which are things he greatly delights in, sometimes they prevail to have the country they have invaded, and he to have the honour. Yet at other times, upon better consideration, he will not be flattered, but falls upon them at unawares, and does them great damage †."

* Knox, part iv. ch. 13. Valentyn, vol. v. p. 201. Philalethes, chap. xv.

† Historical Relation of the Island of Zeilan, part ii. chap. ii.

Such was the posture of affairs in Ceylon, when a new European power attempted a settlement upon the island. In 1672, a French fleet of fourteen sail, commanded by the viceroy of Madagascar, M. de la Haye, appeared upon the coast, and, anchoring at Trincomalee, three envoys were despatched to the Candian court. These Singha received with every demonstration of respect; and hoping that they might become embroiled with the Dutch, and that thus some good might possibly result to himself, permission was granted for the erection of a fort. This they immediately commenced, and De Haye being obliged to depart shortly after for the Coromandel Coast, left a garrison in the fortification, at the same time sending M. de Lanerolle with six attendants to Candy, to assure the king of their intention speedily to return, and of their unalterable devotion to his service. De Lanerolle, however, was totally unfitted for his situation. Thinking it derogatory to the *grandeur* of his nation to comply with the observances of Singha's court, he madly outraged them *, and, like his Dutch predecessors, was detained a prisoner. De Haye was unable to fulfil his engagement. Being met on his return by Admiral Van Goens of the Dutch service, four of his vessels were captured, the rest dispersed, and the fort which they had erected was taken. Thus ended the first and only formidable attempt of the French upon the island of Ceylon.

From this period till the death of Singha, which happened in 1684 or 7, after a lengthened reign of upwards of fifty years, nothing is recorded worthy of notice. He was, in his person, a well-made, corpulent, but muscular

* *Vide* Knox, part iv. chap. 14, for a particular account of his egregious folly.

man, of a blacker tinge of colour than most of his countrymen, and with sharp and active eyes always in motion. "He bears his years well," says Knox, who frequently conversed with him, "being between seventy and eighty years of age; and, though an old man, yet appears not to be like one, neither in countenance nor action." Almost a mountebank in dress, he was fond of display and magnificence, and, like most eastern monarchs, seemed to measure his importance by the jewels and gold which adorned his person *. He was temperate in his diet and chaste in his manners, nor would he permit the slightest irregularity amongst his nobles in the latter respect. "Many times when he hears of the misdemeanours of some of his nobles, he not only executes them, but severely punisheth the women, if known; and he hath so many spies, that there is but little done which he knows not of. And often he gives command to expel all the women out of the city, not one to remain; *but, by little and little, when they think his wrath is appeased, they do creep in again* †."

Although vigorous and warlike in his early manhood, Singha seems to have resigned himself to sloth and inactivity during the latter years of his reign; or perhaps his kingdom, worn out with incessant wars, and harassed for so long a period by foreign invasion, could not support him in his designs with sufficient supplies. His entrance upon the stage of his country as a private character certainly gave promise of a greatness, which his subsequent

* Οὐ γὰρ ἀπο τῶν φαινομένων φαίνεται βασιλεὺς, οὐδε ἀπὸ τῶν πεπηγμένων αὐτῷ λίθων, καὶ ὧν περίκειται χρυσίων οφείλει κρίνεσθαι ὁ βασίλευς, (St Chrysos. Hom. iv.) was a sentiment utterly unknown to the Ceylonese monarchs.

† Historical Relation of Ceylon, part ii. chap. ii.

career (from whatever cause it arose) did not realise, nor were his predatory inroads upon the territories of his enemies either important in their end, or vigorous in their execution. Singha neglected the ordinances of Buddhism, and was probably, like his uncle Don John, an atheist and an infidel in reality. He was peaceably succeeded by his son, Wimala Dharma Suria the Second, whom he warned on his death-bed to remain at peace with the Dutch. Wimala was naturally of a religious and peaceable temper, so that he found no difficulty in acceding to the directions of his father. His reign of twenty-two years consequently passed away without the occurrence of any event of importance, save that of his endeavour to restore the ordinances of Buddhism to their original splendour. By the assistance, and with the concurrence of the Dutch, he despatched an embassy to Siam, requesting that a member of the highest order of priests might be sent to him to revive the rites of neglected Buddhism. Twelve Upasampada, or chief priests, were accordingly procured, and the remainder of the sovereign's reign was occupied in aiding their endeavours to reform the faith.

In 1707, Wimala was succeeded by his eldest son, Kundisāla, (also called Srivira Prackrama Narendra Singha,) who, following the example of his father, left the Dutch to enjoy their maritime advantages in peace, during his lengthened reign of thirty-two years. Some men attain notoriety by their fortune, others by their valour, a few by their virtues, and more by their vices. Kundisāla must be ranked amongst the last of these. Addicted to cruelty and drunkenness, ignorant, and regardless of any restraint upon his passions, he insulted, by his vices, the highest of his nobles, and was, in consequence, not far from losing his throne by a rebellion which they incited. But their enterprise failed, and, with the object of their exertions, they also lost their lives. The Dutch, having heard in 1721 of the death of Kundisāla's queen, resolved to despatch an embassy of condolence to that monarch, as a token of their friendship; and, in pursuance of that object, Cornelius Takel was sent as ambassador by Rumph, the then governor. Arrived at Candy, Takel informed his Majesty that he had been sent to condole with him on account of the death of his late "high-born, excellent, and all-accomplished queen," and to implore the Almighty to comfort his Majesty on this trying occasion *. In this manner they flattered the man whom they were detaining as a prisoner in his own possessions, and whose subjects they were plundering with shameless rapacity.

The short and uninteresting reign of Sri Wejaya Singha, the successor of Kundisāla, was one of mildness, lenity and good government. For eight years a breathing time was allowed the Candian provinces, uninvaded either by civil commotion or external war. In 1747 he was succeeded by his brother-in-law, Kirtisree Singha, in whose reign that war was commenced between the Candians and Dutch, which was, probably, the remote cause of the final expulsion of the latter.

The first care of Sri Wejaya was to purify and reform the religion of the state. The resource of obtaining priests and ministers from Siam was once more resorted to, and once more the genius of Buddhism lifted its venerable head above the trammels of infidelity. The king himself, whose early youth had been one of unrestrained

* The memoir, which Takel composed of his embassy is to be found in Valentyn's voluminous work. By Zondere Zaaken van Zeylon, p. 352.

licentiousness, was the most distinguished of their disciples, and now become as remarkable for virtue as his early years had been for vice.

He next cast his eyes upon the Dutch, and resolved at least to attempt their expulsion, in the full hope of a favourable result. The contest was sluggish and uninteresting. Neither side acted with becoming energy; and, after some successes in the maritime provinces, the king was obliged to evacuate *them*, just as the Dutch, after occupying Candy, were obliged to retire from *it*, (A. D. 1763.) The result of the contest was, however, on the whole favourable to the latter, and the king, in the treaty which ensued, was obliged to yield to them Putlam and Batticaloa, as well as to abolish, for the future, the humiliating prostrations which the proud court of Candy exacted from the Dutch ambassadors.

The character of Sri Wejaya was splendid and dazzling, but without the more solid advantages of talent and perseverance. With a fine person and a noble air, he won the hearts of those around him, and few could compete with him in martial and elegant accomplishments. He died in 1778, and the crown devolved to his brother, Rajadhi, whose reign will ever be memorable in Ceylonese history as the period of the British occupation of the country, and as the era of the expulsion of the Dutch.

These events, however, will require a more lengthened recital than those of the preceding reigns, and we shall now take leave of the administration of the Dutch, with a few remarks on their policy and conduct.

We need not be surprised at the anxiety of the Ceylonese for the expulsion of the Dutch, when we hear that one of the governors of that nation, Stephanus Versluys *, impelled by avarice, raised the price of rice to such an extent as to cause all but a famine amongst those already impoverished by his rapacity; and that another, Petrus Vuist †, in the prosecution of his schemes to render himself an independent sovereign, had recourse to a system of barbarity fortunately rare in the annals of civilised nations.

Such, however, was not the character of all the viceroys sent from Holland. There were, indeed, honourable exceptions; but the very fact of a just administration being an exception shews us what was their usual character. Of these the government of Van Goens, Van Imhoff, and Falck, (A. D. 1664, 1736, and 1765,) merit particular attention. During the first years of Dutch jurisdiction, cinnamon was alone attended to, and the island was profitable and valuable, or the reverse, precisely according to the amount of cinnamon which it produced. The more talented of their commanders, however, occasionally turned their attention to the amelioration of the country and the introduction of other articles of commerce. During these halcyon periods, pepper, coffee and cardamoms were introduced, not without success, whilst the vine and mulberry completely failed. But unfortunately the good commenced in one administration was frequently annihilated by the next; and "the petty interests of functionaries, the egotism, folly, and the want of energy of the general government, formed almost continual obstacles to a settled plan of amelioration ‡."

* A. D. 1729 to 1732.

† A. D. 1726 to 1729.

‡ From the translation of the Dutch Memoir of M. Burnand.—Ceylon Miscellany, vol. i. p. 49.

Bent on enriching themselves, the Dutch entirely neglected the natives, and regarded their residence in Ceylon not as a responsible situation, but as an opportunity of enriching themselves by all the means in their power. Carrying this maxim into their public transactions, as well as into their private speculations, they regarded every war, in which the plunder did not reimburse the expense, as a total loss, and hence arose that fertility of flattery, and that baseness of adulation with which they continually approached the Ceylonese monarchs. Falck was a noble exception, however, to the usual character of the Dutch governors,—enterprising, active and benevolent, he exerted all his powers, during his lengthened administration, to improve the country. Agriculture made a rapid progress under so long an administration (twenty years); the probity and order introduced into the different departments augmented the revenue of Ceylon; but averse, from prudence, to every innovation which might have created troubles in the country, M. Falck was the first who more especially busied himself with the cultivation of cinnamon, and carried it so far that he almost freed the company from dependence on the Candians for supplies *. Van de Graff, the successor of Falck, was worthy of his predecessor, and pursued his schemes with liberality and ability, but his government was of too short a duration to produce any decisive result.

On the whole, however, we may reasonably doubt, whether the mercantile avarice of the Dutch was one whit more advantageous to the colony than the military cruelty and religious bigotry of the Portuguese, and if

* Memoir of M. Burnand, p. 50.

they left behind them the glimmerings of a simpler and a purer faith, they left behind them also their grasping selfishness deeply impressed upon the effeminacy and instability of the native character *.

* The following is the list of Dutch Governors, with the dates of their appointment, from the evacuation of the country by the Portuguese, to its occupation by the British, *i. e.* from March 1640 till February 1796.

AT GALLE.

Willem Jacobson Coster,	1640
Jan Thyss, . .	1640
Joan Matsuyker, .	1646
Jacob Van Kittenstein, .	1650
Adrian Van Der Meyden,	1653

COLOMBO.

Adrian Van Der Meyden,	1656
Ryklof Van Goens, .	1660
Jacob Hustaar, .	1663
Ryklof Van Goens, .	1664
Lourens Van Peil, .	1680
Thomas Van Rhee, .	1693
Paulus De Rhoo, .	1695
Gerrit de Heer, .	1697
Cornilis Johannes Simousz,	1703
Hendrick Becker, .	1707
Isaak Augustin Rumph, .	1716
Arnold Moll, . .	1723
Johannes Hertenberg, .	1724
Jan Paulus Schagen, .	1725
Petrus Vuyst, . .	1726
Stephanus Versluys, .	1729
Gualterus Woutersz, .	1732
Jacob C. Pielaat, .	1732
Diederick Van Domburg,	1734
Jan Maccara, . .	1736
Gustaff W. Baron Van Imhoff,	1736
William Mauritz Bruinink,	1740
Daniel Overkeek, .	1742
J. V. Stein Van Golnesse,	1743
Gerrard Van Vreeland,	1751
Jacob de Jong, . .	1751
Ivan Gideon Soton, .	1752
Jan Schreuder, .	1757
Subhert Jan Baron Van Eck,	1762
Anthony Mooyart, .	1765
Iman Willem Falck, .	1765
Willem Jacob Van de Graff,	1785
Joan Gerrard Van Angelbeeck, . .	1796

Under whom Colombo, and, with it, the entire coast, was delivered to the British.

CHAPTER XVI.

STATE OF CEYLON IN THE SEVENTEENTH CENTURY.

I. Habits and condition of the Ceylonese in the seventeenth century—Their religion—State of the arts—Political condition—Prevalence of bribery.

II. Introduction of Roman Catholic Christianity by St F. de Xavier—Bigotry of the Portuguese—Avarice of the Dutch—Philalethes' remarks.

I. THE advancement of the arts and sciences in Europe was coëval with their decline in Ceylon. In the early ages of the history over which we are traversing, we have seen abundant proofs that this island must have then been great and flourishing, prosperous and happy. The picture is miserably reversed, when we survey it under the blighting influence of European rapacity. An increasing population, a flourishing commerce, a free communication with other nations, and a large share of prosperity, characterise the former period; a gradual depopulation, no commerce, and a nation confined within a circle of enclosing mountains, are the prominent features of the latter era. This decline, however, we have also seen, is not solely to be attributed to the arrival of the Portuguese and Dutch; the seeds of dissolution had long been sown, and that event but accelerated their growth. The causes of this decline we have formerly investigated, and it only remains for us now to add to these causes foreign invasion, civil war, constant commotion, Portuguese injustice and Dutch rapacity, and to consider, in addition, in what that increased decline consisted. Fortunately we are not left to mere conjecture and uncertain inference to discover the state of Ceylon at this period; we have a clear account of it given by one who lived amongst its inhabitants for nearly twenty years *.

During Rajah Singha's reign, the government was absolute, in the widest extent of the term. The council appointed by law †, and used by his predecessors to aid in their deliberations, was totally disregarded, and, from the era of Don John, there can be little doubt that each successive prince was entirely regardless of any thing but his own will. Excessive cruelty in the monarch, and an utter prostration of the people, were the immediate consequences. Ever afraid of the invasion of their maritime foes, the sovereigns were more anxious to destroy the roads, than to render them open and easy of access, and under such a state of things, we surely cannot wonder that the country should become barbarous and wretched. That such, however, had not always been the state of the country, the ruins of ancient temples were sufficient to convince Knox (as they have been in all other cases.) " The pagodahs, or temples of their gods, are so many, that I cannot number them. Many of them are of rare and exquisite work, built of hewn stone, engraven with images and figures; but by whom, and when, I could not attain to know, the inhabitants themselves being ignorant

* Knox.

† Knox says (part iii. chap. 9,) that they had no laws, but the fact of the compilation of a code, mentioned in the preceding history, and the existence of a code at present in Singhalese (translated by Mr Armour) prove the contrary.

therein; but sure I am they were built by far more ingenious artificers than the Ceylonese that are now on the land; for the Portuguese, in their invasions, have defaced some of them, which there is none found that hath skill enough to repair to this day *." Besides this, however, many of their customs and implements evidently shew that the habits of more improved days had descended to an inferior people.

To give a rapid sketch of their customs, as described by Knox, will perhaps be the best way to exhibit the state of the country under the reign of Singha the Second and his successors.

Rice being almost the only food of the inhabitants, its cultivation composed their husbandry, and this they conducted in a manner which seemed to their English resident well suited to the country. Their ploughs consisted of a crooked piece of wood shod with iron, rude, indeed, to an European eye, but, according to Knox, "proper for this country †." "At reaping," he adds, "they are excellent good, just after the English manner." At this season the whole village generously assisted the farmer, he supplying them with provisions during the occupation. The separation of the corn from the stalk was effected according to the eastern custom, by the treading out of it by bullocks. "This," says Knox, "is a far quicker and easier way than threshing ‡," an opinion not likely to be adopted by an English farmer.

Their rents were brought to the king three times in the year, and were chiefly in kind, not money. "Besides these, however, whatsoever is wanted in the king's house,

* Part iii. chap. 3. † Part i. chap. 3. ‡ Ibid.

and they have it, they must, upon the king's order, bring it." This simple circumstance may afford us a lively proof of the absolute jurisdiction of the king. Although despisers and disregarders of their religion, yet they knew perfectly well their duty, and failed, like most others, in the performance, not from want of knowledge, but from their inherently bad propensities. The character which their describer gives them, as being free from a propensity to steal, is certainly not that which we should now feel inclined to apply to them, yet as he had the most ample opportunities of knowing them thoroughly, we can scarcely doubt his correctness. " Of all vices they are least addicted to stealing, the which they do exceedingly hate and abhor, so that there are but few robberies committed amongst them. They do much extol and commend chastity, temperance, and truth in words and actions, and confess that it is out of weakness and infirmity that they cannot practise the same, acknowledging that the contrary vices are to be abhorred, being abomination both in the sight of God and man; they do love and delight in those men that are most devout and precise in these matters; as for bearing witness as confirmation in any matters of doubt, a Christian's word will be believed and credited far beyond their own, because they think they make more conscience of their words *."

The difference in the characters of those who inhabited the lowlands or maritime provinces, compared with those of the more hilly districts, was observed by Knox, although he seems to give a different account of this distinction from that with which we generally meet. That

* Part iii. chap. i.

the inhabitants of the lowlands are a much more gentle race, approaching indeed to pusillanimity, he asserts, but opposes to this, not the bravery and hardihood which the highlanders unquestionably possess, but says that they are ill-natured, false, and unkind, though outwardly fair and hypocritical. This we may, perhaps, ascribe to the circumstance of his having been kept in durance by the latter, whilst the former aided him in his escape; or it may not be impossible, that the constant wars of the Candians may have rendered them all that he declares. "In carriage and behaviour," says the same accurate describer, "they are very grave and stately, like unto the Portuguese; in understanding quick and apprehensive; in design subtle and crafty; in discourse courteous, but full of flatteries; naturally inclined to temperance both in meat and drink, but not to chastity; near and provident in their families; commending good husbandry; in their dispositions not passionate, neither hard to be reconciled again when angry; in their promises very unfaithful; approving lying in themselves, but disliking it in others; delighting in sloth; deferring labour till urgent necessity compel them; neat in apparel; nice in eating, and not much given to sleep.

"As for the women their habit is a waistcoat of white calico, covering their bodies, wrought into flourishes with blue and red, the cloth hanging longer and shorter below the knees, according to their quality; a piece of silk flung over their heads; jewels in their ears; ornaments about their necks and arms and middles. They are in their gait and behaviour very high, stately in their carriage after the Portuguese manner, of whom I think they have learned; yet they hold it no scorn to admit the meanest to come to speech of them. They are very thrifty, and it is a disgrace to them to be prodigal, and their pride and glory to be accounted near and saving; and to praise themselves they will sometimes say that scraps and parings will serve them, that the best is for their husbands. The men are not jealous of their wives; for the greatest ladies in the land will talk and discourse with any man they please, although their husbands be in the presence. And, although they be so stately, they will lay their hand to such work as is necessary to be done in the house, notwithstanding they have servants and slaves enough to do it *."

In estimating the degree of refinement which any people possess, Europeans naturally look at their habitations as one of the surest indications of their condition. In this, however, great latitude must be allowed when we are considering the population of a tropical country. The most fragile materials are there sufficiently substantial, as the vegetable kingdom gratuitously supplies them with a renewal of materials well suited for their construction. Still, however, the decline of their excellence in the formation of their temples would naturally be coëval with a similar decline in the structure of the houses of their nobility.

"Their houses are small, low thatched cottages, built with sticks daubed with clay, the walls made very smooth; for they are not permitted to build their houses above one story high, neither may they cover with tiles, nor whiten their walls with lime †, but there is a clay which is as

* *Ut supra.*

† The excessive rigour of these arbitrary regal commands afford a surprising example of the despotism under which they groaned.

white, and that they use sometimes. They employ no carpenters or house builders, unless some few noblemen, but each one buildeth his own dwelling; in building whereof there is not so much as a nail used; but instead of them, every thing which might be nailed is tied with rattans and other strings, which grow in the woods in abundance, whence the builder hath his timber for cutting. The country being warm, many of them will not take pains to clay their walls, but make them of boughs and leaves of trees. The poorest sort have not above one room in their houses, few above two, unless they be great men; *neither doth the king allow them to build better*. The great people have handsome and commodious houses. They have commonly two buildings, one opposite to the other, joined together on each side with a wall, which makes a square court-yard in the middle; round about against the walls of their houses are banks of clay to sit on. Their slaves and servants dwell round about without, in other houses, with their wives and children *."

Excellent as the system of Buddhism must originally have been, it had now become much degenerated, and had little or no hold on the minds of its professors. They believed, according to Knox, in one superior Deity, the creator of heaven and earth. From this supreme God they held that others of an inferior character were continually despatched, who executed his designs and directed the affairs of man. To Buddhu, however, they ascribed the salvation of souls, and to him their most imposing ceremonies were constantly dedicated. A belief in the immortality of the soul, and in a future state of rewards

* Knox, part iii. chap. 6.

and punishments, was still current amongst them, but with little influence upon their principles and conduct. Their images they believed, according to the Roman Catholic tenets, not to be objects of reverence in themselves, but merely the means of recalling and "representing their gods to their memories;" and it was only on this account that they paid them homage or devotion *. They had certain ceremonies instituted in honour of these deities, which were but imperfectly attended to, and whither they went, (like too many Christians of our own times,) more "to see and to be seen," than to offer up praise and prayer. In all this it is plainly apparent that a comparatively pure and spiritual religion had, in the lapse of ages, lost its hold on the public mind, and the consequence was an extent of immorality and licentiousness not often equalled perhaps elsewhere. Although esteeming and praising chastity as a virtue, their actions shewed their utter disregard of it, and the natural consequence was, that the women entirely lost their most precious ornament, modesty. On this subject we cannot shock the delicacy of modern refinement by quoting the observations of Knox, and we must therefore be contented with referring our readers to his work †, only remarking, that the women fled from contact with a man of an inferior rank, as much as she sought it with her equals or superiors. That they had a full knowledge of their duty, however, is apparent from the fact of their praising extremely the moral virtues, however incapable they might find themselves of practising them. Instead of this, they substituted easy ceremonies, and an ostentatious refrainment from certain kinds

* Knox, part iii. chap. 3.

† *Vide* part iii. chap. 7.

of diet, which they found themselves better able to perform than the more trying virtues of brotherly love and lives of purity.

"They reckon the chief points of goodness to consist in giving to the priests, in making pudgiahs, sacrifices to their gods, and in forbearing from shedding the blood of any creature; which to do they call *pau boi*, a great sin; and in abstaining from eating any flesh at all, because they would not have any hand or any thing to do in killing any living thing. They reckon herbs and plants more innocent food. It is religion (a good work) also to sweep under the bogahah, or god-tree, and to keep it clean. It is accounted religion also to be just and sober, *and chaste and true*, and to be endowed with other virtues, as we do account it.

"They give to the poor out of a principle of charity, which they extend to foreigners, as well as to their own countrymen: but of every measure of rice they boil in their houses for their families, they will take out a handful as much as they can gripe, and put it into a bag, and keep it by itself, which they call *mittahaul;* and this they give and distribute to such poor as they please, or as come to their doors.

"Nor are they charitable only to the poor of their own nation; but, as I said, to others, and particularly to the Moorish beggars, who are Mahometans by religion: these have a temple in Candy *."

The last two paragraphs may suffice to prove that a remnant of that purity inculcated by the religion of their forefathers still remained, and that the last sweeping obliteration of all their virtue did not occur before their final

* Knox, part iii. chap. 5.

subjugation to their Christian conquerors. The account of their learning, as given by Knox, exhibits the depth of degradation into which they were sunk when compared with the days of Tisso, Kumara Dhas, or Prackramabahu the Great. "Their learning is but small; all they ordinarily learn is to read and write; but it is no shame to a man if he can do neither; *nor have they any schools wherein they might be taught and instructed in these or any other arts.*" Under such circumstances we cannot wonder at their rapid relapse into barbarism, a relapse at first unquestionably produced by their own defective institutions, but which was fearfully accelerated by the constant wars which they maintained against their European foes, and which had almost reached the lowest point to which it was probable it would go, when their government was overturned, and their institutions remodelled by the "generous British."

The fact of their being able to extract iron from the ore, and afterwards to manufacture it, proves at least that they were still a step from utter barbarism. Having informed us that the ore was found extensively throughout the country, and that it lay not very deep in the ground, but about four, five or six feet from the surface, our frequently-quoted guide proceeds to describe the manner of its manufacture. We extract the account as one of the best indications of the state of the arts at the period of his captivity.—"*First*, they take these stones and lay them in a heap, and burn them with wood, which makes them softer and fitter for the furnace; when they have so done, they have a kind of furnace made with a white sort of clay, wherein they put a quantity of charcoal, and then these stones on them, and on the top more charcoal; there is a back to the furnace, (such as that in a smith's forge,) behind which the man stands that blows; the use of which back is to keep the heat of the fire from him. Behind the furnace they have two logs of wood placed fast in the ground, hollow at the top, like two pots; upon the mouths of these two pieces of hollow wood they tie a piece of a deer's skin, on each pot a piece, with a small hole as big as a man's finger in each skin; in the middle of each skin, a little beside the holes, are two strings tied fast to as many sticks stuck in the ground, like a spring, bending like a bow; this pulls the skin upwards. The man that blows stands with his feet, one on each pot, covering each hole with the soles of his feet; and as he treads on one pot and presseth the skin downwards, he takes his foot off the other, which presently, by the help of the spring, riseth; and the doing so alternately conveys a great quantity of wind through the pipes into the furnace; for there are also two pipes, made of hollow reed, let into the sides of the pots that are to conduct the wind, like the nose of the bellows, into a furnace. For the ease of the blower, there is a strap that is fastened to two posts, and comes round behind him, on which he leans his back; and he has a stick laid crossways before him on which he lays both his hands, and so he blows with greater ease. As the stones are thus burning, the dross that is in them melts, and runs out at the bottom, where there is a slanting hole made for the purpose so big as the lump of iron may pass through; out of this hole runs out the dross like streams of fire, and the iron remains behind; which, when it is purified as they think enough, so that there comes no more dross away, they drive this lump of iron through the same sloping hole, then they give it a chop with an axe half through, and so fling it into the water: they so chop it that it may be seen that it is good iron, for the satisfaction of those that are minded to buy."

Having thus run rapidly over their social condition, we shall now proceed to their political state, under the tyranny of Singha the Second, and his successors. At this period the entire Candian nation was nothing more than a nation of slaves. Not only did all the land over which his dominion extended belong personally to the king, but even the persons who cultivated it, and all their effects, were equally portions of his property. The chief officers next in rank to the king were two Adigars or prime ministers, in whom was nominally vested an extensive and important trust. To these, any, who conceived their causes were not justly decided by the governor of the province to which they belonged, might appeal, and from them a final appeal might be preferred to the king.

Next to the Adigars came the Dissaves or governors of provinces and counties, some of whom had under their command a certain proportion of the royal troops, otherwise they were included in an inferior designation. The peace of the provinces, and the tribute of the king, were the more immediate objects of their controul, and from the common occurrence of bribery, they were always ready to defend the usurpations and tyranny of the rich. The power of capital punishment, however, did not rest with them, but with the king alone, who frequently took away life on the most frivolous pretences *. Each of these offi-

* The following anecdote of Singha the Second is related by Knox, (part ii. chap. iii.) "Once, to try the hearts of his attendants, and to see what they would do, being in the water a swimming, he feigned himself to be in extremity, and near drowning, and cried out for help; upon which two

cers, being solely dependent on the favour and will of the sovereign, would naturally concur, from self-interest, in all his measures, and thus his most arbitrary and diabolical commands would never want a fit person to execute them. Even the appointment of these officers was in itself but an idle ceremony, as they were never allowed to leave the court *, and were thus incapable of becoming personally acquainted with the affairs of the provinces. This extraordinary regulation was perhaps originated by the constant fear of attacks from their enemies of the maritime provinces, and the consequent wish to be, at all times, prepared for regular or desultory warfare.

Beneath the Dissaves, a number of inferior officers, who obtained their places by the most shameless bribery, composed the country courts of judicature, from which the plaintiff or defendant (if sufficiently rich) might appeal to the governor who dwelt at court. His ear he was sure to reach, and his favour he was certain of gaining, if the

young men, more venturous and forward than the rest, immediately made way and came to his help, who, taking hold of his body, brought him safe to land, at which he seemed to be very glad; putting on his clothes he went to his palace—then he demanded to know who and which they were that had holpen him out of the water; they, supposing by his speech that he was to give them a reward for the good service they had so lately done him, answered, we were they; thereupon he commands to call such a great man (for it is they whom he appoints always to see execution done by his soldiers) to whom he gave command, saying—' Take both these, and lead them to such a place, and cut off their heads, who dared to presume to lay their hands on my person, and did not prostrate themselves rather, that I might lay my hand on them for my relief and safety.' And accordingly they were executed! "—Such is despotism!

* "Neither are they permitted to enjoy their wives; but they are day and night to stand guard in certain stations where the king appoints them." Knox, part ii. c. 5.

length of his purse was sufficient to render him an object of attention, otherwise he had no resource but submission, and no redress but in probably seeing that very governor displaced and beheaded; a circumstance too common to render it surprising or unlikely. Shew and ceremony are the constant attendants of eastern power, and accordingly the travelling of these great officers was attended with every pomp. Before the Adigars, however, a large whip was carried, which the bearer occasionally sounded to warn the passengers of his excellency's approach, a circumstance which may faintly recal to our minds the fasces and lictors of ancient Rome: "But there is something comes after (says the faithful pourtrayer) that makes all the honour and wealth of these great courtiers not at all desirable; and that is, that they are so obnoxious to the king's displeasure; which is a thing so customary that it is no disgrace for a nobleman to have been in chains; nay, and in the common gaol too. And the great men are as ready, when the king commands, to lay hold on one another, as he to command them; and glad to have the honour to be the king's executioners, hoping to have the place and office of the executed." With so great eagerness would ambition rush to almost certain destruction, when that destruction was softened by the empty titles of power, and the unavailing solace of wealth!

Thus rapidly was Ceylon approaching the precipice of barbarism, and thus fearfully had she declined from the flourishing, enterprising, and powerful Lanka of former days.

II. The connection of the Portuguese with Ceylon, as we have formerly remarked, was of no advantage, but fatally the opposite, to that island and its inhabitants.

Nor could the introduction of Christianity (introduced as it was by them) at all compensate for the reckless despotism which they exercised over the natives whom they subdued. The zealous and indefatigable labours of Francis St Xavier were attended with the most brilliant success, so far as the number of his proselytes was concerned, but with the most lamentable failure when we regard the improvement of their conduct. The wily natives easily perceived that the wearing of a cross, and prostration before a host, were not incompatible with the service of Buddhu, and they could easily transfer their adoration of a statue of their own saint to that of the Saviour or of the immaculate Virgin. Hence arose that anomalous class of inhabitants, designated by their fellows as Buddhist-Christians, who, determined to gain heaven by some means, worship, with equal honour, the gods of the Hindoos, the devos of the Buddhists, and the saints of the Roman Catholic calendar, imagining that in a multitude of deities there must be safety.

The following description of some of this class may not be uninteresting,—" There is, holding nearly the same rank as the Goewansè, and liable to the same services, though not strictly belonging to the caste, a certain description of Singhalese Christians, who have been discovered lately at Wayacotté in Matelè, and at Galgomua in the Seven Korles, about two hundred in each village. In their dress, colour, general appearance, and manners, these people do not perceptibly differ from the rest of the Singhalese. Their religion, there is reason to believe, is in a very rude and degenerate state. Their only minister is called Sachristian—an ignorant man who cannot read, and who knows only a few prayers by heart. They worship the Virgin

Mary, and pray before an image of Christ on the cross; they baptise their children, and marry and bury according to the forms of the Roman Catholic Church, conformably with whose doctrine they believe in a purgatory. To what extent their faith is contaminated by the superstitions of the surrounding people, it is not very easy to determine: I have heard it said, that they occasionally visit the temples of Buddhu, and make offerings of flowers at his shrine; which it is easy to believe, knowing that their religion is not founded on judgment and reason, but on mere credulity,—the basis of all superstition. There can be no doubt that they are descendants of the numerous converts to Christianity made by the Portuguese, at the time they had so much influence in the interior *."

Xavier, a native of Navarre, born in 1506, arrived in Ceylon in 1542, and commenced his labours in the district of Manaar and Jaffna with the adjacent islands. There he found a considerable number of Nestorian Christians, whose existence we have formerly mentioned, and who were quite willing, notwithstanding the disparity of their opinions, to follow a man of such austerity and holiness. His exertions to make the natives repeat the Lord's Prayer, the "Hail Mary," and the Creed, were attended with the most complete success, and forty thousand converts attested the power of his ministry. The Malabar chief of Jaffna, however, unwilling to allow a further progress to his religion, took the advantage of Xavier's absence to raise a persecution. The apostle of the Indies, fired with indignation, returned with carnal as well as spiritual arms, but in his attack upon the prince was wholly

* Davy's Ceylon, part i. chap. 4.

unsuccessful. In 1549 he departed for "jealous China" and "strange Japan," where his extraordinary life was at length concluded in 1552. He claims no miracles for himself, nor did his cotemporaries ascribe any to him, so that it is unfair to relate the puerile anecdotes added by later writers. As a Roman Catholic missionary he was eminently successful; as a preacher of faith in Christ and of brotherly love he was as eminently useless. On becoming, subsequently, the masters of the entire maritime district, the Portuguese had ample opportunities for propagating their faith, and they did not neglect them *; since which period Christians of the Roman Catholic persuasion have ever been numerous in the island †.

The Dutch were not less zealous in the inculcation of their peculiar faith, and unfortunately their exertions were still less influential. By refusing to allow any but Christian natives situations in their offices, they took certainly a direct way to make numerous hypocrites; but they were far from giving the Ceylonese a favourable impression of their religion, so that on their departure their religion departed with them, and has left but a small impression upon

* About the time that the Portuguese government ceased in the island, there were, in the fort of Colombo, two parish churches, one of Our Lady, and the other of St Lawrence. There were also five religious houses, viz. Convents of the Cordeliers, the Dominicans, the Augustines, and the Capuchins, and the College of the Jesuits. Without the fort were seven parishes, some of which places retain their ancient names, as St Sebastian's, &c. There were two churches near the present custom house; St Francis and St Cruz, and two others, St John and St Stephen, near the racket-ground.

† In 1843 they had twenty-two missionaries.

the body of the natives *. The following excellent remarks from Philalethes' History of Ceylon admirably characterise the two nations, as they exhibited themselves in their connection with the island.

"The Portuguese were under the influence of a sentiment of bigotry, which, when it becomes a predominant feeling in the human breast, equally disregards the suggestions of caution, the admonitions of prudence, and the higher considerations of humanity. It is a blind impulse, and it has all the effect of blindness, both visual and mental, in the strange deviations which it causes from the straight path of virtue and of truth, and, consequently, of the best policy and the most stable interest. The Dutch did not bend before the grim Moloch of religious bigotry, nor did they worship at the shrine of superstition; but *cent. per cent.* was their faith, gold was their object, and Mammon was their god. But the idol of the Dutch is as unfavourable to the growth of the softer virtues, and to all that tends to humanise the exercise of power, as that of the Portuguese. Avarice is a cold calculating feeling, and where it totally pervades the bosom, absorbing the affections, and concentrating the desires in a single object, it renders the heart as impenetrable as a stone to those moral considerations which are more particularly associated with a benevolent regard for the happiness of those who are placed in subjection to our will, or within the sphere of our influence. The insensate avarice of the Dutch proved as unfavourable to the happiness of the people of Ceylon as the enthusiastic bigotry of the Portuguese."

* There is, I believe, but one clergyman of the Dutch Church at present in the island.

CHAPTER XVII.

1796 TO 1815.

Embassies of the English—Trincomalee taken by the English—Negombo and Jaffna taken—Stewart advances to Colombo—Colombo surrendered—Pusillanimity of the Dutch—Death of Rajadhi—Intrigues of Pilame Talawe—Arrival of Mr North—Embassy to Candy—Candy invaded and taken—Treaty concluded—Major Davie's conduct—Mootu Sámy delivered to the king—Barbarity of the natives—Desultory warfare—Pilame beheaded—Rebellion against Wickrama—Eheylapola flies to the British—His wife and children—Candy again occupied—Wickrama deposed.

The British appear to have cast their eyes upon Ceylon with a desire of conquering it, for the first time in 1766. Their power had now become formidable in the east, and the advantages which the Dutch derived from the possession of the harbour of Trincomalee could not be hidden from the presidential governments of India. The motive for their interference during that year is obvious and plain; but no sense of interest should have blinded them to the injustice of such a proceeding. The Dutch were then involved in a bloody and destructive war with the native prince, but they were at peace with England, and there was therefore no excuse for the interference of the latter power. Interest and justice, however, are not always combined in the operations of powerful kingdoms, and accordingly, in 1766, Mr Pybus arrived at the court of Candy, on a mission from the British Government of Madras. He was instructed to assure the king of the friendship of the English; to represent, in lively terms, the rapid growth, and wide extent of their Indian territories, and to offer him suitable supplies to conduct the war against the Dutch. The subsequent neglect of this treaty by the Madras government, however, defeated the intentions of the embassy, and left no favourable impression on the Candian mind of our fidelity or justice.

Towards the conclusion of the American war, in 1782, another, and a more formidable attempt was made by the British governor of Madras upon the island. A fleet under the command of Admiral Sir Edward Hughes, and a body of land forces under that of Sir Hector Munro, were accordingly despatched by Lord Macartney to reduce the Ceylonese possessions of the Dutch, a war then raging between us and that power. An ambassador to the Candian court, Mr Hugh Boyd *, was also despatched with the expedition, to enter into a treaty of peace with the king, and to remove, if possible, his unfavourable opinion of the British.

The fort of Trincomalee was quickly taken on the morning subsequent to their arrival, and Mr Boyd was shortly after despatched on his mission. In the meantime, the admiral thought it necessary to sail for Madras, in order to execute some repairs, and on again reaching the noble harbour which he had so lately left, he perceived French colours flying on the fort, and a French fleet in possession of the bay, in which position he was obliged to leave it.

* One of the reputed authors of Junius' Letters.

Mr Boyd has left us in his works * a particular account of this extraordinary embassy. Such was the inaccessible

* Miscellaneous Works of Hugh Boyd, vol. ii. pp. 105, 262. London. 1800. The following is a copy of the letter addressed by Mr Boyd to Rajadhi Rajah Singha, previous to his departure from Trincomalee:

To the King of Candy, &c. &c., from Hugh Boyd, Esq., &c.

I have the honour of acquainting your Highness, that I am appointed ambassador to your Highness' Durbar, by his Excellency the Right Honourable Lord Macartney, the Governor, and the Presidency of Madras; and that I am charged with a letter to your Highness, from the Governor, in order to explain to you their favourable sentiments, and assure you of their friendship. I suppose your Highness has already heard of the great successes of the English against their enemies, particularly the Dutch, whom they have now driven entirely from the coast of Coromandel, having taken from them their last settlement there, Negapatam.

To carry on the victories of the English against the Dutch, Vice-admiral Sir Edward Hughes, commander-in-chief of the king of England's ships and marine forces in India, is now arrived with the fleet and force under his command at Trincomalee, in conjunction with the troops of the English East India Company. He has already taken one of their forts from the Dutch, called Trincomalee fort, with many prisoners, and without opposition. And he is proceeding with equal vigour, and with certainty of equal success against their only other fort, called Ostendburgh, which must also yield to the great superiority of the British arms.

This will certainly have been effected long before your Highness can have received this letter. But in the character with which I have the honour of being invested as ambassador to your Highness, I am desirous to take the earliest opportunity in transmitting to you these happy particulars, to assure you that it is only against their enemies, the Dutch, that the arms of the English are directed; and that the highest respect and attention will be shewn to your Highness' rights and dignity, and that your subjects will be treated with the utmost kindness and friendship, according to a declaration which his excellency, Sir Edward Hughes, Admiral and Commander-in-Chief, has already published. I am happy in communicating these matters to your Highness, not doubting that it will give you pleasure to hear of the success and power of your friends.

As many more English ships and troops are expected soon to be here, and as some great further operations will probably be soon carried on by nature of the country, that, although travelling with all the speed circumstances would allow, he did not reach Candy, distant 172 miles from Trincomalee by the route which he took, till the fourth of March, having left the latter fort on the fifth of February. The country in that direction was, as it still is, in a wretched condition. Occasionally a tolerable pathway was to be met with, but generally they had to force their way through an almost impervious forest, inaccessible even to the light of heaven. Scenes of the richest and most sublime character were not wanting, however, to diversify the journey, but every where a lamentable deficiency of inhabitants exemplified the almost ruined state of the country. Arrived at Candy, he was met with tedious conferences, and vexatious delays, and it was not till the seventeenth of March that he was released from attendance in the Candian court, to fall into the hands of the French on his return.

To enter into the minutiæ of his communication with

them, for the destruction of their enemies, and the advantage of their friends, I am ordered by his Excellency, the Governor of Madras, to communicate to your Highness, as soon as possible, the letter from him which I have the honour of being charged with.

I shall be happy, therefore, to deliver it to your Highness in person, with every explanation and friendly assurance which you can desire, as soon as I shall know in reply to this that you have given the necessary orders for my accommodation on the road to Candy, and that you have sent proper persons to conduct me thither. And this, I hope, your Highness will be pleased to do immediately, as there ought to be no delay in transactions of so much importance.

I am also charged with a letter to your Highness, from his Highness Walah Jah, Nabob of the Carnatic, which I shall be happy to deliver to you.

I only wait to have the honour of hearing from your Highness, as I have desired; I shall then immediately proceed to enter on all these important matters, on the most friendly and satisfactory ground to your Highness.

(Signed) HUGH BOYD.

the Candian court would be tedious and unnecessary. Accustomed to bad faith and perfidy from Europeans, the courtiers of Rajadhi naturally treated his offers and professions with distrust. "Twenty years ago," said they, "you sent an ambassador to us when we were at war with the Dutch; your proffers of assistance were answered with unsuspicious openness, and on the departure of your ambassador we heard no more of you or of your offers. *Now* you are at war with that nation; anxious to injure them you come to offer us your assistance to drive them from our island, and you profess to be about to yield us that assistance from the most disinterested motives." Boyd appealed to the known integrity of British proceedings, but all his pleading was in vain, and, although he flattered himself that he had removed their prejudices against his nation, he was unable to conclude a treaty or to persuade them into an alliance. Such was the result of this second interference with Ceylon.

The Dutch, as we have previously seen, did not acquire their possessions in the island without the exercise of much bravery and perseverance. At Colombo, at Galle, and at Jaffna, the reception which the Portuguese gave them, with their reduced forces, was honourable and manly. There seems no reason, therefore, for the imputation frequently cast upon them, that they had degenerated from the Portuguese of former days. Such, however, cannot be said of the Dutch. They acquired the island by valour and perseverance; they lost it by want of discipline, by turbulence, and pusillanimity. Nothing could be more favourable for the success of the British arms in 1795 than the disorganised state of the Dutch troops. Divided into parties, disunited and mutinous, they filled the different forts which they possessed with debauchery, conspiracies and rebellion, so that it would have been utterly impossible for the Dutch commanders, had they possessed the courage, to make any effectual resistance. On the union of Holland with the French republic in 1795, war having been declared with that country, the English prepared for a more effectual and certain means of reducing the island. General Stewart was, in that year, sent by the government of Madras with a pretty considerable force to attempt the reduction of Trincomalee. His operations were conducted with great vigour; and after a regular siege of three weeks, the fortress was delivered up by the Dutch commander, just as the invaders were preparing to storm it. Such was the only attempt at resistance made by the Dutch to the British invaders of Ceylon. After refreshing his wearied troops in Trincomalee, General Stewart next advanced round the north of the island to Jaffna, which was surrendered by its commandant on the first summons.

Early in 1796, the indefatigable general appeared before Negombo, and it, too, like Jaffna, was at once surrendered.

His eyes were next turned upon Colombo, the strength of whose fortress, and the extent of whose garrison, seemed to promise a lengthened siege. With three regiments of the line *, three battalions of sepoys, and a detachment of Bengal artillery, Stewart set out for its reduction. Dangerous woods and rapid rivers were to be crossed before they reached their destination, but not an ambuscade obstructed their march, not an attempt was

* The 52d, 73d and 77th.

made to interrupt their advance. At the river Kalany, four miles from the fort, where the stream was broad and deep, and defended by a fort erected on its southern bank, the English halted, expecting the commencement of a difficult and bloody struggle. Two days had scarcely elapsed, however, ere they heard, to their astonishment, that the guns were dismounted, the fort evacuated, and that its defenders had retreated to Colombo. With caution and anxiety the river was crossed, an encampment formed, and the siege planned. The cowardly occupants of Colombo made but one attempt to defend it: *a body of Malays, headed by a Frenchman,* were sent against the invaders, but were obliged to retreat with precipitation after the loss of their commander. In a few days a capitulation was concluded, and the capital of the maritime provinces was surrendered without a struggle *, whilst the other forts in the island speedily followed the example of the capital.

The total want of discipline amongst the Dutch troops, and their mutinous insubordination, were perhaps the most powerful aids which the British possessed. Even the life of their commander and governor was often endangered by the outrageous conduct of his troops. To this cause, then, and to a total want of energy and courage in their commanders, we must attribute the easy conquest and occupation of Ceylon by the British troops.

Such was the conclusion of the third great act in the drama of Ceylonese history.

* The Dutch force consisted of two battalions of Hollanders, the French regiment of Wirtemberg, with some native troops, forming in all a force equal to that of the invaders. Percival, p. 92.

The coasts having thus come into the possession of the English, no time was lost in endeavouring to conciliate the native prince, and to establish a peace on a sure and secure foundation. An ambassador was at once despatched to the Candian court, whilst Rajadhi, in his turn, sent one to Madras. The Government of Fort St George, through the medium of Mr Andrews, offered to the Candians privileges and advantages which they had not quietly enjoyed for the preceding two hundred years. The leways or salt marshes of Putlam were to be delivered into their hands, and ten vessels were to be allowed his Candian majesty for foreign and domestic commerce, exempt from all European supervision. The treaty, thus apparently concluded, was ratified and signed by the governor of Fort St George, but Rajadhi, with that inexplicable caprice so common in the proceedings of the Ceylonese monarchs, refused to sanction it *.

A slight alteration in the system of jurisdiction on the coast, introduced by the Madras government, had well nigh produced a simultaneous and resolute revolt of the conquered provinces. Malabar Dubashes, or agents of the executive, were placed by the Collectors of the Civil Service in the situations formerly occupied by the head men of the Ceylonese, a measure which caused numerous petty insurrections and revolts, which immediately ceased, however, on the restoration of the native officers.

In 1798 the death of Rajadhi Rajah Singha, after a peaceful reign of twenty years, produced an important revolution in the Candian court: "He bore the character of an indolent, voluptuous man, addicted to love and

* Cordiner's Ceylon, vol. ii. part ii. ch. 1.

poetry, and devoted to nothing else *." The following is the description of him given by Mr Hugh Boyd in his account of the embassy in which he was engaged: "He is about thirty-six or thirty-seven years of age, of a grand majestic appearance; a very large man, and very black, but of an open intelligent countenance, as I found afterwards on a nearer approach. On the whole, his figure and attitude put me much in mind of our Harry the Eighth. He wore a large crown, which is a very important distinction from the other princes of the East †." Though he had five queens, he died childless.

The overweening influence of Pilámè Talawé, the first Adigar, or Prime Minister, enabled him to place upon the throne a Malabar youth of inferior rank ‡ to the exclusion of all the royal family. This measure the second Adigar resolutely opposed, and generously sacrificed his life to what he was convinced was his duty. The principal queen of Rajadhi, with many of his relations, were immediately thrown into prison, whilst others, including the queen's brother, Mootu Sámy, fled to the English, and were protected at Jaffna. Sree Wickrama Rajah Singha, as the young prince was styled on his accession, was, as we may easily conceive, but a puppet placed upon the throne, the wires of which were held and directed by the ambitious Talawé.

In 1798, Mr North § arrived from Madras to undertake the government of the island, and early in the following

* Davy's Ceylon, p. 310.

† Miscellaneous Works, vol. ii. p. 213.

‡ He was, however, a kind of half-nephew to Rajadhi, being a son of a sister of a concubine of that prince.

§ Afterwards the Earl of Guildford.

year he had an interview with the Prime Minister. At first Talawé had not the effrontery to unmask his treasonable and vicious designs, but in a subsequent conference, he openly offered, if assisted by the English, to take away the life of his sovereign, and to rule the country in subjection to his coadjutors. The infamous proposal was treated with merited scorn, and several subsequent communications to the same effect shared the same fate.

These representations, however, were not without their effect on Mr North's mind; although decency forbade his openly harbouring the design, interest urged him to prosecute a similar one in a more secret manner, and by apparently an honourable line of conduct. This fully appears from the instructions with which General Macdowall was deputed to the Candian court. "In order to elude the arts of the Adigar," says the Reverend Mr Cordiner, "the governor promised that Major-General Macdowall should be sent as an ambassador, if the consent of the king were previously obtained to his carrying with him a sufficient military force to maintain his independence. *It was at the same time proposed that, if the king should approve of it, he should transport his person and his court, for greater safety, to the British territories, there to enjoy all his royal rights, and to depute to Pilamè Talawé, the Adigar, the exercise of his power in Candy.*" All this, then, was proposed "to elude the arts of the Adigar!"

The embassy was, with the permission of the Candian court, accordingly despatched. More like a military expedition * than a friendly deputation, it was frequently

* The escort consisted of the light company and four battalions of his Majesty's 19th foot, five companies of the second battalion of the 6th regiment of coast sepoys, five companies of the Malay regiment, a detachment

obliged to quell the rebellious natives who opposed its progress, and, after an ineffectual and protracted discussion, it returned without having effected the slightest alteration in the connection between the two powers.

In April 1802, a pretext was found for sending troops into the Candian dominions. Some Mahommedan merchants having been plundered of a quantity of areka nuts by a party of Candians, a demand was made by the British governor for restitution. This the court of Wickrama Singha, or his director, Pilámè Talawé, promised to give, but after repeated evasions of the demand, Mr North resolved to extort it by force. Major-General Macdowall was therefore put at the head of a considerable force *, and left Colombo for Candy on the last day of January 1803. On the 4th of February, Colonel Barbut † set out from Trincomalee with the same intention, and both detachments, after an unresisted march, arrived, "almost at the same moment," at the capital of Ceylon. This they found totally deserted; and accordingly, the combined forces, consisting altogether of upwards of 3000 men, took peaceable possession of it.

They found the palace partly destroyed by fire, those

from the Bengal artillery, with four six pounders and two howitzers, and part of the Madras pioneer and Lavar corps. Percival, p. 376.

* This force consisted of two incomplete companies of the Bengal artillery, with the usual proportion of gun lascars, two companies of his Majesty's 19th regiment of foot, the entire 51st regiment, (625 strong,) 1000 Ceylon native infantry, one company of Malays, and a small corps of pioneers."

† The force under Col. Barbut comprehended " one company of the Madras artillery, five companies of the 19th foot, the greater part of the Malay regiment, and a necessary proportion of lascars and pioneers." Cordiner, vol. ii. part ii. ch. i.

apartments which remained being ornamented with "sets of glass and china ware, and a few golden cups adorned with silver filagree." There were also pier-glasses and statues, particularly of Buddha, and the arsenals were well supplied with warlike instruments of the most heterogeneous kind *.

The Candian court being resolutely bent on resistance, the next proceeding of Mr North was to send Mootu Sámy (whom we formerly mentioned as having fled to his protection) to Candy, and there to have him formally crowned king. A treaty was then entered into with him, which, as may be readily conceived, was not very disadvantageous to the British interests. This treaty stipulated that full indemnity should be done the British for all the losses hitherto sustained by its merchants and soldiers; that a tract of land, stretching directly through the centre of his Candian Majesty's dominions, should be yielded to the invaders, for the purpose of constructing a road between Colombo and Trincomalee, doubtless with a disinterested desire for the improvement of the country; that the district of the Seven Korles, a tract along the western coast, should be given up in perpetuity to the English, his Candian Majesty's dominions being already more extensive than he could well govern; and that the king should enter into treaty with no foreign power without his Britannic Majesty's consent; whilst the British, on their part, generously promised, in return for these concessions, to keep a European force continually in Candy, for the greater security of his Candian majesty's person. "In this manner, arrangements were made *with*

* For a particular description of the palace, see Davy's Ceylon, part. ii. ch. 2; and Cordiner, *ut supra*.

the most sincere cordiality between the British Government and Mootu Sámy *."

The operations of Pilámè in opposition to the English were cunning and efficacious. Aware of the great inferiority of his troops in a regular engagement, he kept hovering about Candy, with the design of starving the invaders, or of reducing them to distress by stratagem. By artful representations he succeeded in getting a detachment sent under the command of Col. Barbut to Hangramketty, a fortress situated sixteen miles south-east of Candy, in a hilly and inaccessible district; and were it not for the timely apprehensions of the commander, probably not a man would have returned to recount the disaster. Candy was now a blockaded town. All communication with Colombo and Trincomalee was cut off; the mail from the former town was intercepted, and a detachment sent out to conciliate the neighbouring noblemen was narrowly saved from destruction by a precipitate retreat. Ten rupees were offered by the politic Talawè for the head of every European which might be brought him, and half that sum for that of any of the auxiliaries. In this state matters continued for some time, (the English occasionally breaking through the lines of the Ceylonese, and conveying food to the garrison of Candy,) without either party gaining any signal advantage. About the commencement of the rainy season in March and April, negotiations were again opened between the belligerent parties, Talawè's intention apparently being to keep the troops as long as possible in Candy, well aware that sickness would, sooner or later, thin their ranks. In these renewed conferences,

* Cordiner, *ut supra*, ch. 2.

the Adigar promised to deliver up the so-called king to the British, and to allow a suitable maintenance to Mootu Sámy at Jaffna, on condition that the chief power and viceroyalty of Candy might be vested in himself, under the title of Ootoon Komarayan, or Great Prince. This infamous proposal was agreed to by General Macdowall, the British commander, who, relying upon the honour of the faithless and perjured Pilámè, left Candy for Colombo with a considerable detachment of the troops, another party directing their march to Trincomalee, leaving the garrison of Candy under Major Davie, about 1000 strong. Such a measure was evidently exceedingly reprehensible: why should so small a force have been left in the midst of a hostile country under such a commander? and how could the British expect, that he who was neither faithful to his country nor his king, would be faithful to his enemies?

The next attempt of the first Adigar was, to get possession of the person of Mr North. For this purpose, a conference was proposed at Dambadiva, formerly the royal residence, fifty-six miles east of Colombo, to which Mr North, anxious to promote peace, at once acceded. He went, however, attended by a strong guard, whilst another of 300 men unexpectedly met him from Candy. This circumstance probably saved him from confinement; Talawè was afraid to put his treacherous project into execution in the face of such an escort, and, after a fruitless ratification of the former treaty, the two commanders separated.

The troops in Candy were suffering daily from fever and desertion. Large parties of the Candian forces were continually hovering in their vicinity; and towards the latter end of June, a formidable attack was made upon the enfeebled garrison. Major Davie, unable effectually to resist, proposed an armistice, and a truce was agreed to, on condition that he should at once deliver up Candy, with all its military stores, to the Adigar, whilst the British troops, retaining their arms, should march to Trincomalee. During this and the previous transactions, we cannot ascribe too much praise to the noble conduct of Captain Nouradeen, the native commander of the Malay forces. Tempted with the most flattering offers by the native princes in the opposite army, he still maintained his integrity, and has left a noble instance of the faithfulness and fidelity of his nation.

On the evening of the day on which the surrender had been made, Major Davie and Captain Nouradeen marched from Candy at the head of upwards of four hundred men, fourteen of whom were British officers, leaving 120 sick Europeans to the tender mercies of their savage enemies. Scarcely had they advanced two miles, when the Mahavelli-ganga, a rapid and considerable stream, then swollen with the rain, opposed their progress. There were no means of crossing it: it had been completely forgotten in the capitulation, and the destitute followers of Major Davie stood in irresolution, whilst their taunting enemies occupied the neighbouring hills. Their attempts to provide rafts on the following morning were totally unsuccessful; and at length some Candian chiefs entered into communication with Major Davie and his baffled fellow-officers. The degrading proposal was made to them of delivering up the unfortunate Mootu Sámy to his enemies, on which condition alone boats would be provided. After some delay and hesitation this base, this infamous proceeding was agreed to, and Major Davie himself communicated the tidings to the unhappy prince. "My God," was his exclamation, "is it possible that the triumphant arms of England can be so humbled, as to fear the menaces of such cowards as the Candians." His expostulations were lost upon the pusillanimous officer whom he addressed, and Mootu Sámy was accordingly delivered to his enemies, a human sacrifice offered up by British soldiers to the demon of Candian cruelty.

Led before Wickrama Singha, he was asked, "was it proper for you, being, as you are, of the royal family to join the English?"—"I am at the king's mercy," was his humble reply. A few more questions were asked and answered, after which this unfortunate victim of British cowardice suffered the most dreadful and barbarous of all deaths—impalement.

It would have been strange, indeed, if this act of Major Davie's had benefited his troops. That cowardice and cruelty usually go hand-in-hand was fully proved in the present instance. Conscious of their power from the two previous submissions, the next demand of the Candians was that the British troops and their allies should return unarmed to Candy. Every thing was agreed to,—Major Davie and his officers were separated from the troops,—the latter were marched into a narrow defile,—they were then taken out two by two, and, in cold blood, massacred by the Caffres in the Candian service, each successive pair being led to a distance from the larger company, and then murdered. The entire body of helpless sick left in the hospital soon after shared the same fate. But three European officers were spared alive *, and these ended their lives afterwards in miserable captivity.

Such were the fearful effects of the misconduct of Major Davie, misconduct fortunately rare in the annals of British warfare, and which was awfully visited on his own and his brother-officers' heads. To attempt any palliation of his conduct would be futile and useless. That death is ever, and under all circumstances, preferable to infidelity and dishonour, is a maxim of which every soldier should be convinced, and without which no man has a right to take upon him a military command. What might not resolution and decision have accomplished under the circumstances in which he was placed? † And if victory or death had been steadily placed before his mind would he not have gained immortal honour in either case? In the former, respect and admiration during life, and an honourable name in the pages of history after it; in the latter, a no less honourable death, and the same reward subsequently.

The darkest shades, however, are seldom without some bright spot to relieve them; and it is grateful to turn from the pusillanimity of one officer, (although a Briton,) to the devotion and heroism of another, and a Malay. We have already noticed the decision and fidelity of Captain Nouradeen, in his former transactions with the Candians, as an enemy; and as a captive, we shall find the same consistency persevered in with admirable strength of mind.

* Major Davie, Captain Rumley and Captain Humphreys.

† That this is not merely an unmeaning rhetorical flourish, the example of Major Johnson in 1804, on a similar emergency, to be afterwards alluded to, incontestably proves.

Life, service, honours and command were offered to him if he would desert the English standard and join that of Wickrama Singha, but he resolutely refused, declaring that he was already the servant of a great king, and that he could not serve two masters. He was accordingly beheaded.

Elated by these successes, the king now meditated the entire expulsion of the English, and prepared forces for a general and simultaneous attack upon the various provinces under their dominion. Even Colombo itself was threatened, but his Candian Majesty found that even the inconsiderable fort of Hangwelle, when resolutely defended, was more than sufficient to embarrass all his designs. Amidst the mass of petty actions continued during the years of 1804 and 1805, which it would be equally tedious and uninteresting to particularise *, the expedition of Major † Johnson into the interior alone deserves our attention. With a body of 300 troops, attended by a large train of coolies and servants, he fought his way from Batticaloa to Candy, was there surrounded by the Candian forces, and thence marched with continual skirmishing to Trincomalee, thus triumphantly exhibiting what valour and perseverance could accomplish when headed by talent and decision.

The war which continued during these years was carried on with great cruelty on both sides. It was, in fact, a system of retaliation and reprisal which no country could long endure. Accordingly, in 1805, the king,

* The curious reader will find every incident of this war related in Cordiner's Ceylon, vol. ii. part ii. chap. 4.

† Subsequently Lieutenant-Colonel. He published a narrative of this expedition. London, 1810.

doubtless finding himself unable to prosecute it, made overtures for an armistice, which, without any formal treaty, was continued from that year till 1814 *. The ten years which intervened, however, were by no means without producing important events in the government of Candy.

The terms on which Pilámè Talawé and Wickrama Singha had so long acted together, during a protracted war, could not be continued on the same footing, during the lengthened peace which succeeded it. The authority which the minister had possessed during the previous part of the reign he could not reasonably expect to enjoy during a time of profound peace. Scarcely had a year elapsed ere circumstances intervened to disturb their co-operation; and although they did not then come to an open rupture, the seeds of dissension and animosity were sown, and required but time to bring forth their pernicious fruit. The king was determined on governing with absolute power, and Pilámè, on his part, was *as* determined to maintain his influence. A censure passed on the works in which the sovereign was engaged called forth from him some angry words, which raised the fears and excited the hatred of the minister. A few years passed in this state of mutual jealousy, when a request of Pilámè to be allowed to marry his son to the illegitimate daughter of the last king excited the apprehensions of the king. Unable to repress his indignation at what he conceived to be an open attempt at the

* In 1805, the Honourable F. North, to whose abilities the English are indebted for Ceylon, was succeeded by Sir Thomas Maitland in the government of the island, who, in 1812, was, in his turn, succeeded by Sir Robert Brownrigg.

sovereignty, the king assembled the chiefs, brought several charges against the minister, and having fully condemned him, expressed his unwillingness to injure one to whom he was so much attached, and accordingly forgave him. Whether this latter measure was dictated by a spirit of crafty subtlety, or whether it was the generous emotion of a mind not wholly abandoned, cannot now be determined. Certain it is, that the enmity of the king was soon rekindled, and Pilámè, deprived of all his honours and offices, was sent to live as a private individual in his own province.

The resentment of Pilámè, for this treatment, was not long in exhibiting itself. Malay assassins were hired to despatch the king, a rebellion was fomented, and, on the failure of both enterprises, the ex-minister and his nephew * were beheaded, (A. D. 1812.) Pilámè was succeeded in the office of prime minister by Eheylapola, formerly the second Adigar. No conduct on the part of the minister, however faithful and devoted, could allay the suspicions of the monarch. Eheylapola had scarcely been raised to the vacant dignity ere the fears of Wickrama exhibited themselves. Those districts which he considered tainted with the leaven of rebellion were treated with a harshness and severity sufficient to excite it, in subjects the most loyal. All priests, and the Moors or merchants, were ordered to leave them by a stated time, whilst, with a needless rigour, no women who were not natives of the provinces were allowed to remain in them. The effect of this order may easily be conceived:

* His son, who was spared from an accidental delay, we shall afterwards find actively engaged against the English.

"wives were separated from their husbands, mothers from their children; the young bride and the aged parent, all, indiscriminately, were torn from the bosom of their families, and driven from their homes; producing scenes of distress and feelings of anger, which might well shake the firmest loyalty *."

The enmity of the king towards his prime minister was not long in displaying itself. The trifling occasion of the presentation of a gift was sufficient to make him display his resentment and jealousy, and on the return of Eheylapola to his own district, Saffragam, †, (where he was almost adored,) his conduct left no doubt on the mind of the king of his rebellious intentions. Saffragam was soon in a state of open rebellion, a correspondence was carried on with Colombo, and active measures taken to procure the dethronement of the tyrant. Wickrama Singha was not idle on hearing of these proceedings. The second Adigar, Molligodde, was at once despatched against Eheylapola with a competent force, and, before his departure, he was formally installed in all the honours of the rebel. Eheylapola was obliged to betake himself to Colombo, his adherents were dispersed, and Molligodde returned in triumph to Candy.

Nothing could exceed the fury of the king on this second rebellion of his chief officer, and his anger was fearfully visited on the heads of all those suspected of the slightest misdemeanours. Impalements, tortures, and beheading, succeeded each other in quick rotation, and scarcely had one been executed ere another was doomed to succeed him. The final scene of this domestic barbarity was horrible in the extreme, and if we wound the

* Dr Davy's Ceylon, p. 319.

† In the southern province.

feelings of our readers by relating it, we must be excused by our strict adherence to truth, προς ταυτα κρυπτε μηδεν. The unfortunate wife and children of Eheylapola were still in Candy, and under the power of the inhuman tyrant whose actions we are relating. They were condemned to die. Before one of the temples of the gods, in the market-place of Candy, they were doomed to suffer, and were led forth by the gaoler who had them in charge. The lady advanced to meet her fate with resolution; she proclaimed the legality of her lord's conduct, and her own innocence, and hoped that the present sacrifice might be for his good. She then told her eldest boy, a lad of eleven years old, to submit to his fate; the poor infant recoiled with horror from the sacrifice, when his noble brother, two years younger, stept forwards with a determined mien, and told him that *he* would shew him how to die. One blow was struck and the head of the youthful hero was rolling at their feet. The barbarity was not to end here however. The severed head was thrown into a rice mortar, the pestle was placed in the hand of the unfortunate mother, and she was told that if she refused to use it *she should be disgracefully tortured.* The poor woman stood for a moment in irresolution, but disgrace was worse than any inward struggle. She lifted the pestle up, and once she let it fall. The unfortunate woman's sufferings did not end here. One by one the same harrowing scene was repeated, until all were gone, and at last the poor infant at her breast was torn from its resting place, where, in unconscious innocence, it knew nothing of the awful scene that was transacting around it. It too was beheaded, and the milk which it had just received flowed forth to mingle with its blood.

For the honour of human nature we must add, that "during this tragical scene, the crowd who had assembled to witness it wept and sobbed aloud, unable to suppress their feelings. Palihapanè Dissava was so affected that he fainted, and was expelled his office for shewing such tender sensibility. During two days the whole of Candy, with the exception of the tyrant's court, was as one house of mourning and lamentation; and so deep was the grief, that not a fire (it is said) was kindled, no food was dressed, and a general fast was held."

To relate particular instances of the further cruelty of the king would be useless, if not disgusting. The above is but a fair specimen of this Candian reign of terror.

The English were not uninterested regarders of these events. Towards the conclusion of 1814, the year in which the barbarity just related was executed on the wife of Eheylapola, the British forces were prepared for an invasion of the Candian territories, and a cause for declaring war was not long wanting. Some merchants from the British territories trading to the interior were shamefully treated by the Candian tyrant, and came in a mutilated condition to complain to the Government at Colombo. Accordingly, on the 10th January 1815, (a year memorable in Ceylonese as in European history,) a proclamation of war was sent forth, not against the Candian territory or nation, but "against that tyrannical power which had provoked, by aggravated outrages and indignities, the just resentment of the British nation, which had cut off the most ancient and noble families in the kingdom, deluged the land with the blood of its subjects, and, by the violation of every religious and moral law, had become an object of abhorrence to mankind."

The troops were at once marched from all quarters upon the territory of the tyrant; a series of desultory and uninteresting combats ensued; the Candians fought, not as men defending their country and their liberty from hostile invasion, but as men compelled by the sovereign fiat of a cruel tyrant to take arms against their friends. The result of such a contest could not be doubtful; but it was rendered indisputably in the favour of the English, by the desertion, from the king, of the only able general whom he possessed. As long as his wife and family remained in Candy, Molligodde, warned by the fate of Eheylapola, could not desert, but no sooner had they made their escape than he hastened to present himself to the British, as a hater of the tyrant, and a friend of any who would dethrone him *. This event happened on the 8th of February, and on the 14th of the same month the head quarters of General Brownrigg were established in Candy. The king had, unfortunately, fled thence a few days previous, and it was generally believed that his flight had been directed towards the Dombera province, ten or twelve miles distant. This supposition amounted to certainty, on Major Kelly's division, which was advancing to the capital from that quarter, having fallen in with two of the king's wives and a large treasure, on the same day that Candy had been entered. Plans were now proposed and adopted for the capture of Wickrama, the great end of all the previous measures. Detachments from Major Hook's and Colonel O'Connell's divisions were sent to scour the country around; but had not the natives inte-

* *Vide* a "Journal and Narrative of the Military Operations in Ceylon in 1815, by an officer employed in the expedition." Ceylon Miscellany, vol. i. p. 33.

rested themselves in the capture, probably all the exertions of the English had been vain. A party of Eheylapola's followers, assisted by some of the inhabitants of the district, at length succeeded in discovering and securing the refugee prince. He was well defended by the Malabar escort which he carried with him, but they being finally overpowered, he was captured on the 18th February 1815, the day from which we may date the extinction of Ceylonese independence, an independence which had continued, without any material interruption, for 2357 years *.—*Sic transit gloria mundi.*

* The king was conveyed early in the following year to Madras, whence he was subsequently removed to Vellore, where he died on the 30th January 1832, of dropsy.

CHAPTER XVIII.

Deposition of Wickrama Singha, the last sovereign of Ceylon—A rebellion crushed, and the complete establishment of the British power over the whole island—Conclusion.

THE treatment which the Candian monarch received from the party who captured him was disgraceful in the extreme. They bound him hand and foot, reviled him as a monster and a tyrant unworthy to draw another breath; dragged him to a neighbouring village with every mark of disgrace; and, to crown the ignominy which he endured, spat upon him as he went. On being delivered to the English, however, he was treated with suitable respect, and he felt grateful for it. Two different accounts have been handed down to us of his appearance and character, neither of which appears in unison with what his actions would lead us to expect. An officer engaged in the embassy to Candy in 1800 has left us the following portrait of him: "The king seemed very vain of his dress, and very uneasy on his throne; he kept constantly shaking his head to display the precious stones in his crown, and pulled down his vest or armour to shew off the jewels with which it was studded. He seemed particularly fond of a large round ornament which is suspended from his neck.*" From this portrait of an idiot, we turn with surprise to the following: "Wickrama Rajah Singha is, in his person, considerably above the middle size; of a corpulent, yet

* Cordiner, vol. ii. p. 305.

muscular appearance, and with a physiognomy which is at all times handsome, and frequently not unpleasing. His claim to talent has been disputed by many who have had an opportunity of conversing with him, but he is certainly not deficient in shrewdness or comprehension *." He had certainly disappointed the expectations of his first prime minister, Pilámè Talawè, a man who had raised him to the throne in the hope of governing him as he pleased, but who found himself fatally mistaken. That he was a cruel savage, a heartless tyrant, and a haughty despot, is plainly proved by his history; and we can now only regret that he should have been so long allowed to rule a generous and ancient people.

A fortnight subsequent to the capture of the king, he was formally dethroned by a convention held on the 2d March 1815, between his Excellency, the Governor and Commander-in-chief of the forces, and the Chief Officers of the Candian empire. "This day" (says the official bulletin published on the occasion,) "a solemn conference was held in the audience hall of the palace of Candy, between his Excellency, the Governor and Commander-in-chief of the forces, on behalf of his Majesty and of his Royal Highness the Prince Regent, on the one part, and the Adigars, Dissaves and other principal chiefs of the Candian provinces, on the other part, on behalf of the people, and in presence of the Mohottales, Coraals, Vidaans and other subordinate headmen from the different provinces, and a great concourse of inhabitants.

"A public instrument of treaty, prepared in conformity to conditions previously agreed on, for establishing His

* A Narrative of Events, &c., by a Gentleman engaged in the expedition. Egerton, 1820.

Majesty's government in the Candian provinces, was produced, and publicly read in English and Singhalese, and unanimously assented to. The British flag was then for the first time hoisted, and the establishment of the British dominion in the interior was announced by a royal salute from the cannon of the city."

By the second article of the treaty then entered into, Sri Wickrama Rajah Singha was formally declared to be deposed; his family and relations for ever debarred from the throne, and all the claims of his race to be "extinguished and abolished."

By the fifth, the religion of Buddha was declared "inviolable, and its rights, ministers and places of worship, were to be maintained and protected." By the eighth, the laws of the country were to be still recognised and acted on, "according to established forms, and by the ordinary authorities." And, lastly, by the eleventh, the royal dues and revenues were to be levied as before, for the support of Government.

Such were the principal heads of the treaty entered into on the submission of the entire island to the arms of England.

For two years every thing progressed favourably, the natives appeared contented with the government of their new commanders, whilst, on the part of the English, the terms of the agreement were strictly adhered to. A breathing time was thus allowed to the exhausted country, which proved, however, but the lull before the tempest, or the important calm that precedes the sudden attack. One final struggle was still to be made for that independence which Malabars, Malays, Moors, Portuguese and Dutch had all failed to extinguish. The desire was natural, although ungrateful; for as they had assisted the invaders to depose their king, so neither had they expressed the slightest resentment at the treaty that had been concluded. The chiefs, we may easily conceive, would be the first to excite such a revolt. They had no sympathy with their subduers; they had lost their influence; they were now but on a level with their countrymen, and they could become but little less, whatever might chance to be the result of the war. In October 1817, a spirit of insubordination first exhibited itself in Uva, a hilly district in the south-eastern part of the island. The agent of Government stationed there rode forth to repress it, but fell in the attempt, and his escort escaped with difficulty to Badulla *. A priest of Buddha had already thrown off his yellow robes and aspired to the sovereignty, nor was he long without numerous supporters.

The most enterprising chief by whom he was joined, Kapittipola, was the brother-in-law of Eheylapola, and a man of considerable influence in the country. His example, and that of some other influential and powerful leaders, quickly spread the flame just excited, and before six months had elapsed, only a few inconsiderable districts still maintained their allegiance. "During the three following months our affairs assumed a still more melancholy aspect. Our little army was much exhausted and reduced by fatigue, privation and disease; the rebellion was still unchecked; all our efforts had been apparently fruitless; not a leader of any consequence had been taken, and not a district subdued or tranquillised. This was a melancholy time to those who were on the scene of action;

* Pronounced Bădjula.

and many began to despond and augur from bad to worse; and to prophesy (what indeed was far from improbable) that the few districts still attached to us would join the enemy; that the communication between Colombo and our head quarters at Candy would be cut off, and that we should be very soon obliged to evacuate the country, and fight our way out of it *."

All things end in their contraries, said Socrates, and the present narration does not disprove his assertion. That "union is strength" seems to have been forgotten by the Ceylonese chiefs. Dissensions arose amongst them of a serious nature. Their general, Kapittipola, was defeated in several engagements; and to crown their discomfiture the pretender was seized by an opposing party, who immediately erected another as their chief. Under such a state of things it was impossible that their measures could succeed; and whatever successes they met with at first, were more than counterbalanced by their subsequent misfortunes. No conduct on the part of the Ceylonese, however, could justify the cruelty of the English. A district was declared rebellious. Detachments were sent to scour the country, to butcher all whom they found with arms in their hands, to destroy and lay waste every thing that came in their way. Dwellings were burned; fruit-tree plantations were cut down, and martial law proclaimed throughout the district. Such proceedings as those may have been politic and successful, but they are not those on which a humane mind can dwell with pleasure, and we may reasonably question, whether it would not have been more just and wise altogether to

* Davy's Ceylon, chap. x. p. 328.

evacuate the interior than to allow such a state of things to continue for nearly two years *.

The loss of the British troops was very severe, nearly a fifth part of their forces having perished by disease alone. The Candians resorted to every species of attack which they could devise, and left no effort untried to bring about the destruction of their foes. Pits were dug with concealed spikes in their road; snares of all kinds, and ambuscades in every practicable place were planted to harass their enemies, and neither mercy nor quarter was given on either side. It was in fact nothing more or less than a war of extermination.

Fortune at length openly declared for skill and discipline. The leaders of the insurrection were captured one by one ; and, deprived of their commanders, it was utterly impossible that the natives could support the contest. An event of still greater consequence than even the apprehension of the rebellious princes occurred shortly afterwards,—the capture of the sacred tooth (or Dalada relic) of Buddha. " Whoever obtain that relic," says an old Ceylonese tradition, " obtain with it the government of Ceylon;" and, on the information being diffused throughout the country, resistance was at an end, the natives returned to their allegiance, and British rule was once more recognised throughout the entire island. A new convention was at once entered into between the Candian chiefs and Sir R. Brownrigg, stipulating, 1*st*, That all personal services, excepting those required for making and repairing roads and bridges, should be abolished, and that all

* Dr Davy asserts that these " evils " or " irregularities " were not by any means sanctioned by Government ; but if not directly sanctioned they certainly must have been winked at, or they had never occurred.

taxes should be merged into one,—a tax of one-tenth of the produce of the paddy lands; 2*d*, That justice should be administered by the Board of Commissioners in Candy, and by the agents of Government in the different provinces, aided by the native Dissaves, who were henceforth to be remunerated, not by the contributions of the people, but by fixed salaries. Such was the gratifying conclusion of a struggle which at first threatened the most disastrous consequences; and that the peace which was then concluded may be perpetual is, we trust, the confident hope of every resident in Ceylon.

The history of Ceylon has now been brought down to the conclusion of the last war: we have seen it rising into affluence and power under its first dynasty: we have seen its gradual decay: we have seen it the scene of a bloody and a long-continued contest between the natives and the Portuguese: we have seen it wrested from the latter by the Dutch: we have seen it become the theatre of their rapacity and of their degeneracy, and we have seen it at last come into the possession of the British, and the effects of their misrule. It only now remains for us briefly to consider the improvements which they have introduced into its political and social condition, its present state and prospects.

A few partial attempts at rebellion diversify the history of the succeeding years, but they were too inconsiderable to merit a detailed account.

So early as the year 1802, a court of judicature was established to relieve the governor of the responsibility and inconvenience of judicial superintendence; but it was not till 1833 that the judicial establishment of the island was placed on an efficient and regular footing. Another event of great importance to the colony was the re-establishment of all the schools instituted by the Dutch; but such was the parsimony of the home Government, that Mr North was soon obliged to desist from the endeavour; and in order to effect a saving of about £.3000 *per annum*, the British Government resolved to leave its subjects in Ceylon without the means of improvement. The arrival of missionaries from various religious bodies counteracted the evil to a certain extent; but even at the present day, (1844,) the salaries of all the schoolmasters supported by Government throughout the entire island amount to no more than £.4139, whilst the entire ecclesiastical expenditure is beneath £.8000.

In other departments of government, and in none more than the judicial, improvements of the greatest consequence have been introduced. So early as 1811, trial by jury was established, and three years previously a Chief and Puisne Justice had been appointed, measures which evinced, that, however careless the Government might be with respect to the prevention of crime, they were not disposed to allow its commission to pass unpunished.

The construction of an excellent carriage road between Colombo and Candy, and the establishment of a mail-coach in 1832, were but the preludes to the civilisation of the interior; and English capitalists soon found that few other colonies offered the same opportunities for the investment of capital as Ceylon.

In 1834, the Legislative Council * held its first sitting at Colombo, and by the addition of two unofficial members in 1837, (since increased to six,) it was assimilated

* At present consisting of fifteen individuals.

somewhat to the Parliament of England. The Executive Council, consisting of five members *, is first consulted by the Governor, whence he introduces the measures necessary for the regulation of the colony into the Legislative, and thence, if passed, they are finally sent to England for the ratification of the Sovereign.

The granting of the great charter of Ceylon by the British Parliament in 1833 was one of the most important measures adopted for the regulation of the colony. By this minor courts of Civil Jurisprudence and Criminal Jurisdiction were appointed in the several districts of the island, (hence called District Courts,) in which minor causes were to be tried and judged by the District Judge and three Assessors, and from which the more important or intricate cases were to be sent to the supreme court of Colombo. The supreme court (composed of the Chief-Justice, and two Puisne Judges) was appointed as a court of Appellate Jurisdiction for the correction of all errors committed by the District Courts, and for the trial of those cases in which the Judge and Assessors of the other might have been unable to agree.

It is not our intention to enter minutely into the present state of the island †. The operations of the planters in the interior are changing the entire aspect of the country, and where inaccessible forests but lately covered the ground, the bungalow of the planter may now be seen, the coffee bush or the sugar cane is rearing its head, roads are being formed for the conveyance of the produce of the estates, and a complete revolution is slowly advancing

* The Governor, the Commander-in-Chief, the Colonial Secretary, the Queen's Advocate, and the Auditor-General of the Colony.

† In Appendix II. will be found some details respecting its present condition.

amongst the natives. Religion, we are sorry to say, however, is not advancing hand-in-hand with commerce; and as the people are learning to disbelieve in Buddhu, they are not being led to embrace the purer system of Christianity. This state of things requires new exertion on the part of the Legislature of the Island; for if the want be not noticed there, is it likely to be felt in Britain?

It is true, indeed, that Ceylon now nearly pays its own expenses, that it is but a slight burden on the mother country, compared with her other Colonies; but if this advantage be obtained at the price of the demoralisation of the inhabitants, better would it have been had it remained in the hands of its native chiefs, and England would have remained without the guilt of its ruin. Even now, however, the English nation is awakening to a sense of its duty in this respect; and we may hope that ere long, Ceylon will feel the benefit of its exertions for the religious improvement of its colonies, and that it may become in a moral, what it is in a natural point of view, "the Eden of the Eastern wave,—the "pearl drop of India," and the "Emerald gem" of the Oriental world *.

* The following is the list of English Governors up to 1844.

1.	The Honourable the Governor of Madras in Council,	Feb. 1796.
2.	Hon. Frederick North,	12th Oct. 1798.
3.	Lieut.-General Right Hon. Sir Thomas Maitland,	19th July 1805.
4.	Major-General John Wilson, Lieut.-Governor,	19th March 1811.
5.	Gen. Sir Robert Brownrigg,	11th March 1812.
6.	Major-Gen. Sir Edward Barnes, Lieut.-Governor,	1st Feb. 1820.
7.	Lieut.-Gen. Hon. Sir Edward Paget,	2d Feb. 1823.
8.	Major-Gen. Sir James Campbell, Lieut.-Governor,	6th Nov. 1823.
9.	Lieut.-Gen. Sir Edward Barnes,	18th Jan. 1824.
10.	Major-Gen. Sir John Wilson, Lieut.-Governor,	13th Oct. 1831.
11.	Right Hon. Sir Robert W. Horton,	23d Oct. 1831.
12.	Right Hon. J. Alex. Stewart Mackenzie,	7th Nov. 1837.
13.	Lieut.-Gen. Sir Colin Campbell,	5th April 1841.

APPENDIX.

I. BUDDHISM AND THE PHILOSOPHY OF GREECE.

FROM THE "CEYLON MISCELLANY" FOR MAY 1844.
BY W. K. ESQ.

FEW who have considered with attention the respective claims of Buddhism and Brahminism to priority, can, I imagine, rise from the investigation without being convinced that the former is the more ancient of the two. This conclusion (which, in the following remarks, is assumed as granted) I rest chiefly on the four following facts: 1. The total absence of all allusion to Brahminism *as a distinct religion*, in the earlier writings of Gotamo and his disciples; an omission perfectly inexplicable on any other supposition than that of the non-existence of the faith at the periods referred to; 2. The connected history of Buddhism afforded in its annals from the most remote antiquity; 3. The absurdity of the Puranine and Vedie tales of the Hindus, which, although they lay claim to an incomprehensible period, give us no *connected* recital of any events before the Christian era; and, 4. The remains of Buddhistical edifices and Buddhistical inscriptions, which exhibit the prevalence of that religion over the whole of India before its destruction by Brahminism.

P

Had we no other ground for the supposition, we might have reasonably concluded, from the conquests of Sesostris, that a communication had been established between India and Egypt at a very remote period. The allusion to such an intercourse found by Mr Prinsep, however, in one of the ancient inscriptions translated by him *, establishes the supposition on a firm foundation, and leaves no doubt of such a communication having been regularly carried on. Indeed, the very supposition of two powerful kingdoms, such as India and Egypt were in very remote times, remaining in total ignorance of each other's existence is almost impossible, and obviously improbable. At the period when this connection subsisted, Buddhism was the dominant faith of India, and its disciples were actively engaged in its promulgation and extension. The consequence of that activity is apparent, even to the present day, in the prevalence of their faith in China; and as they gave their faith to that country, so do they also appear to have given their philosophy to Egypt. Buddhism is essentially a philosophical religion. Its virtue is meditation, and its perfection an entire victory over the senses and passions. Its teachers were also philosophers of no mean attainments; they inculcated and practised the moral virtues; whilst the universe itself was hinged, not on fate or chance, but on the merit or demerit of its professors. Being, then, essentially a philosophical system, its votaries naturally endeavoured to introduce that philosophy into the coun-

* "The fruit of this discovery" (that of the Deva Nāgara alphabet) "has been the important fact of a connection between the sovereigns of India, and those of Greece and India. Continuing his examinations of these inscriptions, Mr Prinsep has found an allusion in them, equally authentic and distinct, to one of the Ptolemies of Egypt." Foreign Quarterly Review.

tries which they visited, and as they left their religion in philosophical China, we must now see whether they did not also leave their philosophy in religious Egypt.

The visits of Thales, Pythygoras and Plato into Egypt shew us that, in their time, it was famous for its learning, whilst the absence of celebrated men of that nation in those early times naturally leads us to the conclusion that the philosophy which they possessed was not their own, but that they merely retained it, as a jewel of which they knew not the value, to be afterwards handed, without regret, to the more penetrating and energetic Greeks.

That some communication must have taken place with regard to philosophy between India and Egypt, I shall now attempt to prove, by shewing that the doctrines of the Pythagorean school were little more than a *resumé* or a *rifacimento* of the philosophy of Buddhism.

1. The doctrine of the metempsychosis is the grand distinguishing feature of both systems. When introduced by Pythagoras into Europe, it seems to have been eagerly caught at by all who heard of it, as a doctrine of a very extraordinary, as well as of a very satisfactory nature. It was then a perfectly new doctrine to Greece, however trite it might have become in India. It will scarcely be considered necessary, I imagine, that I should formally prove its existence as one of the distinguishing features of Buddhism. Whether personal identity, consciousness or recollection, was maintained or not by Kappalo * or Gotamo and their disciples, is a point of little importance in the present inquiry. The doctrine of a transmigration of the soul, after its separation from the body, into

* The Buddhu who preceded Gotamo.

that of some other animal, is one allowed to Buddhism by all who have written on the subject. The Pythagoreans received the doctrine, but refined on the application, "As we cure diseases of the body by unpleasant medicines, if they will not yield to the more agreeable, so do we correct the evil propensities of the soul by false terrors, if they will not yield to true," is the excuse of Timaeus the Socrian for asserting the doctrine to which I have just referred. "*On this account it is*" (he proceeds) "that we threaten them with punishments to be endured in other bodies. Thus do we declare to the cowardly that they shall become women, and be dedicated to disgrace; to murderers, that they shall become wild beasts; to the libidinous, that they shall assume the forms of goats or swine; to the heedless and rash, we threaten aërial bodies, doomed to eternal wanderings; and, lastly, to the slothful and luxurious, the careless and the obstinate, we consign the stupid minds and awkward forms of the aquatic fowls *." Such are the sentiments of one of the most eminent of the disciples of Pythagoras,—sentiments, which would lead us to infer that the metempsychosis, although numbered amongst the exoteric, was, by no means, one of the esoteric doctrines of his master.

2. The concurrence of a single tenet, however, is far from being sufficient to establish a connection between the two systems. In the discourses of Gotamo, (so far, at

* ὡς γαρ τα σωματα νοσωδεσι ποκα ὑγιαζομες, εικα μη εικῃ τοις ὑγιεινοτατοις ουτω τας ψυχας απειργομες ψευδεσι λογοις, εικα μη αγητα αλαθεσι. λεγοιντο δ' αναγκαιως και τιμωριαι ξεναι, ὡς μετενδυομεναν ταν ψυχαν, των μεν δειλων, ες γυναικεια σκανεα, ποθ' ὑβριν εδιδομενα· των δε μαιφονων, ες θηριων σωματα, ποτι κολασιν· λαγνων δ' ες συων ηκαπρων μορφας· κουφων δε και μετεωρων, ες πτηνων αεροπορων· αργων δε και απρακτων, αμαθων τε και ανοητων, ες ταν των ενυδρων ἰδεαν. Περι ψυχας, κοσμω, και φυσιος. Opuscula Mythologica, Amstelodami, 1688.

least, as they have been made accessible to the English reader,) we find that he almost invariably waves the question of primeval existence, and allows, without asserting, the eternity of matter. He was eminently a practical philosopher, and only dived into the thickets of metaphysics to cull thence some flower to adorn the virtuous, or arrest the heedless. The chain of existence, which he gives us in the discourse entitled " Paticha Samupada *," runs thus: " On account of ignorance, priests, merit and demerit are produced; on account of merit and demerit, consciousness; on account of consciousness, body and mind." But if there be ignorance, there must be also persons to be ignorant, and if beings, there must have been a world in which they existed. That the eternity of matter was one of the doctrines of his followers is evidently proved by their account of the earth, which represents it as being destroyed and re-produced in an endless succession of series. That this tenet was held by several Buddhists anterior to himself, he declares, in one of his discourses †, designating them as " those holding the eternity of matter and spirit."

This doctrine we also find holding a prominent place amongst those of the Italic School. " The universe," (says Ocellus Lucanus,) " as I imagine, is both indestructible and without beginning ‡." And again,—" From all these reasons it may be easily perceived that the world had no beginning, and can have no end §."

* Friend, April 1839.

† The Brahma Jala. Friend, Sept. 1838.

‡ *Δοκει γαρ μοι το παν ανωλεθρον ειναι και αγεννητον.*

§ *Εκ τουτων ουν ἁπαντων σαφως πιστευται, ὁτι ὁ κοσμος αγεννητος και αφθαρτος. Περι του παντος*, ch. i. From the Opuscula, &c. *ut supra*.

3. One of the ten fundamental precepts of Buddhism, and the first of those precepts, is " Abstain from destroying animal life." No less emphatic was the command of Pythagoras neither to kill nor eat. " He rigidly abstained," (says his biographer, Iamblichus,) " from the destruction or devouring of any thing endued with life." Again, " they," (the Pythagoreans,) " were accustomed to abominate the killing of animals as utterly unjust, and contrary to every principle of nature *."

In these three fundamental doctrines, then, the metempsychosis, the eternity of matter, and the abstaining from the destruction of animal life, there was what every one will at least allow to be a very extraordinary coincidence between the Buddhistical and Pythagorean tenets. The accordance of the systems, however, by no means ends here.

4. " Abstain from all intoxicating drinks " is the fifth of the commandments, as delivered by Gotamo. " He ate nothing which had life," (says Iamblichus of Pythagoras,) " *he drank no wine* AT ALL, (ὅλως,) nor did he sacrifice any animals to the gods † ;" assertions which, if we but substitute Gotamo for Pythagoras, will hold equally true.

5. " If any priest shall eat or take food at an improper

* Τουτο μεν γαρ αποχη εμψυχων ἁπαντων, και προσετι βρωματων τινων αγχιστο γενναιως.

Again, εθιζομενοι (οἱ Πυθαγορειοι) γαρ μυσαττεσθαι φονον ζωων ὡς ανομον, και παρα φυσιν. Περι του Πυθαγορειου βιου, ch. xxx. In Bibliopolio Commeliniana, 1598.

† Μητε εμψυχον μηδεν μηδε ποτε εσθιειν εισηγουμενος, μητε οινον ὁλως πινειν, μητε θυειν ζωα θεοις, chap. xxiv. Vita. Iam.

hour of the day, it is Paehittiyan *, *i. e.* a sin requiring confession and absolution for its atonement. The foregoing was the command of Gotamo to his priests; the following that of Pythagoras to those initiated into the esoteric mysteries. "*Let no one eat but at the proper hour of the day* †."

6. "A man subject to his own passions," (says Gotamo,) "applauding the Tatagata ‡, may, say some sages, supported by the alms of the faithful, live in the use of articles for personal adornment, such as ointments, oils, *baths*, &c. But the sage Gotamo abstains from all such personal adornments §." In this extract I desire more particularly to draw the reader's attention to the fact of his abstaining from the bath. In other parts of his discourses, (Winiya Pitaka, for instance, sec. Pāehiti,) he absolutely forbids the indulgence of the bath to his followers, on the ground of its being an incentive to sensuality, and inconsistent with that purity inculcated by his precepts: "Let no one walk in the public ways, or be sprinkled from the font, *or be washed in the bath* ‖," was the no less imperative injunction of the Grecian.

7. The priests of Gotamo and his predecessors bore some resemblance to the esoterics (if I may be allowed the expression,) of Pythagoras. The two classes were initiated into all the mysteries of their respective masters,

* Winiya Pitaka, Sec. Pāehiti. Friend, Feb. 1840.

† Και τουτοις χρονον τινα ὡριζε της λποχης ωρισμενον, ch. xxiv. Idem.

‡ *I. e.* applauding himself, Gotamo. In his discourses, he speaks of himself in the third person as "*the Tatagata.*"

§ Brahma Jala, or the Brahminical Net; for a manuscript translation of which I am indebted to the kindness of the Rev. D. J. Gogerly.

‖ Ουδει τας λεωφορους βαδιζειν ὁδους, ουδει εις περιρραν τηριου εμβαπτειν, ουδε εν βαλανειῳ λουεσθαι. Vita. cap. xvii.

and in several of the injunctions delivered to each, we have just seen how great was the similarity between the two systems. There was one important distinction however. The initiated of Pythagoras were men engaged in the common concerns of life. They lived, indeed, like the priests of the other sect in common, but they were intended not as teachers, but as examples, of the doctrine. They were, therefore, allowed to marry, whilst the others were prohibited from doing so. All kinds of sexual debauchery and irregularity, however, were not more strictly prohibited by Gotamo than by Pythagoras. The former allowed the priests, if unable to keep their rigid and frigid vow of chastity, to put off their yellow robes and marry. The sin, then, consisted not in the unchaste action, but in its performance *with* the yellow robes, thereby proving that this absolute command of Buddhu was not intended as an universal exaction. By a comparison of the 27th chapter of the life of Pythagoras according to Iamblichus, with the rules which regulated the intercourse of priests and females * many striking points of similarity will be observed, which I forbear to transcribe.

8. The excellency of the moral code of Buddhism has long been a subject of admiration to its admirers. What can be more beautiful, for instance, than the following?

" Conquer anger by mildness, *evil by good*, covetousness by liberality, and falsehood by truth.

" Know, O man, that sinful actions cannot be hid; but that pride, covetousness and wrath, will bring long suffering upon you.

" Religion is the path to immortality, irreligion the

* Friend, Oct. Nov. Dec. 1839, and Jan. Feb. 1840.

path to death. The righteous die not, but the irreligious are even as now dead.

"*As the solid rock stands unshaken by the storm, so is the wise man unmoved by contempt or applause.*

"He is a more noble warrior who conquers himself, than the warrior who, in the field of battle, overthrows thousands of thousands *."

Such are a few of the incomparable maxims of Buddhism,—maxims almost literally transferred to the moral code of Pythagoras †. "It will not appear wonderful," says an accurate and learned writer, "when we consider the morality of Pythagoras, that his disciples were so much respected and revered as legislators, and imitated for their constancy, their friendship, and their humanity."

9. Few of the philosophers of antiquity allowed themselves to be addressed or treated as gods. Gotamo and Pythagoras were, however, exceptions to the rule; not only did they allow, but they also encouraged, this species of adulation. The former, indeed, did not assert himself to be a god, but merely declares that he was endowed with all wisdom; that he was *the great* teacher, the saviour, and the object of worship. He did not assume the title of god, because he thought it too mean a thing to be the rival of Brahma, Iswara or Sakraia; he placed himself above them as the very perfection of existence. The ambition of Pythagoras was neither so boundless nor so successful. Alive, he was treated as and styled a deity; dead, he became *the man*. "So wonderful did he appear," says Iamblichus, "that it was truly affirmed by many that he

* Friend, articles Buddhism, passim.

† Vidend. Δημοφιλου, εκ των Πυθαγορειων, ὁμοια, η βιου θεραπεια, et Δημοφιλου γνωμαι Πυθαγορικαι. In Opusculis Mythologicis, &c. Apud Gale.

was the son of God." And, again, "it was a custom amongst the Pythagoreans that no one should call him Pythagoras; when they wished to designate him, they addressed him as *the Divine*; after his death, however, they declared him to have been *the man* *."

10. Buddhism instructs us that there are three orders of beings in the universe,—gods, inhabiting the various heavens; men, inhabiting the world; and demons or yakkhos, inhabiting the air and the great rock Maha Meru †. In this description we have an exact account of the Pythagorean notions on the same subject. This will be easily proved by a reference to Ocellus Lucanus and his treatise *Περι του παντος*. "In each part of the universe, then," says he, "there is collected a distinct race of existences; in heaven, the gods; on the earth, man; and in the elevated region, demons ‡."

I have dwelt thus minutely upon the system of Pythagoras, because it was evidently the most influenced by the tenets of Buddhism; and I may surely be allowed to ask, whence this extraordinary coincidence between the two, if there were no connection between them? An agreement in so many tenets cannot be considered as a merely fortuitous event. If we suppose, with many who have written on the subject, that Pythagoras visited India, the

* *Προσβλεψας θαυμαστως εφαινετο, ωστε υπο των πολλων εικοτως βεβαιουσθαι, τε του θεου παιδα αυτον ειναι.* Cap. ii.

Επι μεν γαρ τω μηδενα των Πυθαγορειων ὀνομαζειν Πυθαγοραν, αλλα ζωντα μεν, ὁποτε βουλοιντο δηλωσαι καλειν αυτον θειον· επειδε ετελευτησεν, εκεινον τον ανδρα. Vita Iambli. cap. xxxv.

† Mr Upham's Buddhism, passim.

‡ *Εστι ουν καθ ἑκαστην αποτομην ὑπερεχον, τι γενος εντετακται των αλλων, εν μεν ουρανῳ το των θεων, εν δε γη ανθρωπος· εν δε τῳ μεταρσιῳ το των δαιμονες.* Cap. iii.

difficulty is solved at once; for we cannot surely conceive it possible that he could visit that country without hearing of the celebrated teacher and sage so lately dead *, a teacher whose tenets so soon spread over the whole of the east.

If, however, we maintain with others, that such was not the case, but that his doctrines were solely derived from Egypt, we must allow that some communication had taken place with regard to philosophy between the two countries, or how can we account for the metempsychosis; the eternity of matter; the abstaining from the destruction of animal life; the abstaining from all luxuries; the prohibition of sexual intercourse; the excellency of the moral code; the similar assumptions of Pythagoras and Gotamo; and, finally, the threefold division of creation, appearing in the one sect precisely as they did in the other?

But Plato also visited Egypt; and if we can discover no traces of Buddhism in his system, our former conclusions are likely to be very doubtfully received. Plato, however, we must remember, was a very different character from Pythagoras—

Nullius addictus jurare in verba magistri,

he thought and decided for himself; reasoned on what he heard; weighed the doctrines of Egypt with the nobler

* The Ceylonese chronology fixes Buddha's death at 543, A. C. The Indian and Chinese, however, declare it to have occurred in 1087; and as we account for the wish of the former to postdate the era, (through the desire of making it coincide with the landing of Wijeya,) I am inclined to give credence to the latter. Pythagoras died (according to the most common account) 497, A. C.

system of Socrates, and, from the two, compiled that beautiful and ideal edifice, which has been the admiration of all succeeding ages. To expect, then, a similarity between Gotamo and Plato, similar to that which we have just illustrated, would be unreasonable ; nor, I must confess, am I sufficiently well acquainted with his voluminous writings to seize on many points of resemblance. Those which have come under my observation, however, are both striking and interesting, and appear to me quite sufficient to prove an intimate connection between the two systems.

Perhaps the most striking points of resemblance between the two are, 1*st*, in those doctrines which relate to the origin of the earth, its primeval condition, its history, and its destination; and, 2*dly*, the origin, history and destination of the human soul.

1. The eternity of matter and spirit, and their independent existence, I have formerly shewn to be a tenet of Buddhism; and from the following observations it will be apparent that it was also the opinion of Plato: "In this dialogue, (the Timæus,) which comprehends his whole doctrine on the subject of the formation of the universe, matter is so manifestly spoken of as eternally co-existing with God, that this part of his doctrine could not have been mistaken by so many and able writers, had they not been seduced by the desire of establishing a coincidence of doctrine between the writings of Plato and Moses. It is certain that neither Cicero, nor Apuleius, nor Alcinous, nor even the later commentator Chalcidius, understood their master in any other sense, than as admitting two primary and incorruptible principles, God and matter * ".

* Enfield's History of Philosophy, book ii. ch. viii. sec. i.

2. The primeval condition of the human race and of the world is thus described by Gotamo: "Living beings first appeared by an apparitional birth, subsisting on the element of felicity, illuminated by their own effulgence, moving through the air, delightfully located, and existing in unity and concord *." An eminent Buddhistical work, (the Janawanso) thus describes the same period: "The Brahmins from the Brahma world descended to the newly-formed world, which they illuminated universally by the effulgence of their bodies, and they fed on the most delicious food, and were able to soar through the air †." Let us now regard the description of the same period afforded us by Plato: "God was then the prince and common father of all; he *now* governs by inferior deities, but he *then* governed it himself; cruelty and hatred were then unknown; war and sedition were unheard of. God himself guarded man; he was his supporter and shepherd. They had no magistrates, no civil polity. In those happy days, man sprung from the bosom of the earth, which spontaneously yielded him flowers and trees. The fertile fields generously yielded him untilled corn and fruit. He had no need of raiment, for changes of temperature were then unknown, whilst the perennial verdure formed his downy bed. * * Every thing there was beautiful, harmonious and transparent; fruits of an exquisite flavour grew naturally; it was watered with rivers of nectar. They there breathed the light as we do the air, and their water was purer than air ‡."

* Suttrapitaka, sec. Dighaniko.

† Friend, September 1843.

‡ Τοτε γαρ αυτης πρωτον της κυκλησεως ηρχεν επιμελουμενης όλης ὁ θεος, ὡς νυν κατα τοπους ταυτον τουτου υπο θεων αρχοντων παντη τα του κοσμου μερη διειλημμενα

3. One of the most peculiar doctrines of Buddhism, and one which I am not aware is to be found in any other system of religion, is the constant destruction and reproduction of the world. "That which is destroyed and re-formed is loka, the world," (says the Janawanso.) "It is denominated loka, from being destroyed and reformed *in a never-ending series of successions* *." This doctrine we also find holding a prominent place in the tenets of Platonism. So diffuse are his descriptions, however, that I prefer inserting the following pithy observations of one of his most learned commentators, Tiedemann, to confusing the reader with a host of extracts from the Dialogues Politicus, Timæus and Critias, to which it is sufficient to direct the curious reader: "Platonem accedere eorum sententiae, qui mundum, *non semper manere eundem, sed magnas ejus esse conversiones, ac ruinas, ut refici eum interdum ac in prostinum redigi ordinem,* sit necesse, ante eum docuerunt, idque non simulante, aut disputandi causa, sed ex animo, cum e firmissimis hæc ejus de materiæ natura initiis sequantur, hinc est manifestum †."

4. If we suppose the Indian philosopher to have taught the non-existence of a Supreme Being, we must suppose that he considered the human soul as a part of an extensive whole, or of a kind of intellectual and spiritual world,

ώστε ουτ' αγριον ην ουδεν, ουτε αλληλων εδωδαι· πολεμος τε ουκ ενην, ουδε στασις το παραπαν· το δ' ουν των ανθρωπων λεχθεν αυτοματου περι βιου, δια το τοιονδε ειρηται· θεος ενεμεν αυτους, αυτος επιστατων· εκ γης ανεβιωσκοντο παντες· καρπους δε αφθονους ειχον απο τεδρυων και πολλης ὑλης αλλης, ουχ ὑπο γεωργιας φυομενους, αλλ' αυτοματης αναδιδουσης της γης· γυμνοι δε και αστρωτοι θυραυλουντες ταπολλα ενεμοντο, το γαρ των ὡρων αυτοις αλυπον εκεκρατο· μαλακας δε ευνας ειχον, ανα φυομενης εκ γης ποας αφθονον, &c. Πολιτικος, vol. vi. Bipont. p. 34.

* Friend, *ut supra.*

† Dialogorum Platonis Argumenta, p. 157.

as he certainly taught its absolute existence. If, on the other hand, we acknowledge, as a part of his system, the existence of a God, we must suppose the human soul to have been a part of that being, as it certainly returned to him at death. On either of these suppositions, and I cannot easily conceive any other which we can make to harmonise with his opinions, the doctrine of Gotamo was but a shade different from that of Plato. "To account for the origin and present state of the human soul Plato supposes, that when God formed the universe, he separated from the soul of the world inferior souls, equal in number to the stars, and assigned to each its proper celestial sphere; but that these souls (by what means, or for what reason does not appear) were sent down to the earth into human bodies, as into a sepulchre or prison *."

5. The history of the human soul in the tenets of Buddhism is contained in one word,—metempsychosis; and its ultimate destination in another,—nirwana. Gotamo himself speaks of this nirwana as being a state of "exalted felicity †." Others represent it as a complete cessation of existence; whilst others maintain that it is an absorption into the soul of the universe; for which state (whatever that state was) all are agreed the soul was to be fitted by the extinction of all evil, and the acquirement of a perfect equanimity. "My mind is detached from all existing objects; I have attained to the extinction of desire," said Gotamo in the verses spoken by him when he became a Budhu ‡. The doctrines of

* Enfield, *ut supra.*

† Pansiga-panas-jataka-groto. Friend, August 1838.

‡ Friend, April 1839. In this hymn he says, "I have seen the architect, and said you shall not build me another house," *i. e.* my transmigra-

Plato on the same subject are extremely similar. How near he comes to the doctrine of the metempsychosis in his Phæda and Timæus, every one who has read those beautiful dialogues must know; but as we have his whole doctrine on the subject succinctly stated by Enfield, in continuation with the last quotation, I think it preferable to insert it, instead of appending a number of lengthened quotations to this already too-extended essay. "He (Plato) ascribes to this cause (the entrance of the soul into the body) the depravity and misery to which human nature is liable, and maintains, that *it is only by disengaging itself from all animal passions*, and rising above sensible objects to the contemplation of the world of intelligence, that the soul of man can be prepared *to return to its original habitation* *." If, then, there was no transmigration of the soul in his doctrines, what became of it before its being fitted to return to its primeval abode?

6. Another of the peculiar doctrines of Buddhism is its inculcation of a plurality of heavens. Almost every deity has a separate abode, all differing in height, in glory, and in majesty. This tenet we cannot of course expect to find in monotheistic Platonism; but in one of his dialogues we find Plato putting the following question into the mouth of one of the followers of Socrates: "Whether shall we say that there is one heaven, or is it more correct to declare that the heavens are many and infinite? †" From this it is plain that he had heard of such a doctrine;

tions are over; now, if there be no God in Buddhism, who is this architect?

* Enfield, loc. cit.

† Ποτερον ουν ορθως ἑνα ουρανον προσειρηκαμεν, η πολλους και απειρους λεγειν ην ορθοτερον.—Timaios. vol. vii. p. 259.

and if so, where *had* he heard of it? Not in Greece; for we find it not in their poets, and not from Socrates, who believed in the unity of God. It must have been in Egypt, and either thence conveyed to India, or *vice versa*.

In those doctrines, then, which relate to the origin, history, and destination of the universe, as well as in those which treat of the origin, history, and destination of the human soul, we cannot but allow that the coincidence between the systems of Gotamo and Plato is striking and extraordinary; nor, I imagine, when we take into consideration the still more striking analogy between Gotamo and Pythagoras, can be doubt but that all are parts of one system, and all based upon the same foundation. The question that next presents itself is one which we cannot *yet* answer,—What was that foundation, and where was it laid? Many will point to the Bible; others to India; others to Egypt; and I confess many considerations may be advanced in support of each of these suppositions. I have already hinted that I imagine the philosophy proceeded from India to Egypt; but the supposition is based on such slight grounds, that I cannot pretend to assert it as a well-supported and probable one. If, in the present essay, I have succeeded in shewing that some such supposition must be adopted, my object will have been attained; and the decision of the question just proposed, must be left to more imaginative, or to more learned, heads.

II.—SINGHALESE SOVEREIGNS FROM 543 B. C. TO 1815, A. D.

No.	Name.	Length of Reign.	Date of Accession. B. C.
1.	Wijeya,	38 years,	543
2.	Upatissa I.	1 do.	505
3.	Panduwāsa,	30 do.	504
4.	Abhaya,	20 do.	474
	Interregnum,	17 do.	454
5.	Pandukābhayo,	70 do.	437
6.	Ganatissa,	13 do.	367
7.	Mutasēwo,	47 do.	354
8.	Devananpiatisso,	40 do.	307
9.	Utteya,	10 do.	266
10.	Mahasēwo,	10 do.	256
11.	Suratisso,	10 do.	246
12.	Sena and Gutika, (Malabars.)	22 do.	236
13.	Asela,	10 do.	214
14.	Elala, (a Malabar,)	44 do.	204
15.	Dutu-Gaimono,	24 do.	164
16.	Saidatisso,	18 do.	140
17.	Toohl or Thulathanāka,	1½ months,	122
18.	Laiminitisso I.	9½ years,	122
19.	Kaluna,	6 do.	112
20.	Walagambahu I.	5 months,	104
21.	Several Malabar Princes,	14½ years,	104

No.	Name.	Length of Reign.	Date of Accession.
			B. C.
22.	Walagambahu I. (restored,)	12½ years,	89
23.	Mahachula,	14 do.	77
24.	Chora Naga,	12 do.	63
25.	Koodatisso,	3 do.	50
26.	Anula, (Queen)	5 do.	47
27.	Makalantisso,	22 do.	41
28.	Batiatisso,	28 do.	19
29.	Maha Dailiya,	12 do.	A. D. 9
30.	Addagaimono or Amanda-Gaimono,	9½ do.	21
31.	Kinihirridaila or Kanijani Tisso,	3 do.	30
32.	Choolabhayo,	1 do.	33
33.	Seewali, (Queen,)	4 months,	34
34.	Ellona or Ilanaga,	6 years,	38
35.	Sanda Muhuna,	8½ do.	44
36.	Yasa Siloo,	7½ do.	52
37.	Subho,	6 do.	60
38.	Wahapp or Wasabho,	44 do.	66
39.	Waknais,	3 do.	110
40.	Gajabahu I.	12 do.	113
41.	Mahalamāna,	6 do.	125
42.	Batiatisso II.	24 do.	131
43.	Chulatisso,	18 do.	155
44.	Koohuna,	10 do.	173
45.	Koodanāma,	1 do.	183
46.	Kuda Sirinā,	19 do.	184
47.	Waiwahairatisso or Wairatissa,	22 do.	209

No.	Name.	Length of Reign.	Date of Accession. A. D.
48.	Abha Sen,	8 years,	231
49.	Siri Naga II.	2 do.	239
50.	Weja Indoo or Wijaya II.	1 do.	241
51.	Sangatisso I.	4 do.	242
52.	Dahama Sirisangabo,	2 do.	246
53.	Golu Abha,	13 do.	248
54.	Mekalan Dethu Tisso I.	10 do.	261
55.	Mahasen,	27 do.	271
56.	Kitsiri Majan,	28 do.	298
57.	Dethu Tisso II.	9 do.	326
58.	Bujas or Budhadaso,	29 do.	335
59.	Upatisso II.	42 do.	364
60.	Mahanamo,	22 do.	406
61.	Sengot or Sotthi Sena,	1 day,	428
62.	Laimani-tisso II.	1 year,	428
63.	Mitta Sena or Karalsora,	1 do.	429
64.	Several Malabar Chieftains,	24¾ do.	430
65.	Dhatu Sena,	18 do.	456
66.	Kasiapo I. or Sigiri Kasumba,	18 do.	475
67.	Mogallano I.	18 do.	493
68.	Kumara Dhas,	9 do.	512
69.	Kirti Sena,	9 do.	521
70.	Maidi Siwu,	25 days,	530
71.	Laimini Upatisso III.	1½ years,	531
72.	Ambaherra Salamawan,	13 do.	*534
73.	Dapulo I.	6½ months,	547

* Error one year six months.

No.	Name.	Length of Reign.	Date of Accession. A. D.
74.	Dalamagalan or Mugallano II.	20 years,	547
75.	Kuda Kitsiri Maiwan I.	19 do.	567
76.	Senewi or Maha Nāga,	3 do.	586
77.	Aggrabodhi I.	34 do.	589
78.	Aggrabodhi II.	10 do.	623
79.	Sanghatissa II.	2 months,	633
80.	Buna Mugalan,	6 years,	633
81.	Abhasiggahaka,	9 do.	639
82.	Siri Sangabo II.	6 months,	648
83.	Kaluna Detutisso,	5 do.	648
84.	Siri Sangabo II. (restored,)	16 years,	649
85.	Dalupiatisso I.	12 do.	665
86.	Kasiapo II.	9 do.	677
87.	Dapulu II.	7 do.	686
88.	Dalupiatisso II.	9 do.	693
89.	Siri Sangabo III.	16 do.	702
90.	Walpitty Wasidata,	2 do.	718
91.	Hatthadatha,	6 months,	720
92.	Mahalaipamu,	6 years,	720
93.	Kasiapo III.	3 do.	726
94.	Aggrabodhi III.	40 do.	729
95.	Aggrabodhi IV.	6 do.	769
96.	Mihindo I.	20 do.	775
97.	Dapulo III.	5 do.	795
98.	Mihindo II.	4 do.	800
99.	Aggrabodhi V.	11 do.	804
100.	Dapulo IV.	16 do.	815
101.	Aggrabodhi VI.	3 do.	831
102.	Mitwella Sen,	20 do.	838

No.	Name.	Length of Reign.	Date of Accession. A. D.
103.	Kasiapo IV.	33 years,	858
104.	Udaya I.	35 do.	891
105.	Udaya II.	11 do.	926
106.	Kasiapo V.	17 do.	937
107.	Kasiapo VI.	10 do.	954
108.	Dapulo V.	7 months,	964
109.	Dapulo VI.	10 years,	964
110.	Udaya III.	3 do.	974
111.	Sena II.	9 do.	977
112.	Udaya IV.	8 do.	986
113.	Sena III.	3 do.	994
114.	Mihindo III.	16 do.	997
115.	Sena IV.	10 do.	1013
116.	Mihindo IV.	36 do.	1023
	Interregnum,	12 do.	1059
117.	Wijayabahu I.	55 do.	1071
118.	Jayabahu I.	1 do.	1126
119.	Wickramabahu I. }	20 do.	1127
120.	Gajabahu II. }		
121.	Prackramabahu the Great,	33 do.	*1153
122.	Wijayabahu II.	1 do.	1186
123.	Mihindu V.	5 days,	1187
124.	Kirti Nissanga,	9 years,	1187
125.	Wirabahu,	1 day,	1196
126.	Wickramabahu II.	3 months,	1196
127.	Chondakanda,	9 do.	1197
128.	Leelawatee, (Queen,)	3 years,	1197
129.	Sahasamallawa,	2 do.	1200

* Error 6 years.

No.	Name.	Length of Reign.	Date of Accession.
			A. D.
130.	Kalyanawati, . .	6 years, . .	1202
131.	Dharmasoko, . .	1 do. . .	1208
132.	Nayanga, . .	17 days, . .	1209
133.	Leelawatee, (restored,)	1 year, . .	1210
134.	Lokaiswera I. .	9 months, .	1210
135.	Leelawatee, (restored,)	7 do. . .	1211
136.	Prackramabahu II.	3 years, . .	1211
137.	Māgha, (Malabar usurper,)	21 do. . .	1214
138.	Wijayabahu III. .	24 do. . .	1235
139.	Prackramabahu III.	35 do. . .	1266
140.	Wijayabahu IV. .	2 do. . .	1301
141.	Bhuwaneko Bahu I.	11 do. . .	1303
142.	Prackramabahu IV.	5 do. . .	1314
143.	Bhuwaneko Bahu II.	24 do. . .	1319
144.	Prackramabahu V.	not stated, .	1343
145.	Bhuwaneko Bahu III.	do. . .	
146.	Wijayabahu V. .	do. . .	
147.	Bhuwaneko Bahu IV.	14 years, . .	1347
148.	Prackramabahu V.	10 do. . .	1361
149.	Wickramabahu III.	7 do. . .	1371
150.	Bhuwaneko Bahu V.	20 do. . .	1378
151.	Wijayabahu V. .	12 do. . .	1398
152.	Prackramabahu VI.	52 do. . .	1410
153.	Jayabahu II. .	2 do. . .	1462
154.	Bhuwaneko Bahu VI.	7 do. . .	1464
155.	Prackramabahu VII.	14 years, . .	1471
156.	Prackramabahu VIII.	20 do. . .	1485
157.	Prackramabahu IX.	22 do. . .	1505
158.	Wijayabahu VII. .	7 do. . .	1527
159.	Bhuwaneko Bahu VII.	8 do. . .	1534

No.	Name.	Length of Reign.	Date of Accession. A. D.
160.	Don Juan or Dharmapala,	39 years,	1542
161.	Rajah Singha I.	11 do.	1581
162.	Don John or Wimala Dharma I.	12 do.	1592
163.	Senerat,	30 do.	1604
164.	Rajah Singha II.	50 do.	1634
165.	Wimala Dharma II.	22 do.	1684
166.	Narendra Singha,	33 do.	1706
167.	Wijaya Singha,	8 do.	1739
168.	Kirtisree Singha,	33 do.	1747
169.	Rajadhi Singha,	18 do.	1780
170.	Wickrama Singha,	16 do.	1798
		Deposed by the British,	1815

III. NOTES ON THE PRESENT STATE OF THE ISLAND.

Few portions of the British territories have advanced from barbarism to civilisation with so rapid a progress as Ceylon. In 1815, the entire of the interior of the island had sunk into the most degraded state; the greater part of the country was covered by impervious forests, in which the elephant, the cheetah and the wild cat roamed undisturbed; there was not a single road of any extent in the territories of the native princes, save a few pathways; the people were degraded and uncivilised, a degradation to which every year was adding, and the vast natural capabilities of the kingdom were unimproved. Even the sea-shore, which had been for nearly four centuries under European control, was only known by the line of forts which encircled it, and, from its perpetual disturbances, was almost as barbarous as the interior. Since that period but twenty-nine years have elapsed. Eleven lines of public carriage roads now traverse the country in almost every direction, of which one completely encircles the island *. Another, " the Simplon of the East," runs from Colombo, the seat of Government, to Candy †, the capital of the interior, and the centre whence civilisation and cultivation are gradually radiating in every direction. Another extends in a north-eastern direction from Co-

* A length of 764 miles.

† Seventy-two miles.

lombo to Trincomalee, a distance of 160 miles, through the wildest part of the country, which it will be a powerful instrument in improving. By these three, all the chief towns of the island (Colombo, Jaffna, Trincomalee, Matura and Galle) communicate with each other; and by the others * the most improved districts are easily accessible.

Ceylon was anciently divided into a number of petty districts, denominated *Korles*, of which the boundaries were exceedingly irregular, and are now unknown. It has been divided by the British Legislature into five provinces,—the northern, southern, eastern, western and central. Of these, Jaffna, Galle, Trincomalee, Colombo † and Candy are the respective capitals; and in each of these an agent of Government and an assistant reside. The other chief towns of the island are, Manaar, Mantotte and Anuradhapoora in the northern province; Negombo, Chilan, Putlam, Kurnegalle, Caltura and Bentotte in the western; Matura, Tangalle and Hambantotte in the southern; Batticaloa and Bintenne in the eastern; and Gampola, Dambool, Nuwera Ellia and Badulla in the central. The capitals of the various provinces have populations varying

* The remaining eight are,—

From Negombo to Candy, sixty-six miles.

From Putlam, through Kurnegalle to Candy, eighty-five miles.

From Aripo, through Anuradhapoora and Dambool, to Candy, 137 miles.

From Colombo, through Ratnapoora to Adam's Peak, eighty-one miles.

From Colombo to Ruanwelle, thirty-six miles.

From Candy to Trincomalee, 113 miles.

From Candy to Badulla, (through Gonegamme,) fifty-three miles.

Do. do. (through Nuwera Ellia,) eighty-four miles.

† In Colombo, two newspapers (each issuing two numbers weekly,) and a Government Gazette are published.

from ten to forty thousand, and the other villages are proportionately less.

The increase of the population (partly caused by the influx of labourers for the coffee estates from the Continent,) is an evident proof of the advancement of the island. In 1832, the entire population scarcely amounted to 1,000,000, of whom 6500 were whites; in 1842 it had increased to 1,337,000, of whom about 7500 were whites; whilst in 1843, it is stated at 1,442,000, being an increase, in a single year, of 105,000. This amount of population gives but fifty-nine individuals to a square mile, in the excessively fertile and productive Ceylon; whilst in comparatively barren England, there is a proportion of 259 to the same area.

In ancient times there can be no doubt that the island supported a population at least five times as great as it now does, and that, too, when it was exporting grain to the Continent; now, however, large annual importations of rice meet a rapid sale, at very fluctuating prices, an evil which the Government could prevent by renewing the embankments of a very few of the tanks, and, in a short time, Ceylon, instead of importing, would be exporting, large quantities of grain. Not only are these tanks useless now, but from the saturation of the soil, by the abundant rains, they become the nests of pestilence and malaria, a truth fatally confirmed by the present unhealthiness (almost deadliness, indeed,) of the climate of Anuradhapoora, the former capital of the island.

The revenue of Ceylon consists chiefly of customs, duty on cinnamon, land rents and customs, licenses, salt farms, judicial stamps, taxes on lands and houses, &c.

The largest items of the expenditure are of course the civil, judicial and revenue charges, the military maintenance, and the expense of building. From the pearl-fishery in the Gulf of Manaar large sums have been drawn by the British Government, which makes the returns of income somewhat irregular, as an interval of a few years sometimes elapses between the successive fishings. Annexed is the return of these sums.

1797,	A pearl-fishery yielded,		£.144,000
1798,	do.	do.	192,000
1799,	do.	do.	30,000
1803,	do.	do.	15,000
1804,	do.	do.	75,000
1806,	do.	do.	35,000
1808,	do.	do.	90,000
1809,	do.	do.	25,000
1814,	do.	do.	64,000
1828,	do.	do.	29,000
1829,	do.	do.	37,000
1830,	do.	do.	21,000
1831,	do.	do.	28,000
1832,	do.	do.	3,800
1833,	do.	do.	25,000
1835,	do.	do.	40,000
1836,	do.	do.	26,000
1837,	do.	do.	10,500

Few of the colonies of the United Kingdom have been less expensive to the mother country than Ceylon. In the twenty years which elapsed between 1821 and 1841, the expenditure exceeded the revenue only by £.260,000, and on many of these years there was a large excess of the latter. The following table gives the returns for every third year between 1821 and 1842.

Year.	Revenue.	Expenditure.	Excess of Revenue.	Excess of Expend.
1821	459,699	481,854	—	22,155
1824	387,259	441,592	—	54,333
1827	264,735	411,648	—	146,913
1830	403,475	347,029	56,446	—
1833	437,555	331,764	105,791	—
1836	406,787	352,986	53,801	—
1839	369,084	383,592	—	14,508
1842	322,369	327,103	—	4,734

Several sources of income are increasing at a rapid rate; but as the improvement of the country demands an increased expenditure, it is probable the utmost the Colonial Government can do for a series of years yet to come will be to make the revenue equal it; and if that be accomplished, Ceylon will be the only colony of England which entails no expense on its parent.

The ecclesiastical establishment of the island bears a great disproportion to its size and importance. For the instruction of nearly a million and a half of subjects, there are maintained by Government, one archdeacon, nine European colonial chaplains *, two Singhalese and one Malabar, *i. e.* an average of about 100,000 souls for the cure of a single clergyman! The whole of the ecclesiastical expenditure of 1842 amounted to £.7734, the judicial to nearly £.50,000. Fortunately, however, where Government is remiss, patriotism and piety step in to supply the deficiency. The Gospel Propagation Society maintains three missions. The Church Missionary So-

* Six of the Established Church, one of the Scotch Church, and one of the Dutch Reformed Church.

ciety maintains four stations and eleven missionaries. The Wesleyan Society has nineteen missionaries and assistants, the assistants being likewise styled "Reverend." To the honour of this society we must mention, that two useful monthly publications issue from its press, the Friend, and the Lanka Nidhāna, (the Treasure of Ceylon,) the latter in Singhalese. The Baptist Mission maintains three clergymen and sixteen assistants, and from its press issues a monthly work in English and Singhalese. The American Ceylon Mission has eleven missionaries and three assistants. It also maintains two boarding schools, and sends forth a bi-monthly paper in English and Tamil (Malabar.) The Roman Catholic Church maintains twenty-two missionaries, a vicar-general, and a bishop.

With regard to education much has been done, and much remains to do. Fifty schools, containing 2300 scholars, are maintained by Government, of which the Colombo academy is the most important, and will probably be chartered as a college at some future period. The Church Mission maintains ninety-eight schools, containing about 3000 scholars, and the other religious bodies in proportion. An improved system of scholastic superintendence, and a regular educational plan, are greatly wanting throughout the entire island; and until these are provided, its education must continue imperfect.

In a commercial point of view Ceylon is rapidly improving. In 1831, the value of the exports from the island to Great Britain was £.60,000, to other parts of the world £.92,000. During the same year the value of imports from Great Britain was £.28,500, and from other places £.354,000. Ten years afterwards, in 1841, the exports to Great Britain equalled £.247,000, to other parts of the world, £.97,000, whilst the imports from Great Britain had increased to £.162,000, and from elsewhere to £.401,000. In 1842, the rate of increase was nearly doubled, the following being the returns.

EXPORTS.

To Great Britain, £.327,000, elsewhere, £.94,000.

IMPORTS.

From Great Britain, £.204,000, elsewhere, £.417,000.

The increase in the value of the exports is chiefly caused by the quantities of coffee now produced in the island, almost the whole of which finds a profitable market in the mother country. New estates are, however, continually being commenced, and there can be little doubt that in ten years more the exports will have doubled their present value, and sugar will have become nearly as important an item as cinnamon, coffee, and cocoa nut oil.

Perhaps no country in the world is better adapted for the growth of coffee, and the sugar cane, than the interior and maritime provinces of Ceylon; and the rapidity with which the mountainous districts are coming into cultivation attests that its advantages are not being overlooked. The civil servants of the colony, and those otherwise connected with the island, are at present the most extensive planters, and the returns of the lands sold for a few past years will exhibit the increased desire for embarking in so profitable a speculation. In 1835, the total number of acres sold by Government was 146.

In 1834,	337	acres	sold for nearly £.150,000.
1835,	434	do.	
1836,	3,919	do.	
1837,	3,661	do.	
1838,	10,401	do.	
1839,	9,570	do.	
1840,	30,788	do.	
1841,	78,685	do.	
1842,	48,533	do.	

The rapidly increasing extent of these sales for each successive year may exemplify the rapid improvement of the colony, and the development of its capabilities.

An agricultural society has been formed, which has already been of infinite service to the island, and has introduced almost all the European vegetables into the elevated districts of Ceylon, where the potato and other culinary vegetables flourish almost as luxuriantly as the cocoanut and the plaintain in the valleys beneath.

The improvement which we have just seen exemplified, was ably promoted by the energetic and masterly administration of Sir Edward Barnes. Under his able government, the great road from Colombo to Candy was planned and accomplished, a work which did more to impress the natives with an awe of English ability, than all the bloodshed of preceding governments. The Right Honourable Stewart Mackenzie was as valuable in an intellectual, as Sir Edward Barnes had been in a more material point of view, and the schemes which he planned, for the improvement of the country, (so far as he had time to carry them out,) were important and valuable. Ceylon has now done (we trust for ever,) with war and bloodshed; she requires, then, not the stern rod of military sway, but the gentle, fostering care of a mild government. England would do well to remember a lesson taught her by one of her profoundest poets *, that

> "It is not in the battle-field we train,
> The Governor who must be mild and good,
> And temper with the wisdom of the brain,
> Thoughts motherly and kind as woman-hood."

The following lively description by a friend of a trip into the interior, may afford the reader a better idea of the actual state of the country than any prosaic statements of ours.

COLOMBO TO CANDY.

Having resolved on a trip to Nuwera Ellia †, four of us engaged the Commercial Coach a fortnight before hand, and, on the morning appointed for our drive to Candy, met in Bailly Street, at five o'clock. It was a drizzling rainy morning, such an one as seldom troubles the climate of Ceylon. However, the anticipations of a pleasant journey kept our spirits wonderfully up, and shortly after the morning gun had boomed out its solitary warning we were

* Wordsworth.

† An elevated plain in the south-eastern district of the central province, which enjoys a delightfully cool temperature.

comfortably seated in the coach, and wending our way, with two not overfed horses, through the eastern gate of the fort. The frequent drawbridges and the frowning of the cannon on the rampart above would almost lead one to imagine that they were on the banks of the Rhine, and that the rugged wall before them was the outside of some ancient German castle. The fort and its adjuncts passed, a general running over the various articles of our luggage commenced, and, when it was too late to correct our mistake, we found that our cases of guns had been left behind, and that a few packages of salmon, just arrived from England, had remained to keep them company, the blue bag, the black box, the brown valise, the hams, the cheeses and hat-cases were all right however, and if we had to eat a dinner in the jungle without the orthodox allowance of salmon, why there was nothing for it but contentment. Then commenced all the old jokes which from time immemorial accompany the first ten miles of the road, such as the Highlander's vociferous applause of the little wheel for outdoing the larger one, the counting out of the journey and so forth; and by the time these were concluded, light had again dawned, and in a few minutes the sun peeped out in clouded splendour, (the only splendour one wishes to see in Ceylon,) clearing away the drizzling rain, and enabling us to look about us.

For twenty miles the dreadfully monotonous character of the scenery, so common on the sea-shore, continued, and but for the terraces of the rice (or paddy) fields, there would have been little to interest me. Of these I had a very different idea from what the reality presented. There was nothing of that regular ascent, step by step, which I had fancied. On the contrary, much irregularity prevailed throughout each field as to the elevations and depressions. A small spot raised in the middle was the general character, round which a platform of less height extended, and so on, each level space nearly full of water, and separated from that beneath by low mud walls, through which an aperture allowed the water to descend to the inferior ones. The appearance of the growing rice was beautifully fresh and green, somewhat similar to that of young wheat, with thinner stalks.

As we proceeded, the cocoa-nut trees gradually disappeared, and were succeeded by a great abundance of areka nut and suria trees, the former similar to the cocoa-nut, but more slender and straight, the latter like the English elm, save that it bears a yellow flower.

The costume of the natives and coloured people was now beginning to assume a more decided character, without that extraordinary variety so common in the fort. Parsees were now not to be seen at all; Malabars with their characteristic turban but seldom; the Moors not so common as before; and the elegant comb, petticoats and moustaches of the Singhalese gentry gradually giving way to a simple handkerchief tied round the head, and a much shorter allowance of gown. The priests with their yellow robes and shaven crowns became more numerous, and the umbrella was gradually giving place to the simpler tallipot leaf, as a defence against the sun.

At length we entered upon the region of hills and coffee, a change to me exceedingly agreeable. We passed several huge masses of rock which appeared on the sides of some of the hills, which, had they been in Derbyshire, would certainly have obtained, (in addition to their "local habitation,") "a name" in every "tour," or "sketch," or " ramble," or " wandering" in that celebrated country. But perhaps the time is not very far distant, when " Tours in Ceylon," " Trips to the interior," and " Journeys through the mountainous districts" will be as common and plentiful as Welch " Guide Books," and Derbyshire " Sketches."

The luxuriance of vegetation alone distinguishes the mountain scenery of Ceylon from that of Europe. Every portion of the surface is covered, and the rocks, unless excessively large, are generally hidden by mosses and creepers.

About thirty-six miles from Colombo, we arrived at a rest house, half way between the two termini, where, at half-past ten o'clock, we sat down to an excellent breakfast. The building (called Ambapusse rest-house,) is a somewhat elegant structure, and is situated in a valley formed by a semicircular amphitheatre of hills. Perhaps there is no scene so common in the elevated districts of Ceylon, as that of a number of hills, forming a kind of basin in the midst, and which would doubtless have been the site of elegant and picturesque lakes had they existed farther north. In fact the great desideratum in the views of the interior is the apparent want of water,—I say apparent, because there are rills and rivers rushing along in almost every direction, but so overhung with the superabundant vegetation as to be frequently imperceptible. This want of lakes and ponds gives a kind of sameness and monotony to the views which they would be otherwise far from possessing, and which would be tiresome and uninteresting in a country clothed with less sublimity than Ceylon.

Having breakfasted at Ambapusse, we proceeded on

our way with loaded stomachs and lightened hearts. Between that place and Attumankandy, a distance of eighteen miles, there are some very fine and richly varied scenes chiefly of the cultivated kind, which might bring back to one's recollection the luxuriance of Buckinghamshire, or the level pasturages of Leicester. One can only be said to reach the zone of mountains after passing the latter place; and, perhaps, the world might be searched in vain for a scene of greater sublimity than that to be viewed from the summit of the Kadduganawa pass.

The first view of the stupendous mountains, which seemed to debar farther progress, brought back curious reminiscences to my mind. I thought of all the hills and mountains I had seen in England, Ireland, Scotland and Wales, of my situation then and now, and of my far-distant home, until I became pleasingly melancholy. I shall not trouble you with my reflections, but proceed to notice what I saw. We were at the foot of an exceedingly lofty and enormous chain of mountains, which had long formed the boundary of his Candian Majesty's dominions, and which had for three hundred years resisted the arms of the Portuguese, the Dutch, and the English. On either side appeared successive and extended fields of rice ended by jungle and rocks, whilst behind was seen the regular and level country we had left, stretching far into the distance with gentle undulations.

That it was not impossible, however tedious it might be, to proceed, soon became apparent. We were gradually winding up the side of the mountain, but at an exceedingly slow rate. Fissure after fissure, and ravine after ravine were wound round and passed, affording the most delightful variety and succession of views. At one time, the mountain rose perpendicularly on our left, whilst it descended as perpendicularly on our right. At another a roaring torrent appeared directly over our heads, as though ready to sweep us and our frail machine into the abyss beneath. Now, not a foot of earth was to be seen but that on which we stood; whilst, on turning an angle of the road, a wide-spread view was, perhaps, afforded of the country around. Fearful chasms, frightful abysses, thundering torrents, and hanging rocks succeeded each other with interesting rapidity, whilst the delightful *fraicheur* of the air as we ascended afforded the most pleasing sensations. A well-proportioned column surmounts the pass, erected in honour of the architect of the road; and beyond this the succeeding ten miles which lead the traveller to Candy are comparatively uninteresting, save for the wide-spanning bridge at Paradenia, which crosses the Mahavelli-ganga, and which is almost entirely composed of satin wood.

DESCRIPTION OF CANDY.

Such is the difference between Colombo and Candy, that one might almost fancy himself transported into a different country, when visiting the latter for the first time, after residing in the former. Like most other Eastern capitals, it is situated in a small valley surrounded by rather lofty mountains. From the great number of trees about and in it, it is almost impossible to obtain a full view of the city. These trees, however, when viewed from the adjacent hills, and combined with the artificial lake in the vicinity, form an exceedingly picturesque and highly interesting feature in the landscape. The lake is encircled by a winding road, which, running at the foot of the surrounding hills, forms a delightful promenade for the British residents. In its centre is built an isolated house, rising as it were from the water that encircles it, and giving quite a romantic appearance to the views. This house was formerly the bathing place of the king of Candy's seraglio: it is now under John Bull a—powder magazine! —fit emblem of the luxury of Asiatics, and the iron stubbornness of the nations of the north. Nevertheless, we may be allowed to sigh over the change, and we may reasonably doubt whether the sum of universal happiness is increased by the transmigration.

To what base uses may we come at last, Horatio!

A long and wide street, which forms the central part of the town, gives a stranger precisely the idea he must have formed from the descriptions with which one continually meets of an Oriental town. The small open shops which line each side, tenanted by three or four owners patiently seated awaiting their customers, and enjoying the usual luxury of chewing betel, is even in itself interesting, from its total dissimilarity to anything European; whilst the plantains hanging around, the chillies, rice, pepper, cardamoms and cinnamon exposed for sale on wicker trays, heighten the unique character of the scene. Such is the mid-day appearance; but view it in the morning or evening, and you perceive the street literally crowded with companies of dusky chatterers in every variety of eastern and western * costume, and speaking every variety of Oriental

* The Portuguese and Dutch descendants (mixed with native blood) retain the European dress, and may always be distinguished by the absurd English hat, in every stage of dilapidation.

tongues. Here a group of turbaned Malabars, clothed in their simple ankrika, hold discourse in their native and noble language. There the fierce Malay, with military cap, and accompanied by his really handsome spouse, jabbers in his own rythmic tongue. On this side, the active Portuguese descendant, with hat of miserable brown, discourses lovingly to his mate in Indo-Lusitanian. On that, the able-bodied Candian, with simple kerchief on his head, holds forth in drawling Singhalese, to his jacketed and camboyed * companion. It is a veritable Babel, and he may well be excused who cries out in the midst of it—"Is this the plain of Shinar ?" Of these various classes, the most interesting are unquestionably the females of the Mahommedans. These glide through the streets enveloped, like the tenants of the tomb, in a mass of beautiful drapery, which frequently forms the most elegant combinations. This drapery, being almost invariably white, and often of spotless purity, looks exceedingly picturesque, especially from behind. Often have I wandered, in romantic mood, behind some gliding demoiselle, thus proceeding through the streets, forming the most enchanting visions of the face that appertained to so fair a mass of drapery, until the unlooked-for turning round of the enchanting fair one has dissipated the vision, and left me to saunter on trying to recall to my mind all the wise saws formerly heard about bootless visions, fair outsides, rotten nuts, and so forth. Imagine an English fair with all the clowns and clownesses in masquerade, and you may have some idea of a Candian evening.

* The cloth wrapped round the waist and legs of the Ceylonese is called a camboy.

The most interesting building in the town, to a stranger, is the great temple, containing the tooth-relic of Buddhu, and forming what was once part of the establishment of the king of Candy. The immediate receptacle of this precious deposit is a small temple situated within the other, and approached by a noble flight of steps, lofty arches and imposing colonnades. These are in many places decorated with excellent carving, wrought with surprising skill into the hardest granite, and generally representing processions, in which the elephant forms the most important figure. The small temple, containing the relic, is decorated on all sides with paintings and carvings, whilst the doors and their brazen bars are of the most massive character. The tooth itself is inclosed in six cases gradually increasing in size, of which the outer and larger one is five feet in height, of a conical shape, formed of silver gilt, but all the others are of beaten gold. These cases, with their precious deposit, are placed on a silver table, richly adorned with tapestry and brocade. The tooth itself is of the shape of the extreme end of the elephant's tusk, slightly curved, formed of ivory, and encircled by a golden string. This forms the great object of Buddhistic worship, and is, in the estimation of the votaries of that religion, the most precious thing in the world.

The ruins of the palace are too inconsiderable to merit a particular description. They are chiefly remarkable from the massive and substantial appearance of the walls, and from the excellent carvings visible in various places. By the side of the lake, runs from the palace a beautiful little trellised wall, perforated by holes of all shapes and sizes, and forming a most interesting object from the neighbouring hills. It is gradually crumbling away, however, and John Bull sees no use in the ornamental holes, so that probably ere long, it will be replaced by some structure of brick or stone, permanent as ponderous, and ponderous as ugly.

The tombs of the kings of Candy now afford scarcely any thing worth the trouble of looking at. The hand of rapine has been busy, the carvings and sculptures have been removed, and but a few shapeless stones attest the burial place of the "lion kings."

CANDY TO NUWERA ELLIA.

In proceeding from Candy to Nuwera Ellia, the traveller must retrace his steps to the bridge at Paradenia; thence the road starts off to the hilly district, rendered famous by the legends of Rama, Seeva and Rawana, the Menelaus, Helen and Paris of Indian story. Three rest-houses or inns are very conveniently stationed between the two extremes of the road, a distance of forty-eight miles. The first of these, Gampola, twelve miles from Candy, is a place of considerable resort by the planters and superintendents of the various estates, the latter, for the most part, a moustached and white-coated race, comically combining the attendants of eastern luxury with the simplicity of English agricultural life. Here every reasonable luxury can be procured, and the traveller, in the midst of Ceylon, may stretch his limbs on a couch and call for a bottle of Edinburgh ale or London porter, as may suit his taste or caprice.

Here, with two companions, I enjoyed a substantial and excellent breakfast, a luxury which repays one for all the fatigue of travelling, even without the agreeable additions of views, adventures and variety.

From Gampola to the next station (Paradenia) the road is not wholly uninteresting, but the chief variety of the scenery arises principally from a lamentable devastation, caused by coffee and its cultivators. In all directions, and on all sides, trees of magnificent size and appearance lie strewn around in miserable plight, there left to rot upon the ground. Amongst these a litle green laurel bush rises in all directions, and that bush is coffee. In the eyes of the planter, I have no doubt, the scene will be reviving and pleasant in the extreme, but in those of the hunter after the picturesque, it is desolate and mournful. The rest-house at Paradenia, although very far inferior to that at Gampola, will yet afford a shelter from the sun, and a bottle of English beer, two of the greatest comforts of Anglo-Ceylonese life. From this station to Rambodde, the next rest-house, the road winds along the side of a hill which forms one side of an extensive valley, ended by the hill of Rambodde. Here we remained for the night, intending to perform the ascent of the mountain and the remainder of the journey early on the ensuing morning. The delightful coolness of the atmosphere first attracted our attention, and, for the first time in Ceylon, I enjoyed and relished a blanket on my bed. Next morning we stept forth to view the splendid waterfall adjoining the rest-house, which, glittering, as it was, in the rays of the newly risen sun, appeared as a dashing line of burnished gold. The mountain, at the base of which we stood, was next to be ascended, and this we accomplished by an exceedingly zig-zag road, running like a strung series of Z's up the side of the hill. The air was every moment becoming more refreshing and invigorating, and, on the summit of the mountain, seven degrees from the equator, we enjoyed a temperature delightfully cool, and exceedingly pleasant to those who have been broiling at Colombo for months or years. Here one of the grandest views that I have ever beheld, expands before the traveller, one unequalled, perhaps, in the British islands, save by that from the summit of Snowdon. The wide spread valley beneath, losing itself in gently undulating ground, together with the towering hills which form the sides, resembles some vast amphitheatre hollowed out by a gigantic race. The remainder of the journey was frequently diversified by extensive and magnificent prospects, of which I shall not attempt to give a description; and at length the wide spread plain of Nuwera Ellia was before us, a desert looking district, but diversified with chimnies. Yes! strange though it be, chimnies are one of the most refreshing sights that an Anglo-Ceylonese resident can see in the luxuriant and beautiful Lanka. They recall Old England, and its village hamlets, to our minds, and with these, a host of associations as pleasing as they are old. Nuwera Ellia is a delightful place for a month's residence: here you can walk all day in defiance of the sun, and here too may you see the ghost of ice * in a thin frost, which occassionally covers the grass in the mornings.

* Ice half an inch thick is sometimes obtained here, and the thermometer has been seen during day-light as low as 28° F.

NOTES OF AN EXCURSION TO THE SUMMIT OF ADAM'S PEAK.

I.

The foot impression upon the summit of Adam's Peak has probably had a longer period of reputed sanctity and worship, than any other object of reverence in the East. To the followers of Buddhu and of Mahomet it is equally the centre of attraction, as the monument of the life and existence of an extraordinary man. The former assert that on one of Buddhu's visits to the island, he left that impression as an evidence of his power, and an object of worship for his followers. The latter, that Adam after spending his paradisaical happiness in Ceylon, endured there his penance likewise, subsequently to his fall, by standing on the summit of the Peak on one foot, for a long series of years, and that hence arose the impression. But were there even no traditions of the sort to hallow the mountain, its extreme height, its peculiar shape, and the distance to which it can be seen at sea, would alone render it worthy of attention to all who visit the island. From my first landing I had always a great desire to visit its summit, and to view with my own eyes the holy place which has thrown around it so great an air of sanctity and mystery. To attain that summit, however, is by no means an easy task, and but comparatively few, even of the enterprising Europeans in the island, have succeeded in reaching it. Once balked by floods and accidents in the enterprise, I had determined on accomplishing it the next time, and set out, therefore, with a resolution to be defeated by no dangers, and to be disconcerted by no accidents. The shortest road from Colombo lies from Bolgodde, a village situated at the extremity of the Morottoe lake, through Horona and Nambapanna to Ratnapoora, the usual starting point for the numerous pilgrims who annually swarm to the mountain in the months of January, February and March.

The village of Morottoe, whence the lake takes its name, and whence we started by boat for Bolgodde, lies about eleven miles from Colombo on the road to Galle. Here we determined to embark at four o'clock in the morning, so as to reach Bolgodde before the heat of the day would prevent our advancing to Horona the same morning. The boat consisted of two canoes about five feet apart, connected by a small platform of split bamboos on which we might sit, or lie, or stand, as suited our convenience or our taste. The water was without a ripple on its surface when we commenced our voyage. A full bright moon afforded us abundance of light, whilst a cloudless sky, thickly studded with stars, appeared above and below us, the former in reality, the latter by reflection in the water. It was altogether a curious and a beautiful sight. The swarthy natives, seated at the corners of our equipage, impelled the boat almost noiselessly along with considerable rapidity, our coolies were stretched upon the bamboos asleep, our portmanteaus were beside them, whilst we, stretched upon the scanty deck, lay upon our sides, supported our heads upon our hands, and calculated the dangers and the difficulties of the expedition. The shores all around as we advanced were level as a plain save towards the east, and the thick foliage of cocoa-nut trees appeared almost to lose itself in the water. Towards the east a solitary hill was visible, on which a picturesque Buddhist temple, with its spired dagobāh, glistened in the moon, whilst the repose around us seemed to invite us to that state of torpid abstraction from terrestrial desires, so eloquently inculcated by the prophet of Maghada.

At length the dawn of day gradually extended over the eastern sky, or as Byron beautifully describes it, "morn on the mountains, like a summer bird, expands her purple wings."

Gradually the outline of the range of hills, of which Adam's Peak forms the centre, became distinct, and the extraordinary cone of the summit soon appeared boldly outlined upon a back-ground of the richest golden hue. As we took a turn in the lake, however, we lost the mountains again, and the sun appeared to issue from the centre of an immense level plain. Four distinct lines of light shot through the heaven from the centre point whence we might expect the sun, and these four faithfully reflected in the water, formed a beautiful wheel of fire, such as I had never seen anything resembling before. However, the sun rose, and would have quickly dissipated all our pleasure as we stood unshaded on our little bark, had it not been for some friendly clouds which obscured his beams. We had now had quite sufficient of the lake, and were looking anxiously out for the landing place, when the friendly clouds disappeared and the sun shot forth rays upon us that made us almost forget all the pleasure he had afforded us in rising, in the anxiety we felt to gain a shade once more. However, our patience was not long tested, and about half-past eight we stepped from our frail machine upon terra firma, with a good appetite for breakfast, and a walk of six miles before us to render it sharper. This we soon accomplished, the road winding through paddy fields and some wooded districts to an ugly temple, opposite which, in modest simplicity, rose the humble rest-house.

On procuring the owner we entered with the resolution of men determined to enjoy themselves. The very click of the lock, as we stood in the verandah before the opening of the door, sounded pleasantly in our ears, but imagine our ruminations when, on entering, we perceived not a single article of furniture in the room into which we were first introduced. The second, however, was better. There were a sofa with bamboo bottom, which appeared to be neither of the newest shape nor of the strongest character, a chair with bottom to match, and another without that necessary appendage at all, together with a table beautifully balanced upon three legs. This was luxury. One stretched himself upon the sofa, which, after a little premonitory creaking, gave way in the middle, while the other throwing himself upon the chair, attempted to rest his legs upon the table. This duty that venerable piece of furniture disdained and came down accordingly.

The breakfast, however, we resolved should make up for the furniture, so we commenced a catalogue of those things, which, from time immemorial, have formed the staple of a substantial first meal; beef there was none, but he was sure of eggs, and egg-curry is not to be despised; he thought it possible a fowl might be procured; unfortunately their tea was all out, but coffee was to be had in abundance. "Ah, very well," said we in a breath, "now then, quick and let us have a bottle of beer in the mean-time."—"All done, Sir," was the reply. "Yes, but you have water, and that will do," we answered, anxious not to create a bad impression at first. Water he had, and in due time it was forthcoming, with coffee and rice and curry afterwards. The former without milk or sugar, the latter without spoons. "What! no spoons and no fowls," said we, "No spoons, Sir," said the host, "but I have two ladles." "Ah, those will do admirably well," said we, with the resignation of martyrs,—another pause and the ladles were forthcoming, they being two cocoa-nut shells with handles introduced; and with these (every spoonfull being considerably more than a breakfast cup-full) we went admirably through our savoury dish, preferring the cocoa-nuts at every disadvantage to our hands. The good host was assiduous in his attentions, and was evidently delighted at being able to render two such fastidious individuals perfectly satisfied.

II.

From Horona to the sugar estate, at which we passed the night, was but a distance of six miles, and this we easily accomplished the same evening. Next morning early we set off for Nambapanne, a distance of seven miles, on one of the worst roads ever trodden. The water was frequently up to our knees; the bridges across the streams were almost invariably a single tree, with a slight bamboo hand-rail, and often of considerable breadth; they were such as I have often seen represented in the various accounts of travels in America, and at which I have often shuddered. At Nambapanne there was a repetition of the scene at Horona, with the slightest shade of greater comfort; and on leaving it for Ratnapoora, we found the road to be yet passed if anything worse than that we had accomplished in the morning. One of the bridges, I distinctly remember, over a large branch of the Kallu-ganga. It consisted of four horizontal beams, supported at convenient distances in the stream by perpendicular ones of considerable height. These were stretched in a direction, not across the river, but in a line with the stream; from the bank on which we were standing, to the first of these, an unplaned, rough tree, divested of its branches, was placed so as to meet another supported by that beam and the next. In this manner five distinct divisions were formed into a single bridge by five distinct trees, and at each side a loose chain waved to and fro as a support for the hand. Across this, we luckless travellers, had to pass; the slightest lean to either side, nay, the slightest breath of wind, would have inevitably precipitated us into the stream rolling at a great distance beneath us. Tree after tree was to be passed; the chain at either side yielded to the slightest pressure; there was nothing to save us but the preservation of the nicest balance. However, we crossed, and, at length, weary, tired and wet, we arrived at Ratnapoora, where a much better table awaited us than any we had enjoyed since our departure from Colombo. Ratnapoora, the capital of the Saffragam district, is a fine populous village, surmounted by a fort, and containing a great proportion of coloured inhabitants of European descent. It is situated on the Kallu-ganga, about sixty miles from its mouth; and from the establishment of a district court, and from being the residence of an agent of Government, is gradually rising into consequence. It is situated in a narrow irregular valley, surrounded by mountains, in some cases of considerable elevation. The fort, which was erected in 1816, is at present ungarrisoned, and is used as the seat of the district court, whilst one of its rooms is occasionally converted into a church. From Ratnapoora to the summit of the Peak is a distance of about twenty-four miles, divided about half way by the village and rest-house of Palabatula, the last seat of civilisation which one finds before penetrating into the wild district immediately surrounding the holy mountain, a district of which elephants, cheetahs and monkeys are the sole inhabitants.

Having stopped some time at Ratnapoora to recruit ourselves before proceeding to the more difficult part of our expedition, we at length set forth one fine evening about 3 o'clock, hoping to push on to Palabatula before it became too dark to proceed. The road at first led us along the base of a rather steep hill, along the side of which, a better one had been constructed for the convenience of Prince Waldemar of Prussia on his ascent to the Peak. It was scarcely finished, and probably (as the Prince has gone) it may remain in its present condition for a long time to come. How fortunate would it be for Ceylon if princes were more abundant, even though they were but German! We had gone over about four miles of this road, when we found ourselves on the banks of the Kallu-ganga, even here a wide and rapid stream. How we were to get over was a mystery; for boat there appeared to be none, and the ford (if ford it were, for we could not decide that it was one) was any thing but tempting.

We therefore sat ourselves quietly down awaiting our guide and coolies, that we might see how they would force a passage. In due time they came, and walking boldly into the river, proceeded to fight their way across. We watched the road they took, and were getting quite reconciled to the passage from the shallowness of the water for some time after they had entered, when we at length perceived them stemming the current with considerable difficulty, being in about three feet deep of water. This looked any thing but tempting—for a few moments we saw our pioneers standing irresolute; for the current was really so strong, that it was with considerable difficulty they kept their feet. A bold push, however, was attempted, and they succeeded. It was now our turn to force a passage, and not being much of a swimmer, I contemplated an upset in the stream with any thing but complacency. I looked at the length of my legs, however, and felt re-assured; so, rushing in, I was quickly struggling in the place the coolies had so lately left. I felt that a single instant of irresolution would ruin me; and although thoroughly alarmed at the risk I ran of being carried down, I made a determined push for the shore, and succeeded in gaining it. My companion was equally fortunate, and it was with considerable satisfaction that we found ourselves all safely landed on the other side—drenched of course, but in no other way the worse. The force of the current may be conceived from the fact, that we found it utterly impossible to keep our sticks planted on the bottom as we advanced, and could, in consequence derive from them no assistance.

We were again upon the road, when a few premonitory drops of rain warned us of another approaching wetting from above, that we might be kept *in equilibrio*. The scattered drops, few and far between, were not long in becoming thick and heavy, so that, as we advanced to Ginnemalle, the next station, 7 miles from Ratnapoora, we found it would be necessary to put up there for the night. The rest-house, however, was completely dismantled of its roof, so that, notwithstanding our anticipations of a change of clothes and a dry earthen couch to sleep upon, we were obliged to hold a council in the open air, to decide on our future proceedings. A little inquiry taught us that the best plan we could adopt was to pay a visit to the head man of the place, (a Mohandiram,) and beg for ourselves and followers a resting place for the night. At a short distance from the road we found the great man himself, enjoying a cigar in his verandah, and on making known our wants, very generously received from him possession of the place he then occupied, (the verandah,) whilst he retreated into the house, and there shut himself up. This act of politeness and generosity quite overcame our feelings; and as we pulled off our sodden pith hats, many a drop coursed down our cheeks. A verandah, I can assure the reader, is not a bad place to spend a rainy night in, when there is nothing better to be obtained; so, changing our clothes, and squatting ourselves upon the ground, we looked forth into the sky to bless some star for our good fortune, and then looked at the fire our attendants had just kindled, to see if the coffee, and the fried bacon and eggs were yet ready. In due time these agreeable restaurateurs were fully discussed, and we at length composed ourselves to sleep on as black and uncomfortable a looking night as ever clouded the weather-beaten face of nature.

III.

At day-light we were pursuing our tract again in single file to the Ginnemalle river, a considerable stream, over which we were anticipating as pleasant a passage as that we had effected the preceding evening over the Kallu-ganga. A boat, however, was found to be procurable, with which we made good our transit, and soon found ourselves entering upon the country of leeches and red legs. These troublesome and disgusting vermin are exceedingly numerous about the Muskallawa river, and for about two miles on the other side. On crossing this stream, (which is about a mile and half from the last mentioned,) we found our feet and legs streaming with blood, and being unfortunately unprovided with gaiters, we were obliged to continue in that agreeable condition for about two miles further. However, Palabatula, our resting place, six miles from Ginnemalle, was at length gained, our feet were once more bloodless, our wet clothes once more removed, and breakfast of rice and curry, with coffee, once more enjoyed. The walk from Ginnemalle to Palabatula is by no means an easy one, although much inferior in difficulty and steepness, to that immediately succeeding. We were rather tired when we reached it, indeed I should say very much so under ordinary circumstances, but with the vivid recollection of the succeeding part of the road impressed upon my mind, I must say but partially. Here I was obliged to part from L—, the swelling of his feet, and the badness of his shoes, preventing him from proceeding. This was exceedingly distressing; for I had the remainder, and by far the most difficult part of the journey to undertake alone, meaning by that term, without any one with whom I could carry on a free conversation, or whose remarks might serve to beguile the road. However, there was nothing for it but perseverance; so *putting a stout heart to a stey brae*, I set forth in the afternoon with the coolies and our guide for Deabetme, the next station, about six miles distant. This part of the road is by far the most difficult and precipitous; in fact, much more so considering the extent, than any thing I could have supposed possible. I had ascended Ben Lomond and Snowdon, the latter after a hard day's walk, which I considered no ordinary achievement; but anything like the ascent from Palabatula to Deabetme I had never before dreamt of. It was a constant succession of the most precipitous hills to be climbed, one after the other, with wearisome uniformity and unvarying difficulty, but description can give no idea of the resolution and exertion required—it must be seen and experienced to be appreciated.

St Pierre might have taken it, instead of the "black mountain of Bember," as an illustration of misfortune. The following is the simile to which I refer.—"Le malheur ressemble à la montange noir de Bember, aux extremités du royaume brûlant de Lahor; tant que vous la montez, vous ne voyez devant vous que de stériles rochers; mais, quand vous êtes au sommet, vous appercevez le ciel sur votre tête, et le royaume de Cachemire á vos pieds." The ascent to Deabetme cannot be much less difficult than that of Bember; and neither the sky nor the plains of Ceylon will suffer, I imagine, in a comparison with those of Cachmire. Two resting places are to be met with during the ascent, at one of which, called Neelee Hella, a magnificent echo may be awakened.

The Amblem at Deabetme is a large uncomfortable tiled building, having two rooms surrounded by a kind of walled verandah of peculiarly forbidding aspect. The interior of it, as may be easily imagined, is a damp close uncomfortable cell, the floor being of earth, and so thoroughly saturated with the heavy dews of the district, that the guide informed me it was never known to be dry. The Amblem stands in the corner of a small plain, cleared of its brushwood for a short distance round the building. Immediately opposite, rises the magnificent cone of the Peak surmounted by its tiny temple, which now for the first time becomes visible. The temperature of the place was so refreshing, that I felt comparatively little fatigued by my previous exertion, whilst the poor coolies who accompanied me, sat upon the damp cold earth the very picture of misery and chilliness. Two of the number were busily engaged in endeavours to obtain a spark from the flint and steel, in which however, they did not succeed; and seeming utterly unconscious of any other way of warming themselves, they huddled together in a corner and lay down to sleep. Having dined upon a little bread and cold bacon, which we had fortunately brought with us, washed down with libations from the brandy flask, I wrapped my blanket round me, and endeavoured to compose myself to rest upon the bamboo platform, supported by four rugged sticks, that served me for chair, table, couch and sideboard. This was a vain attempt however; for what with the noise of elephants, cheetahs, monkeys, jungle cats, jungle fowls and crows, it was utterly impossible even to dose, besides the pleasant expectation of having some of the former as visitants (for our mud edifice was without doors) during the long dark night that was approaching. I lay with my walking stick in my hand during that tedious night, listening hour after hour to the roar of the elephants, and the screams of the cheetahs, which were often to all appearance, within a very short distance of the house. However, " it is a long lane that has no turning," and a still longer night that has no end,—morning dawned at last, and the mists which had encircled the mountain on which I stood, the whole of the preceding evening, like a vast sea of quiet foam, gradually wore away, and a magnificent view rewarded us for the tedium of the preceding night. To the south and west was a long succession of irregular hills, terminated by an extended plain, which appeared fading off in the distance till terminated by the sea, whilst in the north a high range of hills abruptly ended the prospect. Having breakfasted, as I had dined on the preceding evening, I once more set off on my pilgrimage, with the pleasant prospect before me, of being obliged to eat raw fowls and rice before returning to Palabatula, as a fire seemed a luxury unattainable.

A descent for a short distance brought us to a brawling stream, over which we passed by leaping from rock to rock, as they lay in irregular groups interrupting the current of the water, and soon after we arrived at the immense mass of almost perpendicular rock, which goes by the name of Durmah Rajah Kande, in which steps have been cut to facilitate the ascent. These steps are in number about one hundred and forty, and about half way up is to be seen the figure of a man roughly outlined on the rock. At this place the guide informed us that the king, whose name it bears, had died whilst on a pilgrimage to the sacred footsteps.

IV.

From Durmah Rajah Kande, a short uneven road leads to another stream of somewhat larger dimensions, flowing beautifully over an immense sheet of granite, which seems as if purposely constructed for the transit of the water. This passed, we entered upon an ascending ravine, the road through which is certainly much less occupied as a pathway than as the bed of a stream. Several immense rocks lie scattered over the country in the succeeding part of the journey, but there is nothing that particularly strikes the attention till we arrive at Andea Malla Tenna, a small plain and amblem immediately at the base of the cone, and whence a magnificent view is obtained of that extraordinary pile. The small temple on the summit may be seen from this position to great advantage, whilst below it, appears the narrow pillar of nature's workmanship covered with rocks and foliage, on which it stands. Looking at the Peak from this station, there appears nothing wonderful in its being esteemed sacred; certainly if there is a convenient spot on earth for ascending to the upper regions, (were such places required) Adam's Peak is that spot. Tapering as it does, to so fine a point, and lofty as it is, it seems precisely the position that one would choose for such a purpose. A short rest on this flat made me feel the difference in temperature more than I had hitherto experienced, and I was soon glad to renew my toil, (for I was still lightly clad,) to keep myself sufficiently warm. We were soon climbing as usual up the bed of a mountain torrent, until, at length, we reached the first of a series of iron ladders, supported by cramp irons in the rock, and placed, not perpendicularly, but in a slanting direction, apparently to diminish the danger by this position, but in reality increasing it. The constant dependence upon the left hand, in mounting these, is anything but agreeable, whilst a glance at the precipice below, is sufficient to prove, *to the most superficial observer*, that he had better mind what he is about. After these, a perpendicular rock was to be scaled by means of two chains, (one at each side,) and which, though a work of considerable difficulty, is by no means so dangerous as the ladder ascent. Next there was an ugly corner to turn, and a few steps conducted me to an entrance in a wall, on going through which, I found myself upon the summit of the Peak. I need scarcely say, that I felt a considerable elevation of spirits at finding myself upon the sacred precincts of the top; and as I turned round to view the ascent I had just accomplished, I considered the satisfaction I felt at my success quite sufficient reward for the difficulties of the road. However as it will not do to say briefly I came down again, I must endeavour to give some description of the *choses à voir* there. The summit is surrounded by a wall about five feet high, in the shape of an irregular hexagon, by the side of which a level path has been formed encircling the rocks, which rise to a height of about eight feet in the centre, (on the top of which is the holy foot-print,) and which are again overtopped by the wooden temple surmounting it. On the outside of the wall, on the southern and eastern side, a number of stunted trees, not unlike the elm, rise to about a level with the summit of the rocks, so that standing in the temple (which consists merely of a roof supported by a paling) you see the irregular points of the rocks, the highest natural object on the summit, irregularly sinking on all sides, till terminated by the level space or footpath, formerly mentioned, immediately within the wall, which latter has three small gateways at its three corners, the one on the west, that by which we ascended; another on the south-east leading down to a small priest's house on the side of the hill, and, if I am not mistaken, being the termination of another road leading to the summit; and a third upon the north, which conducts by a short walk to a spring almost on the summit, which the guide assured me is constantly filled. The water from this spring, I need scarcely say, felt exceedingly cold, and a few draughts of it had a wonderful effect in reviving me. The descent from the outside of the wall is exceedingly steep on all sides, but more especially so upon the west and north. Abundance of moss and a great number of weeds, common in England, which I had not seen before in Ceylon, are to be met with near the summit, but I regret I do not know either their vulgar or their scientific names. The climate at the summit was delightfully refreshing; an east wind was blowing which soon cooled us to a reasonable temperature, and although the thermometer did not fall below 51° of Fahrenheit, I was glad to luxuriate in flannels, cloth clothes and blankets. The attendants fortunately succeeded in kindling a fire, and, in a short time, a most interesting and unique ceremony was in the course of performance. Sitting round the fire, they began to find that it did not heat their backs to the same degree as the fore part of the body; and wisely considering that it would be better to get a little for both parts, than all for one, they commenced, almost simultaneously, a rotatory motion on their heels, which they kept up with admirable uniformity during the remainder of the evening. It was not unlike the voluntary roasting of half a dozen public-spirited monkeys, determined to sacrifice themselves for the welfare of the community.

Here, as at Deabetme, the evening was too cloudy to allow of my obtaining a good view, so I contented myself by taking sketches of the temple and the sacred foot print, hoping better things of the approaching morning.

The impression, like most other natural curiosities of the same kind, is a complete deception. In the rock itself there is no indentation resembling a footstep, and were it not that some judicious devotees have made a good use of mortar and a trowel, the visitor would gaze a long time before he would fancy he saw anything of the kind. Even as it is, were the plastered separations of the toes removed, one would be much more ready to take it for the impression of a door with a semicircular top, than for that of a foot. It is about four feet and a half long, by two feet and a quarter broad. During the months of visitation by the pilgrims, it is preserved from the too-enquiring gaze of unbelieving or wavering sceptics, by a metal cover, glittering with glass diamonds. The border, which makes the outline of the impression, is about four inches broad, made of coarse lime painted brown, and the temple which surmounts the imposition is about six feet by five in extent. It is supported by chains running from the corners of the roof to the outside of the walls, where they are firmly fastened to the rock.

I was impatiently awaiting the rising of the sun long before he appeared, and was rather anxious lest I should miss the scene, which is of all others the most attractive from the summit, and by far the most magnificent of the kind that I had ever beheld. The mists, however, gradually rolled away; I could see indistinctly the country around me at an immense depth beneath, and at length the magnificent sight of his rising began. Gradually the sky was illuminated towards the east, then the summit of the mountain on which I stood, whilst the whole country around remained in darkness. It was as if I were detached from the earth, and had got into an island far above it. Slowly as he advanced, the rays descended on the cone, other hills were touched next, and hundreds of shining summits stood in bright relief from the surrounding blackness. There was a sublimity about the scene, of a character totally different from any other I had ever experienced. In other situations you may admire the works of man and those of nature combined, but here you are the solitary link between the mighty works of Omnipotence and human insignificance. The scene brought to my remembrance a passage from an American work, entitled " Specimens of Foreign Literature," contained in an introductory notice of Theodore Jouffroy, which the reader will perhaps not blame me for transcribing, as a conclusion to these rough and hurried notes.

" In the bosom of cities, man appears to be the principal concern of creation ; his apparent superiority is there signally displayed ; he there seems to preside over the theatre of the world, or rather to occupy it himself. But when this being, so haughty, so powerful, so absorbed by his own interests, in the crowd of cities, and in the midst of his fellows, chances to be brought into a vast and majestic scene of nature, in view of the illimitable firmament, surrounded with the works of creation, which overwhelm him, if not by their intelligence, by their magnitude ; when from the summit of a mountain, or under the light of the stars, he beholds petty villages lost in diminutive forests, which themselves are lost in the extent of the prospect, and reflects that these villages are inhabited by frail and imperfect beings like himself; when he compares those beings and their wretched abodes with the magnificent spectacle of external nature; when he compares this, with the world on whose surface it is but a point, and this world in its turn, with the myriads of worlds that are suspended above him, and before which it is nothing; in the presence of this spectacle, man views with pity his miserable, conflicting passions." . . . . .

Colombo, 18*th January* 1845.